CHAMBERS ENGLISH VOCABULARY

Chambers

English Vocabulary

- Higher studies • Creative writing • TOEFL/IELTS
- Job interviews • Test Prep • Everyday situations
- Office communication

hachette INDIA

First published in 2024 by Hachette India
(Registered name: Hachette Book Publishing India Pvt. Ltd)
An Hachette UK company
www.hachetteindia.com

1

ISBN 978-93-5731-501-2

Hachette Book Publishing India Pvt. Ltd
4th & 5th Floors, Corporate Centre,
Plot No. 94, Sector 44, Gurugram 122003, India

Typeset in Minion Pro 11.5/14.5
by InoSoft Systems, Noida

Printed and bound in India
by Manipal Technologies Limited

FSC www.fsc.org
MIX
Paper | Supporting responsible forestry
FSC™ C043100

Contents

Level 2

Level 3

Preface

COMMUNICATION HAS ALWAYS BEEN IMPORTANT, AND TODAY'S competitive landscape has elevated its significance. Whether you are a seasoned professional or you are just starting out, words have immense power. Words shape ideas, build relationships, close deals, and define success. In today's competitive landscape, being able to communicate clearly, persuasively, and precisely can make all the difference, and this book has been designed keeping those objectives at its core.

Chambers English Vocabulary doesn't have words or phrases that bore you, like 'drill down' and 'deliverables', neither does it have words or phrases that scare you, such as 'logistics management' or 'trade union'. It won't tell you to go to work and impress with your *sesquipedalian* speech, nor does it ask you to go to college and *fatuously boast* of your *novel* talent. This is a book of practical knowledge. Whether you are negotiating contracts or leading a team, whether you are appearing for an exam or looking to communicate effectively with peers, whether you are looking to network within the industry or create stunning presentations, this book will be your guide to elevating your communication in the real world.

From simple words like *aroma*, *bare*, and *ball*, this guide goes on to advanced words like *inchoate*, *timorous*, and *escheat*. It gives you trivia that goes along with the words to make their background and usage comprehensible. It comes with phrasal verbs, phobias, collocations, onomatopoeic words, and subject-specific terms. And the book isn't shy of telling you what the specific cuts of meat are or what words are unpleasant to hear or inform you on the various ways to kill someone.

Finally, it gives you exercises to practise the vocabulary you have learned. Knowing vocabulary is not simply learning new words but mastering their use. Using the words in the right contexts is far more important than relying on difficult or obscure terms to impress others, although the book does not discourage such activity. Effective communication lies in the ability to convey your meaning in a way that resonates with others, builds trust, and strengthens understanding, and *Chambers English Vocabulary* acts as a manual to achieve that goal.

The book has been designed for the sole purpose of helping the reader integrate new words into their daily communication naturally and with confidence. Among other things, this book provides practical tools that can be applied to improve writing and public speaking.

We thank the reader sincerely for choosing this book as part of their language development, and hope that it becomes a valuable resource they can return to time and again.

LEVEL 1

Parts of Speech

BEFORE WE BEGIN, LET'S LOOK AT THE DIFFERENT PARTS OF SPEECH and their significance in the English language. The parts of speech are words categorized based on their function within a sentence and are fundamental to the structure and clarity of the English language. Knowing the parts of speech helps in understanding how sentences are constructed, and their correct use enhances clarity and precision in communication. The parts of speech are key to understanding grammar and syntax, enhancing reading comprehension, improving writing skills and assisting in language analysis. Below is a table summarizing the parts of speech.

Parts of Speech	Meaning	Examples
Noun	Names a person, place, thing or idea	professor, Columbia, table, love
Pronoun	Takes the place of a noun	he, she, it, they
Verb	Expresses action or state of being	run, is, have
Adjective	Describes or modifies a noun	happy, large, green
Adverb	Modifies a verb, adjective or another adverb	quickly, very, well
Preposition	Shows relationship between a noun and other words	in, on, at, over
Conjunction	Connects words, phrases or clauses	and, but, or

There are two types of conjunctions: 1. Coordinating Conjunctions 2. Subordinating Conjunctions	1. Coordinating Conjunctions – these connect words, phrases or clauses that are of a similar meaning. 2. Subordinating Conjunctions – these connect an independent clause with a dependent clause	1. Coordinating Conjunctions – for, and, nor, but, or, yet, so 2. Subordinating Conjunctions – although, because, since, unless, until, while, when, if, as
Interjection	Expresses strong emotion or surprise	oh, wow, ouch
Determiners	Words placed in front of nouns to clarify what the noun refers to. The different types of determiners are: 1. Articles 2. Demonstratives 3. Possessives 4. Quantifiers 5. Numbers 6. Interrogatives	1. Articles – a, an, the 2. Demonstratives – this, that, these, those 3. Possessives – my, his, their, our 4. Quantifiers – some, any, many, few, several 5. Numbers – one, two, second, third 6. Interrogatives – which, what, whose

Recognize the parts of speech below:

1. The painting, created by the local artist, is quite <u>impressive</u>.
2. <u>Having</u> finished their meal, they left the restaurant.
3. <u>Although</u> tired, he completed the marathon.
4. The company announced a new initiative <u>yesterday</u>.
5. <u>After</u> much consideration, they decided to relocate.
6. <u>Amidst</u> the chaos, he remained calm and composed.
7. <u>Oops</u>, I forgot to send the email!
8. <u>She</u> is known for her generosity and kindness.
9. Despite the heavy rain, <u>they</u> continued their journey.
10. <u>If</u> you study hard, you will pass the exam.

LIST OF WORDS:

1. Abandon: (verb) to give up something or someone
2. Abase: (verb) act in a way that is humiliating or degrading
3. Abhor: (verb) to hate something or someone
4. Abode: (noun) house; place of dwelling
5. Abort: (verb) to stop something before completion
6. Abound: (verb) to exist in large quantities
7. Absorb: (verb) to soak up or hold something
8. Abuse: (verb) to use something in a harmful or corrupt way
9. Access: (noun) to be able to use or have something
10. Accompany: (verb) to go with someone
11. Accomplish: (verb) to complete something; to succeed in a planned task
12. Accurate: (adjective) correct; without any mistakes
13. Accuse: (verb) to hold someone responsible for a crime
14. Acknowledge: (verb) to admit or recognize the truth or existence of something
15. Acquaintance: (noun) a person you recognize but are not friends with
16. Acquire: (verb) to obtain or get something
17. Adage: (noun) a phrase or saying that expresses a common or true observation
18. Adapt: (verb) modifying oneself or something to meet existing conditions
19. Adequate: (adjective) having enough of what you need
20. Adjourn: (verb) to discontinue a meeting for a while and have it later again
21. Adopt: (verb) to take in a child; to use something
22. Advance: (verb) to progress; move forward
23. Advantage: (noun) opportunity; a condition that is favourable to success
24. Advise: (verb) to provide solution; tell somebody what they should do
25. Advocate: (verb) supporting a particular course of action

26. Affect: (verb) to influence or change something or someone
27. Affection: (noun) a feeling of liking or loving someone
28. Afford: (verb) able to buy something or spend time on something
29. Against: (preposition) to be opposed to somebody or something
30. Agency: (noun) to be able to choose a course of action to take

> 'Affect' and 'Effect' are often confused due to their similar pronunciation, but they serve different functions in a sentence. 'Affect' is primarily a verb meaning to influence or change something, while 'Effect' is a noun referring to the result of a change. For example, a policy change can affect employee morale, and the effect of this change might be seen in decreased productivity.

31. Aggressive: (adjective) always willing to fight and argue; showing anger
32. Agitate: (verb) to excite or trouble (a person, their feelings, etc.)
33. Alarm: (verb) to frighten, warn someone of danger
34. Algebra: (noun) a branch of mathematics that uses letters and symbols to represent variable quantities and numbers, and to express generalizations about them
35. Allot: (verb) to give to each member of a group
36. Allow: (verb) to permit (someone to do something, something to happen, etc.)
37. Allure: (noun) attractiveness, appeal or charm
38. Ally: (noun) a country, state, etc. that has formally agreed to help and support another
39. Almost: (adverb) nearly but not quite
40. Alone: (adjective, adverb) by oneself; without anyone or anything else
41. Along: (adverb) in some direction
42. Aloof: (adjective) unfriendly and distant
43. Aloud: (adverb) loud enough to be able to be heard
44. Already: (adverb) before the present time or time in question
45. Alternate: (adjective) of two feelings, states, conditions, etc.

46. Although: (conjunction) in spite of the fact that
47. Amass: (verb) to gather or collect (money, possessions, etc.) especially in great quantity
48. Amaze: (verb) to surprise someone greatly
49. Ambit: (noun) range or extent, circumference or boundary
50. Amble: (verb) to walk without hurrying
51. Amenable: (adjective) accommodating, flexible
52. Amend: (verb) to correct, improve or make minor changes
53. Amiss: (adjective) wrong, out of order
54. Amok: (adverb) to rush about violently and out of control
55. Amount: (noun) a quantity
56. Ample: (adjective) more than enough
57. Amuse: (verb) to make someone laugh
58. Anagram: (noun) a word, phrase or sentence is formed by changing the order of the letters of another word, phrase or sentence
59. Analogue: (noun) something regarded in terms of its similarity to something; parallelism to something else
60. Analyse: (verb) to examine the structure or content of something in detail
61. Anatomy: (noun) the scientific study of the structure of plants and animals
62. Ancestor: (noun) someone usually more distant than a grandparent, from whom a person is descended
63. Ancestral: (adjective) belonging to or inherited from one's ancestors
64. Anchor: (noun) a heavy piece of metal attached by a cable to a ship to restrict the ship's movement; anything that acts as a weight to secure something else
65. Ancient: (adjective) dating from very long ago
66. Anger: (noun) a feeling of great displeasure or annoyance
67. Angle: (noun) a corner; a point of view
68. Angst: (noun) a feeling of apprehension or anxiety
69. Anguish: (noun) severe mental distress or torture
70. Ankle: (noun) the joint that connects the leg and the foot
71. Announce: (verb) to make something known publicly

72. Annul: (verb) to declare publicly that a marriage, legal contract, etc. is no longer valid
73. Anoint: (verb) to put oil or ointment on someone's head
74. Anonymous: (adjective) having no name
75. Antelope: (noun) a hoofed mammal, usually with paired horns, found mainly in Africa
76. Anthem: (noun) a song or praise or celebration
77. Anticipation: (verb) to see what will be needed or wanted in the future and to do what is necessary in advance
78. Antidote: (noun) any agent or a drug that counteracts or prevents the action of a poison
79. Anvil: (noun) a heavy iron block on which metal objects can be hammered into shape
80. Anxiety: (noun) a strong feeling or fear or distress
81. Ape: (verb) to imitate (someone's behaviour, speech, habits, etc.)
82. Apology: (noun) an expression of regret for a mistake or offence
83. Apostle: (noun) someone sent to preach about Christ in the early Church, especially one of the twelve disciples
84. Appeal: (noun) an urgent or formal request for help; a request made in a pleading or heartfelt way
85. Applaud: (noun) show approval or appreciate by clapping
86. Appointment: (noun) an arrangement to meet someone
87. Apprise: (verb) to give information about something
88. Approach: (verb) to come near or nearer in space, time, etc.
89. Approve: (verb) to agree or to permit
90. Apt: (adjective) suitable; clever or quick to learn
91. Arable: (adjective) land: suitable or used for ploughing or growing crops
92. Arc: (noun) a continuous section of a circle or other curve
93. Archer: (noun) someone who uses bow and arrow
94. Ardent: (adjective) enthusiastic; passionate
95. Argue: (verb) to put forward one's case especially in a clear and well-ordered manner; to quarrel or disagree
96. Arid: (adjective) of a region or climate: characterized by very low rainfall

97. Arise: (verb) to come into being; to stand up; to come to notice
98. Arm: (noun) in humans: either of the two upper limbs of the body from the shoulders to the hands
99. Armour: (noun) a suit or covering of metal, chain-mail, etc., worn by men or horses to protect them against injury in battle
100. Army: (noun) a large number of people armed and organized for fighting on land
101. Aroma: (noun) a distinctive usually pleasant smell
102. Around: (adverb) on every side; in every direction
103. Arrange: (verb) to put into proper or desired order
104. Arrest: (verb) to take someone into custody
105. Arrive: (verb) to reach a place during a journey or come to a destination at the end of a journey
106. Arson: (noun) the crime of deliberately setting a building on fire
107. Art: (noun) the creation of works of beauty
108. Ash: (noun) the dusty residue that remains after something has been burned
109. Ashamed: (adjective) troubled by feelings of guilt, embarrassment, etc.
110. Assignment: (noun) a task or duty that has been selected for someone to do
111. Assistant: (noun) a person whose job is to help someone of higher rank, position, etc.
112. Associate: (verb) to connect in the mind; to mix socially
113. Assume: (verb) to accept something without proof
114. Athletic: (adjective) of someone or their build: physically fit and strong
115. Atmosphere: (noun) the layer of gas surrounding the planet especially the Earth, and held to it by gravity
116. Attach: (verb) to fasten or join
117. Attack: (verb) to make a sudden or violent attempt to hurt, damage or capture
118. Attain: (verb) to complete successfully
119. Attempt: (verb) to try

120. Attend: (verb) to be present at something
121. Attest: (verb) to be proof of the truth or validity of something
122. Attic: (noun) a space or room at the top of the house under the roof
123. Attract: (verb) to cause (attention, notice, a crowd, interest, etc.) to be directed towards oneself, itself, etc.
124. Attribute: (verb) to think of it as being written, said or caused by them or it
125. Auburn: (adjective) of hair: reddish-brown
126. Audible: (adjective) loud enough to be heard
127. Auger: (noun) a hand tool with a corkscrew-like point for boring holes
128. Aunt: (noun) the sister of one's father or mother
129. Authority: (noun) the power or right to control or judge others
130. Avail: (verb) to help or be of use
131. Awe: (noun) admiration, fear and wonder
132. Awful: (adjective) very bad or unpleasant
133. Axe: (noun) a hand tool with a long handle and a heavy metal blade used for cutting down trees, chopping wood, etc.
134. Azure: (adjective) deep sky-blue in colour
135. Back: (noun) the rear part of the human body from the neck to the base of the spine
136. Bacon: (noun) meat from the back and sides of a pig
137. Bad: (adjective) not good
138. Badge: (noun) a small emblem worn to show rank
139. Badminton: (noun) a game played with rackets and a shuttlecock, which is hit back and forth across a high net
140. Baffle: (verb) to confuse or puzzle

> The word 'aunty' is an informal way of using the word 'aunt'. In Indian culture we use the term 'aunty' to show respect while addressing older women in our family or community. For example: 'Seema Aunty' or 'Neelima Aunty'.
>
> In Western culture the term is used before the name, especially for people related to the family. For example: 'Aunt Samantha'.
>
> Same usage difference can be noticed for the word 'uncle'.

> Pork (pig meat) is divided into various cuts that come from different parts of the pig. Each cut has it own uses in cooking. Some of the parts are:
>
> 1. Pork Butt: This cut comes from the upper part of the shoulder and is well-marbled with fat. It is used for slow cooking methods like roasting, braising or smoking. Pulled pork is commonly made with Pork Butt.
> 2. Tenderloin: A small, tender cut located underneath the loin. It's lean and cooks quickly.
> 3. Pork Chops: These are parts cut from the loin. They include bone-in or boneless varieties and are usually grilled, pan-friend or baked.
> 4. Pork Belly: This is a fatty and flavourful cut and is used to make bacon and pancetta. It is also braised or roasted for dishes like crispy pork belly.
> 5. Ham: This cut comes from the back leg and is sold fresh, cured or smoked.
> 6. Trotters (Pigs' feet): These are used in soups and stews in add richness and gelatin to the dish.

141. Bag: (noun) a container made from soft material with an opening at the top for carrying things
142. Baggy: (adjective) hanging loose or bulging
143. Bail: (noun) the temporary release of a person awaiting trial, secured by the payment of money and/or the imposition of special conditions
144. Bait: (noun) food put on a hook or in a trap to attract fish or animals
145. Bake: (verb) to cook using dry heat in an oven
146. Balance: (noun) a state of physical stability in which the weight of the body is evenly distributed
147. Bald: (adjective) of a person: having little or no hair on their head
148. Bale: (noun) a large tied bundle of a commodity such as hay
149. Baleen: (noun) whalebone
150. Balk: (verb) to hesitate or refuse to go on
151. Ball: (noun) a round or roundish object used in some sports
152. Ballot: (noun) a method or system of voting, usually in secret, by putting a marked paper into a box

153. Balsam: (noun) a pleasant-smelling thick sticky substance obtained from some trees and plants, used to make medicines and perfumes
154. Ban: (noun) an official order stating that something is not allowed
155. Banal: (adjective) lacking in interest or originality
156. Band: (noun) a flat, narrow strip of cloth, metal, paper, etc. used to hold things together or as decoration
157. Bandage: (noun) a strip of cloth for winding round a wounded or injured limb
158. Bandit: (noun) an armed robber, especially a member of a gang
159. Bane: (noun) the cause of trouble or evil
160. Bang: (noun) a sudden, loud explosive noise
161. Banish: (verb) to send someone away from a place
162. Banter: (noun) light-hearted friendly talk.
163. Barb: (noun) a point on a hook facing in the opposite direction to the main point
164. Barber: (noun) someone who cuts and styles men's hair and shaves their beards
165. Bard: (noun) a poet
166. Bare: (adjective) not covered by clothes
167. Barely: (adverb) scarcely or only just
168. Bark: (noun) the short sharp cry of a dog
169. Barn: (noun) a building in which grain or hay is stored
170. Barren: (adjective) of a woman or female animal: not able to bear offspring
171. Base: (noun) the lowest part or bottom
172. Bash: (verb) to strike or smash something bluntly
173. Basic: (adjective) referring to or forming the base or basis of something
174. Basket: (noun) a container made of interwoven twigs, canes, or wire often with a handle across the top
175. Bass: (noun) the lowest male singing voice
176. Baste: (verb) to pour hot fat or juices over when cooking

177. Bat: (noun) a shaped piece of wood with a flat or curved surface for hitting the ball in cricket; any of various small nocturnal flying mammals
178. Batch: (noun) a number of things or people dealt with at the same time
179. Bath: (noun) a large open container for water, in which to wash the whole body while sitting in it
180. Batman: (noun) an officer's personal servant in the armed forces
181. Batter: (verb) to hit something or someone hard and often
182. Battle: (noun) a fight between opposing armies or people
183. Bauble: (noun) a cheap small trinket
184. Bawl: (verb) to cry loudly in distress, pain, etc.
185. Bazaar: (noun) a marketplace or exchange
186. Beacon: (noun) a warning or guiding device for aircraft or ships, e.g., a lighthouse or dio transmitter that broadcasts signals
187. Beak: (noun) the horny projecting jaws of a bird
188. Beam: (noun) a long thick piece of wood used as a main structural component of a building; (verb) to smile broadly with pleasure
189. Bear: (verb) to support or sustain (a weight or load); to put up with or tolerate
190. Beard: (noun) the hair that grows on a man's chin and neck
191. Beast: (noun) any large animal, especially a wild one
192. Beaten: (adjective) defeated or outmanoeuvred
193. Beautiful: (adjective) having an appearance or qualities which please the senses or give rise to admiration in the mind
194. Beckon: (verb) to summon with a gesture
195. Bed: (noun) a piece of furniture for sleeping on
196. Bedeck: (verb) to cover with decorations
197. Beef: (noun) the flesh of a bull, cow or ox used as food
198. Befit: (verb) to be suitable or right for
199. Begin: (verb) to start
200. Beguile: (verb) to charm or captivate
201. Behave: (verb) to act in a specified way

Cow meat too, like pork, has different cuts:

1. Rib: This cut includes ribeye steaks, prime rib roast and short rib.
2. Brisket: This cut if often used for barbecue, corned beef and pastrami. It comes from the lower breast or pectoral muscle of a cow.
3. Shank: This cut usually comes from the leg portion. It is used for soups and stews.
4. Sirloin: This cut comes from the back of the animal and is used for steaks and roasts.
5. Tenderloin: This cut usually comes from the loin and it is a long, narrow muscle located there. It is most famously used for the tenderloin steak or filet mignon.
6. Ox tail: This cut comes from the tail of the animal begins from the base of the spine. It is also used in soups and stews.

202. Behead: (verb) to cut off the head of someone, especially as a form of capital punishment
203. Behold: (verb) to see, to look at
204. Being: (noun) existence: come into being
205. Belated: (adjective) happening or coming late or too late
206. Bellow: (verb) to make a loud deep cry like that of a bull
207. Belong: (verb) to be the right or property of
208. Bemoan: (verb) to express great sadness or regret about something
209. Bend: (verb) to make or become angled or curved
210. Benefit: (noun) something good gained or received
211. Bent: (adjective) curved or having a bend
212. Benumb: (verb) to make numb
213. Berate: (verb) to scold someone severely
214. Bereft: (adjective) deprived of something
215. Beset: (verb) to worry someone or to hamper something
216. Besmirch: (verb) to spoil or stain the reputation or name of someone
217. Bestow: (verb) to give or present (a title, award, etc.) to someone
218. Betray: (verb) to hand over or expose (a friend or one's country, etc.) to an enemy

219. Beware: (verb) to be careful of something
220. Bias: (noun) an inclination to favour or disfavour one side against another in a dispute, competition, etc.
221. Bid: (verb) to offer (an amount of money) when trying to buy something, especially at an auction
222. Bide: (verb) to wait or stay
223. Bigot: (noun) someone who is persistently prejudiced, especially about religion, politics or race
224. Bile: (noun) a thick yellowish-green alkaline liquid produced by the liver to aid the digestion of fats
225. Bind: (verb) to tie or fasten tightly
226. Biped: (noun) an animal with two feet
227. Birth: (noun) the act or process of bearing offspring
228. Bisect: (verb) to divide something into two equal parts
229. Bite: (verb) to grasp, seize or tear with the teeth
230. Bitter: (adjective) having a sharp, acid and often unpleasant taste
231. Bizarre: (adjective) weirdly odd or strange
232. Blabber: (verb) to talk nonsense especially without stopping or without being understood
233. Black: (adjective) having the darkest colour
234. Blade: (noun) the cutting part of a knife or sword
235. Blame: (verb) to consider someone as responsible for something bad, wrong or undesirable
236. Bland: (adjective) of food: having a very mild taste
237. Blanket: (noun) a thick covering of material, used to cover beds or for wrapping a person in for warmth
238. Blessing: (noun) a wish or prayer for happiness or success
239. Blink: (verb) to shut and open
240. Bliss: (noun) a very great happiness
241. Blizzard: (noun) a severe snowstorm with strong winds
242. Blood: (noun) a fluid tissue that circulates in the arteries, veins and capillaries of the body as a result of muscular contractions of the heart
243. Blossom: (noun) a flower or a mass of flowers, especially on a fruit tree; verb: of a plant, especially a fruit tree: to produce blossom or flowers

244. Blow: (noun) a forceful knock with the hand or a weapon; (verb) of a current of air or wind, etc.: to be moving, especially rapidly
245. Blue: (adjective) with the colour of a clear cloudless sky; sad or depressed
246. Blunt: (adjective) of a pencil, knife or blade: having no point or sharp edge; of a person, character or manner: honest and direct in a rough way
247. Blush: (verb) to become red or pink in the face because of shame, excitement, joy, etc.
248. Bluster: (verb) to speak in a boasting or threatening way; of wind or waves: to blow or move roughly
249. Boar: (noun) a mature uncastrated male pig
250. Boast: (verb) to talk with excessive pride about one's own abilities or achievements
251. Boat: (noun) a small vessel for travelling over water
252. Bobbin: (noun) a small cylindrical object on which thread is wound
253. Boil: (verb) of a liquid: to change rapidly to a vapour on reaching a certain temperature
254. Bolster: (verb) to support it, make it stronger or hold it up
255. Bone: (noun) the hard dense tissue that forms the skeleton of vertebrates
256. Borrow: (verb) to take something temporarily
257. Bother: (verb) to annoy, worry or trouble someone or something
258. Bottle: (noun) a hollow glass or plastic container with a narrow neck, for holding liquids
259. Bound: (adjective) tied with or as if with a rope or other binding; on the way or going towards it; (noun) a limit or boundary; a jump or leap upwards
260. Box: (noun) a container made from wood, cardboard or plastic usually square or rectangular and with a lid; (verb) to fight someone with the hands formed into fists and protected by thick leather gloves, especially as a sport
261. Boxing: (noun) the sport of fighting with the fists

262. Brain: (noun) the highly developed mass of nervous tissue that co-ordinates and controls the activities of the central nervous system of animals
263. Branch: (noun) an offshoot arising from the trunk of a tree or the main stem of a shrub
264. Break: (verb) to divide or cause something to become divided into two or more parts because of stress or a blow
265. Breath: (noun) the air drawn into and then expelled from the lungs
266. Breathe: (verb) to respire by alternately drawing air into and expelling it from the lungs
267. Breeze: (noun) a gentle wind
268. Brethren: (noun) plural of brother
269. Brick: (noun) a rectangular block of baked clay used for building
270. Bride: (noun) a woman who has just been married or is about to be married
271. Bright: (adjective) giving out or shining with much light
272. Brisk: (adjective) lively, active or quick
273. Broad: (adjective) large in extent from one side to the other
274. Brook: (noun) a small stream
275. Broom: (noun) a long-handled sweeping brush, formerly made from the stems of the broom plant
276. Brother: (noun) a man belonging to same group, trade union, etc. as another or others
277. Brow: (noun) short form of eyebrow
278. Brush: (noun) a tool with lengths of stiff nylon, wire, hair, bristles or something similar set into it, used for tidying the hair, cleaning, painting, etc.
279. Brute: (noun) a cruel, brutal or violent person
280. Bucket: (noun) a round open-topped container for holding liquids and solids such as sand, etc.
281. Bud: (noun) in a plant: an immature knob-like shoot that will eventually develop into a leaf or flower
282. Buffalo: (noun) a member of the cattle family which has a heavy black or brown body and thick upward curving horns

283. Bulb: (noun) in certain plants, e.g., tulip and onion: a swollen underground organ that functions as a food store and consists of a modified shoot and roots growing from its lower surface
284. Bull: (noun) the uncastrated male of animals in the cattle family; (noun) an official letter or written instruction from the Pope
285. Bullock: (noun) a castrated bull
286. Burn: (verb) to be on fire or set something on fire
287. Burp: (verb) to let air escape noisily from one's stomach through one's mouth
288. Burst: (verb) to break or fly open into pieces, usually suddenly and violently or cause something to do this
289. Bury: (verb) to place (dead body) in a grave, the sea, etc.; to hide something in the ground
290. Bust: (verb) to break or burst something
291. Button: (noun) a small round piece of metal or plastic, etc., sewn onto a piece of clothing, which fastens it by being passed through a buttonhole
292. Cabbage: (noun) a vegetable with a compact head of green, white or red leaves
293. Cabin: (noun) a small house, especially one made of wood
294. Cabinet: (noun) a piece of furniture with shelves and doors, for storing or displaying items
295. Cable: (noun) a strong wire cord or rope
296. Cactus: (noun) any of the numerous plants with sharp spines, which usually store water in fleshy stems
297. Cage: (noun) an enclosure, usually with bars, in which birds and animals are kept
298. Cajole: (verb) to persuade using flattery, promises, etc.
299. Calf: (noun) the young of any bovine animal, especially domestic cattle
300. Call: (verb) to shout or speak loudly in order to attract attention
301. Calm: (adjective) relaxed and in control
302. Camel: (noun) a large mammal with a long neck and legs and one or two humps in the back

303. Candidate: (noun) someone who is competing with others for a job, prize, parliamentary seat, etc.
304. Candle: (noun) a piece of wax or (especially formerly) tallow, formed around a wick, which is burnt to provide light
305. Cane: (noun) the long jointed hollow or pithy stem of certain plants, especially various small palms and larger grasses (e.g., bamboo and sugar cane)
306. Canister: (noun) a container for storing tea or other dry foods
307. Cape: (noun) a short cloak
308. Captain: (noun) a leader or chief
309. Car: (noun) a self-propelled four-wheeled road vehicle designed to carry passengers and powered by an internal combustion engine
310. Card: (noun) a kind of thick, stiff paper or thin cardboard
311. Care: (noun) attention and thoroughness
312. Career: (noun) one's professional life, one's progress in one's job
313. Cargo: (noun) the goods carried by a ship, aircraft or other vehicle
314. Carpet: (noun) a covering for floors and stairs, made of heavy fabric
315. Carrot: (noun) a plant with a large orange root eaten as a vegetable
316. Cartilage: (noun) in humans: a tough flexile material that forms the skeleton of the embryo but is converted into bone before adulthood, persisting in the adults in structures such as the larynx and trachea
317. Case: (noun) often in compounds: a box, container or cover, used for storage, transportation, etc.; a particular occasion, situation or set of circumstances
318. Cash: (noun) coins or paper money, as distinct from cheques, credit cards, etc.
319. Caste: (noun) any of the four hereditary social classes into which Hindu society is divided
320. Castle: (noun) a large, fortified building with battlements and towers

321. Cat: (noun) any of a wide range of carnivorous mammals including the lion, leopard, and tiger as well as the domestic cat
322. Cater: (verb) to supply food for an event
323. Cauliflower: (noun) the firm head of a type of cabbage made up of white florets and eaten as a vegetable
324. Cavity: (noun) a hollow or hole
325. Cedar: (noun) a tall coniferous tree with widely spreading branches, cones, needle-like leaves and reddish-brown bark
326. Censor: (noun) an official who examines books, films, newspaper articles, etc. with the power to cut out any parts thought politically sensitive or offensive or to forbid showing them altogether
327. Ceremony: (noun) a ritual performed to mark a particular, especially public or religious, occasion
328. Chair: (noun) a seat for one person, with a back support and usually four legs
329. Chamber: (noun) a room, especially a bedroom; a hall for the meeting of an assembly, especially a legislative or judicial body
330. Charm: (noun) the power of delighting, attracting or fascinating
331. Chase: (verb) to follow or go after them in an attempt to catch them
332. Cheek: (noun) either side of the face below the eye, the fleshy wall of the mouth; impudent speech or behaviour
333. Cheer: (noun) a shout of approval or encouragement
334. Chemistry: (noun) the scientific study of the composition properties and reactions of chemical compounds
335. Cherish: (verb) to care for lovingly
336. Chess: (noun) a game of skill played on a chequered board, by two people, each with 16 playing pieces, the object of which is to trap the opponent's king
337. Chest: (noun) the front part of the body between the neck and the waist
338. Chew: (verb) to use the teeth to break up food inside the mouth before swallowing

339. Chicken: (noun) the domestic fowl, bred for its meat and eggs
340. Chilli: (noun) the fruit or pod of one of the varieties of capsicum, which has a hot spicy flavour
341. Chilly: (adjective) rather cold
342. Chimney: (noun) a vertical structure made of brick, stone or steel, that carries smoke, steam, fumes or heated air away from a fireplace, stove, furnace or engine

> Chilli, also known as 'chili con carne' is a hearty stew featuring ground meat simmered with beans, tomatoes and a blend of spices, including chilli powder, cumin and garlic. This popular dish originates from Tex-Mex cuisine and is enjoyed for its robust flavours and comforting warmth. It is usually served with toppings such as cheese, sour cream and chopped onions.

343. Chimpanzee: (noun) the most intelligent of the great apes, found in tropical rainforests of Africa
344. Chin: (noun) the front protruding part of the lower jaw
345. China: (noun) articles made from a fine translucent earthenware, originally from China
346. Chirp: (verb) of birds, grasshopper, etc.; to produce a short high-pitched sound
347. Chisel: (noun) a hand tool which has a strong metal blade with a cutting edge at the tip, used for cutting and shaping wood or stone
348. Chivalry: (noun) courtesy and protectiveness, especially as shown by men towards women
349. Cholera: (noun) an acute and potentially fatal bacterial infection of the small intestine
350. Chubby: (adjective) plump
351. Churn: (noun) a machine in which milk is vigorously shaken to make butter
352. Cinder: (noun) a piece of burnt coal or wood
353. Circus: (noun) a travelling company of performers including acrobats, clowns and often trained animals, etc.
354. Citron: (noun) a fruit like a large lemon, with a thick, sweet-smelling yellow rind

355. Civics: (noun) the study of local government and of the rights and duties of citizenship
356. Clamour: (noun) a noise of shouting or loud talking
357. Clang: (verb) to ring or make something ring loudly
358. Clash: (noun) a loud noise, like that of metal objects striking each other
359. Clasp: (noun) a fastening on jewellery, a bag, etc., made of two parts that link together
360. Clatter: (noun) a loud noise made by hard objects striking each other or falling onto a hard surface
361. Claw: (noun) a hard curved pointed nail on the end of each digit of foot in birds, most reptiles and many mammals
362. Clay: (noun) a poorly draining soil consisting mainly of aluminium
363. Cleaner: (noun) someone employed to clean buildings, etc.
364. Clever: (adjective) good or quick at learning and understanding
365. Client: (noun) someone using the services of a professional institution, e.g., a bank
366. Climate: (noun) the average weather conditions of a particular region of the world over a long period of time
367. Cling: (verb) to hold firmly or tightly
368. Clink: (noun) a short sharp ringing sound
369. Clock: (noun) a device for measuring and indicating time
370. Close: (adjective) near in space or time; at a short distance
371. Cobweb: (noun) a web of fine sticky threads spun by a spider
372. Cock: (noun) a male bird, especially an adult male chicken
373. Collapse: (verb) of buildings and other structures to fall or cave in; of people: to drop into a state of unconsciousness
374. Collar bone: (noun) the clavicle
375. Colonize: (verb) to establish a colony in
376. Colt: (noun) a male horse or pony less than four years old
377. Columnist: (noun) someone who writes a regular section of a newspaper
378. Comb: (noun) a rigid toothed device for tidying and arranging the hair

379. Combine: (verb) to join together
380. Comfort: (noun) a state of contentedness or wellbeing
381. Comical: (adjective) funny, humorous, ludicrous
382. Commerce: (noun) the buying and selling of commodities and services
383. Compassion: (noun) a feeling of sorrow and pity for someone in trouble
384. Complain: (verb) to express dissatisfaction or displeasure
385. Conceal: (verb) to place out of sight
386. Conceive: (verb) to become pregnant; to think or imagine
387. Concept: (noun) an abstract or general idea
388. Concerned: (adjective) worried
389. Conclude: (verb) to come or bring to an end
390. Concubine: (noun) a woman who lives with a man and has sex with him, without being married to him
391. Condition: (noun) a particular state of existence
392. Confess: (verb) to own up to a fault, wrongdoing
393. Confident: (adjective) certain; self-assured
394. Confine: (verb) to restrict or limit
395. Congeal: (verb) of a liquid, e.g., blood: to thicken or coagulate, especially through cooling
396. Conifer: (noun) an evergreen tree or shrub with needle-like leaves, which produces its pollen and seeds in cones
397. Conservative: (adjective) favouring that which is established or traditional, with an opposition to change
398. Console: (verb) to comfort in distress, grief or disappointment
399. Consult: (verb) to ask the advice of
400. Consume: (verb) to eat or drink
401. Contain: (verb) to hold
402. Container: (noun) an object designed for holding or storing such as a box, tin, carton, etc.
403. Content: (adjective) to satisfy or make oneself or another satisfied
404. Control: (noun) authority or charge; power to influence or guide; (verb) to exercise authority or influence over

405. Convince: (verb) to persuade someone of something; to make or cause to make them believe it
406. Cookery: (noun) the art of practise of cooking food
407. Copper: (noun) a soft reddish-brown metallic element, which is an excellent conductor of heat and electricity
408. Coriander: (noun) a plant with narrowly lobed leaves and globular aromatic fruits
409. Corn: (noun) the most important cereal crop of a particular region, especially wheat in England
410. Cot: (noun) a small bed with high, barred sides for a child
411. Cotton: (noun) a shrubby plant cultivated for the creamy-white downy fibres which surround its seeds
412. Couch: (noun) a sofa or settee
413. Count: (verb) to recite numbers in ascending order; (noun) a European nobleman
414. Couple: (noun) a pair of people attached in some way, often romantically
415. Courteous: (adjective) polite, considerate
416. Courtiers: (noun) someone in attendance at a royal court
417. Cover: (verb) to form a layer over someone or something
418. Cow: (verb) to frighten something into submission
419. Crab: (noun) a marine crustacean with a hard flattened shell and five pairs of jointed legs, the front pair developed into pincers
420. Crackle: (verb) to make a faint continuous cracking or popping sound
421. Cradle: (noun) a cot for a small baby, especially one that can be rocked
422. Crane: (noun) a machine with a long pivoted arm from which lifting gear is suspended allowing heavy weights to be moved both horizontally and vertically
423. Crash: (verb) to fall or strike with a banging or smashing noise
424. Crawl: (verb) of insects, worms, etc.: to move along the ground slowly; of a human: to move along on the hands and knees

425. Cream: (noun) the yellowish fatty substance that rises to the surface of milk, and yields butter when churned
426. Credit: (noun) faith placed in something
427. Creep: (verb) to move slowly, with stealth or caution
428. Creeper: (noun) a creeping plant
429. Cricket: (noun) an outdoor game played using a ball, bats and wickets, between two sides of eleven players; a species of mainly nocturnal insect related to a grasshopper
430. Crime: (noun) an illegal act
431. Crimson: (noun) a deep purplish red colour
432. Cringe: (verb) to cower away in fear
433. Crisis: (noun) a crucial or decisive moment
434. Crisp: (adjective) dry and brittle
435. Critical: (adjective) fault-finding
436. Crop: (noun) a plant cultivated for food, fodder or raw materials
437. Crow: (noun) a large black bird, usually with a powerful black beak and shiny feathers
438. Crowd: (noun) a large number of people gathered together
439. Crown: (noun) the circular, usually jewelled, headdress of a sovereign
440. Cruel: (adjective) deliberately and pitilessly causing pain and suffering
441. Crumple: (verb) to make or become creased or crushed
442. Crunch: (verb) to crush or grind noisily between the teeth or under the foot
443. Crush: (verb) to break, damage, bruise, injure or distort by compressing violently
444. Crystal: (noun) colourless transparent quartz
445. Cuckoo: (noun) an insectivorous bird which lays its eggs in the nests of other birds
446. Cucumber: (noun) a creeping plant cultivated for its edible fruit
447. Culprit: (noun) someone guilty of a misdeed or offence
448. Cultivate: (verb) to prepare and use for growing crops
449. Cultural: (adjective) relating to a culture

450. Cunning: (adjective) clever, sly or crafty
451. Cup: (noun) a small, round, open container usually with a handle used to drink from
452. Cure: (verb) to restore someone to health or normality
453. Curious: (adjective) strange; eager or interested
454. Curly: (adjective) having curls; full of curls
455. Curse: (noun) a blasphemous or obscene expression, usually of anger
456. Curtain: (noun) a hanging cloth over a window, round a bed, etc., for privacy or to exclude light
457. Cushion: (noun) a fabric case stuffed with soft material, for sitting on
458. Custom: (noun) a traditional activity or practice
459. Customer: (noun) someone who purchases goods from a shop, uses the services of a business
460. Cypress: (noun) any of a family of dark-green coniferous trees or their wood
461. Daisy: (noun) a small flower with heads consisting of a yellow centre surrounded by white petals
462. Damp: (adjective) slightly wet
463. Dark: (adjective) without light
464. Dash: (verb) to run quickly
465. Daughter: (noun) a female child
466. Daunt: (verb) to frighten, worry or discourage someone
467. Dawn: (noun) the time of day when light first appears
468. Daze: (verb) to make someone confused or unable to think clearly
469. Dealer: (noun) a person or firm dealing in retail goods
470. Debt: (noun) something owed
471. Decade: (noun) a period of 10 years
472. Decay: (verb) to make or become rotten
473. Deception: (noun) deceiving or being deceived
474. Deck: (noun) a platform forming a floor or covering across a ship
475. Decorum: (noun) correct or socially acceptable behaviour

476. Deduce: (verb) to think out or judge on the basis of what one knows or assumes to be fact
477. Deer: (noun) mammal, the male of which has antlers
478. Defame: (verb) to attack the good reputation of someone
479. Defence: (noun) the act of defending against attack
480. Definite: (adjective) fixed or firm; not liable to change
481. Deliver: (verb) to carry (goods, letters, etc.) to a person or place
482. Demoralise: (verb) to take away the confidence, courage or enthusiasm of someone
483. Depend: (verb) to trust and rely on something or someone
484. Deposit: (verb) to put down or leave something
485. Derby: (noun) a horse race held annually at Epsom Downs
486. Derive: (verb) to have something as a source or origin
487. Desire: (noun) a longing or wish
488. Desk: (noun) a table, often with drawers, for sitting at while writing, etc.
489. Despair: (verb) to lose or lack hope
490. Destiny: (noun) the purpose or future as arranged by fate or God
491. Detach: (verb) to unfasten or separate
492. Deuce: (noun) referring to the number two, a tie in tennis when both players have 40 points or a playing card with two pips
493. Devote: (verb) to use or give up to a purpose
494. Dialect: (noun) a form of a language spoken in a particular region or by a certain social group
495. Dice: (noun) a small cube with one to six spots on each of its faces, used in games of chance
496. Dictate: (verb) to say or read out something for someone else to write down

> As an Interjection the exclamation 'What the deuce?' is often used to express annoyance or surprise. Similar phrases include 'What the hell?' 'What in the world?' 'What the heck?' 'What the flip?' and 'What the fuck?' (coarse slang)

497. Dig: (verb) to turn up or move (earth) especially with a spade
498. Digestion: (noun) the process whereby food is broken down by enzymes in the alimentary canal
499. Dignity: (noun) stateliness, seriousness and formality of manner and appearance
500. Dilate: (verb) to make or become larger, wider or further open
501. Dim: (adjective) not bright or distinct
502. Dip: (verb) to put something briefly into a liquid
503. Dirt: (noun) mud or dust
504. Disability: (noun) the state of being disabled
505. Disabled: (adjective) having physical or mental handicap
506. Disappear: (verb) to vanish
507. Disaster: (noun) an event causing great damage, injury or loss of life
508. Disbelieve: (verb) to believe something to be false or someone to be lying
509. Disciple: (noun) someone who believes in and follows the teachings of another
510. Discipline: (noun) a strict training or the enforcing of rules, intended to produce controlled behaviour
511. Discomfort: (noun) a slight physical pain or mental uneasiness
512. Discover: (verb) to be the first person to find something or someone
513. Disease: (noun) a disorder or illness caused by infection
514. Disgrace: (noun) a shame or loss of favour to respect
515. Dish: (noun) a shallow container in which food is served or cooked
516. Dismiss: (verb) to refuse to consider or accept (an idea, claim, etc.)
517. Disobey: (verb) to act contrary to the orders of someone; to refuse to obey
518. Dispel: (verb) to drive away or banish (thoughts or feelings)
519. Disperse: (verb) to spread out over a wide area

520. Display: (verb) to put someone or something on view
521. Dispute: (verb) to question or deny the accuracy or validity of (a statement, etc.)
522. Disturb: (verb) to interrupt someone; to upset the arrangement or order of something
523. Dizzy: (adjective) experiencing or causing a spinning sensation in the head
524. Dog: (noun) a carnivorous mammal such as a wolf, jackal or fox
525. Domain: (noun) the scope of any subject or area of interest; a territory owned or ruled by one person or government
526. Dome: (noun) a hemispherical roof
527. Domestic: (adjective) belonging or relating to the home, the family or private life
528. Donate: (verb) to give, especially to charity
529. Donkey: (noun) a hoofed herbivorous mammal related to but smaller than the horse
530. Doormat: (noun) a step in front of a building's door
531. Double: (adjective) made up two similar parts; in pairs
532. Doubt: (verb) to feel uncertain about something; to be suspicious of it
533. Downpour: (noun) a very heavy rainfall
534. Dowry: (noun) an amount of wealth handed over by a woman's family to her husband on marriage
535. Drake: (noun) a male duck
536. Dramatic: (adjective) relating to plays, the theatre or acting in general
537. Draw: (verb) to make a picture of something or someone, especially with a pencil
538. Drawer: (noun) a sliding lidless storage box fitted as part of a desk or other piece of furniture
539. Drill: (noun) a tool for boring holes
540. Drizzle: (noun) fine light rain
541. Drop: (verb) to fall or allow to fall
542. Drought: (noun) a prolonged lack of rainfall

543. Drowsy: (adjective) sleepy; quiet and peaceful
544. Dry: (adjective) free from or lacking moisture or wetness
545. Dull: (adjective) of colour or light: lacking brightness or clearness
546. Dump: (verb) to put something down heavily or carelessly
547. Dung: (noun) animal excrement
548. Dusky: (adjective) partially dark; shadowy
549. Dust: (noun) earth, sand or household dirt in the form of fine powder
550. Duty: (noun) an obligation or responsibility or the awareness of it
551. Dynamic: (adjective) full of energy, enthusiasm and new ideas
552. Dynasty: (noun) a succession of rulers from the same family
553. Eager: (adjective) feeling or showing great desire or enthusiasm
554. Eagle: (noun) any of various kinds of large birds of prey
555. Ear: (noun) the sense organ that is concerned with hearing
556. Earn: (verb) to gain (money, wages, one's living, etc.) by working
557. Earnings: (noun) money earned
558. Ease: (noun) freedom from pain, anxiety or embarrassment
559. Ebony: (noun) a type of extremely hard, heavy and almost black wood
560. Echo: (noun) the repeating of a sound caused by the sound waves striking a surface and coming back
561. Eclipse: (noun) the total or partial
562. Economics: (noun) the study of the production, distribution, and consumption of money, goods and services
563. Edge: (noun) the part farthest from the middle of something; a border or boundary
564. Education: (noun) the process of teaching
565. Effigy: (noun) a crude doll or model representing a person, on which hatred of or contempt for, the person can be expressed
566. Elate: (verb) to make someone intensely happy
567. Elect: (verb) to choose someone to be an official or representative by voting

568. Electricity: (noun) the energy which exists in a negative form in electrons and in a positive form in protons, and also as a flowing current usually of electrons
569. Elite: (noun) the best, most important or most powerful people within society
570. Elusive: (adjective) difficult to find or catch
571. Embrace: (verb) to hold someone closely in the arms affectionately or as a greeting
572. Empire: (noun) a group of nations or states under the control of single ruler or ruling power
573. Enable: (verb) to make someone able; to give the necessary means, power or authority
574. Encamp: (verb) to settle in a camp
575. Enemy: (noun) a person who is actively opposed to someone else
576. Energetic: (adjective) the capacity for vigorous activity, liveliness or vitality
577. Engage: (verb) to take someone on as a worker
578. Enhance: (verb) to improve or increase the value, quality or intensity of something
579. Enormous: (adjective) extremely large
580. Entertain: (verb) to provide amusement or recreation for someone
581. Entry: (noun) the act of coming or going in
582. Epoch: (noun) a major division or period of history or of a person's life, etc., usually marked by some important event
583. Eskimo: (noun) (now often offensive) an Inuit person
584. Evade: (verb) to escape or avoid something or someone by trickery or skill
585. Evidence: (noun) information, etc. that gives grounds for belief; that which points to, reveals or suggests something
586. Examine: (verb) to inspect, consider or look into something closely
587. Except: (verb) to leave out or exclude
588. Excite: (verb) to make someone feel lively expectation or a pleasant tension and thrill

589. Exile: (noun) enforced or regretted absence from one's country or town, especially for a long time and often as a punishment
590. Exist: (verb) to be, especially to be present in the real world or universe rather than in the story or imagination
591. Expel: (verb) to dismiss from or deprive someone of membership of a club, school, etc., usually permanently as punishment for misconduct
592. Expense: (noun) the act of spending money or the amount of money spent
593. Explain: (verb) to make something clear or easy to understand
594. Export: (verb) to send or take (goods, etc.) to another country, especially for sale
595. Expose: (noun) a formal statement of facts, especially one that introduces an argument
596. Express: (verb) to put something into words
597. Extrovert: (noun) someone who is sociable, outgoing and talkative
598. Fabricate: (verb) to invent or make up (a story, evidence, etc.)
599. Face: 1. (noun) the front part of the head, from forehead to chin, 2. (verb) to look at or look in some direction
600. Facility: (noun) an arrangement, feature, etc. that enables someone to do something
601. Fact: (noun) a thing known to be true, to exist or to have happened
602. Faint: 1. (adjective) dim, 2. (verb) to lose consciousness
603. Fair: (adjective) 1. not using dishonest methods or discrimination, 2. having light-coloured hair and skin
604. Faith: (noun) trust, confidence or strong belief, e.g., in God
605. Falcon: (noun) a type of long-winged bird of prey
606. Fall: (verb) to descend, drop or collapse
607. Fame: (noun) the condition of being famous
608. Familiar: (adjective) well known or recognizable
609. Famous: (adjective) well known
610. Fan: (noun) 1. any device that creates air currents, 2. a supporter or admirer

611. Fancy: (verb) to have a desire for something
612. Fang: (noun) a sharp, pointed tooth of an animal
613. Far: (adjective) at, to or from a great distance
614. Fare: (noun) the price paid by a passenger to travel on a bus, train, etc.
615. Fascinate: (verb) to interest strongly
616. Fatal: (adjective) causing death
617. Father: (noun) a male parent
618. Fault: (noun) a flaw or defect in an object; responsibility for something wrong
619. Favour: (noun) a kind or helpful action; an unfair preference
620. Fear: (verb) to be afraid of (someone or something)
621. Feast: (noun) a large rich meal, especially one prepared to celebrate something
622. Feather: (noun) any of the light growths that form the soft covering of a bird
623. Fence: (noun) a barrier, e.g., of wood or wire, for enclosing or protecting land
624. Fenugreek: (noun) a plant with strong-smelling seeds used in cooking
625. Fertile: (adjective) of land, soil, etc.: containing the nutrients required to support an abundant growth of crops, plants, etc.
626. Fervour: (noun) passionate enthusiasm; intense eagerness
627. Fetch: (verb) to go and get something, and bring it back
628. Field: (noun) a piece of open grassland, an area
629. Fig: (noun) a pear-shaped fruit full of tiny seeds
630. Fight: 1. (verb) to attack or engage in combat, 2. (noun) a violent struggle
631. File: (noun) a collection of papers, especially dealing with a particular subject
632. Fin: (noun) a thin wing-like projection on a fish's body for propelling it through the water
633. Fire: 1. (noun) flames coming from something that is burning, 2. (verb) to dismiss someone from employment
634. Fireplace: (noun) a recess for a fire, mostly in homes
635. Fist: (noun) a tightly closed hand

636. Fixed: (adjective) fastened, permanent, immovable, concentrated
637. Flash: (noun) a sudden and short blaze of light
638. Flax: (noun) a plant cultivated for the fibre of its stem and for its seeds
639. Flee: (verb) to run away quickly
640. Flesh: (noun) in animals: the soft tissues covering the bones, the meat of animals
641. Flicker: (verb) to burn or shine unsteadily by alternately flashing bright and dying away again
642. Flock: (noun) a group of creatures, especially birds or sheep
643. Flour: (noun) the finely ground meal of wheat or other cereal grain
644. Flow: (verb) to move along like water
645. Flower: (noun) the structure that bears the reproductive organs in a flowering plant
646. Flush: 1. (verb) to blush or make someone blush, 2. (adjective) level or even with an adjacent surface
647. Fly: 1. (noun) a two-winged insect, 2. (verb) to move through air using wings or similar structures
648. Fodder: (noun) any bulk feed for cattle and other livestock
649. Foe: (noun) an enemy
650. Fog: (noun) a suspension of tiny water droplets or ice crystals forming a cloud close to ground surface
651. Foil: (noun) metal beaten or rolled out into thin sheets
652. Fold: (verb) to double something over so that one part lies on top of another
653. Follow: (verb) to go or come after someone or something
654. Folly: (noun) foolishness, a foolish act
655. Football: (noun) 1. games played with a large ball that players try to kick or head into the opposite team's goal, 2. The ball used in the game
656. Forbade: (verb) past tense of forbid: to command not, to refuse to allow
657. Force: (noun) strength, impact or influence
658. Foreign: (adjective) not belonging where found

659. Forget: (verb) to be unable to remember something
660. Forgive: (verb) to stop being angry with someone
661. Fork: (noun) an eating or cooking implement with prongs for spearing and lifting food
662. Forlorn: (adjective) exceedingly unhappy
663. Form: (noun) 1. shape, 2. A document with printed text and spaces for the insertion of information
664. Fortitude: (noun) uncomplaining courage in pain or misfortune
665. Fowl: (noun) a farm bird, e.g., a chicken or turkey
666. Fox: (noun) a carnivorous mammal of the dog family, with a pointed muzzle, large pointed ears and a long bushy tail
667. Frail: (adjective) easily broken or destroyed
668. Frame: (noun) a structure that surrounds and supports something
669. Fraud: (noun) an act or instance of deliberate deception, with the intention of gaining some benefit
670. Freak: (noun) a person, animal or plant of abnormal shape or form, someone or something odd and unusual
671. Free: (adjective) 1. not restricted, controlled or enslaved, 2. costing nothing
672. Frequently: (noun) recurring at short intervals
673. Fright: (noun) sudden fear
674. Frighten: (verb) to make someone afraid
675. Frost: (noun) a white deposit of ice crystals formed when water vapour comes into contact with a surface whose temperature is below freezing point
676. Frown: (verb) to wrinkle one's forehead and draw one's eyebrows together in worry, disapproval, deep thoughts, etc.
677. Fuel: (noun) any material that releases energy when it is burned and can be used as a source of heat or power.
678. Fulfil: (verb) 1. to carry out or perform a task, promise, etc., 2. to satisfy (requirements)
679. Funds: (noun) a sum of money on which some enterprise is founded or on which the expenses of a project are supported

680. Funnel: (noun) a tube with a cone-shaped opening through which liquid, etc. can be poured into a narrow necked container
681. Fur: (noun) the thick fine soft coat of a hairy animal
682. Furnish: (verb) to provide with furniture
683. Furniture: (noun) movable household equipment such as tables, chairs, beds, etc.
684. Further: (adjective) more distant or remote than something else
685. Fury: (noun) an outburst of violent anger
686. Fuss: (noun) agitation and excitement, eso over something trivial
687. Futile: (adjective) unproductive, foolish, vain or pointless
688. Future: (noun) the time to come, events that still to occur
689. Gain: (verb) to get, obtain or earn
690. Gale: (noun) any strong wind
691. Garment: (noun) an article of clothing
692. Gaze: (verb) to stare fixedly
693. Gear: (noun) a toothed wheel or disc that engages with another wheel or disc having a different number of teeth, and turns it, so transmitting motion from one rotating shaft to another.
694. Gems: (noun) semi-precious or precious stones or crystals
695. Generation: (noun) the act or process of producing something
696. Generous: (adjective) giving or willing to give or help unselfishly
697. Gently: (adjective) lightly and softly
698. Genuine: (adjective) not artificial or fake
699. Geography: (noun) the scientific study of earth's surface, especially its physical features, climate, resources, population, etc.
700. Geometry: (noun) the branch of mathematics dealing with lines, angles, shapes, etc. and their relationships
701. Germs: (noun) micro-organisms, especially bacteria or viruses that cause diseases

702. Ghosts: (noun) the spirit of a dead person when its visible in some form to a living person
703. Giant: (noun) a huge, extremely strong creature of human form
704. Gifted: (adjective) having a great natural ability
705. Giraffe: (noun) a very tall African mammal with an extremely long neck and legs, a small head, and large eyes
706. Girdle: (noun) a belt or cord worn round the waist
707. Gleam: (noun) a gentle glow
708. Glint: (verb) to give off tiny flashes of bright light
709. Glitter: (verb) to shine with bright flashes of light
710. Gloomy: (adjective) 1. dimly lit, 2. sad or depressed
711. Glow: (verb) to give out a steady heat or light without flames
712. Goal: (noun) 1. an aim or purpose, 2. in various sports: a set of posts with a crossbar, through which the ball is struck to score points
713. Goat: (noun) a herbivorous mammal, noted for its physical agility and sure-footedness
714. Gobble: (verb) to eat hurriedly and noisily
715. Gold: (noun) a soft yellow precious metal used for making jewellery, coins, etc.
716. Golf: (noun) a game played on a golf course, the object being to hit a small ball into each of a series of nine or eighteen holes using a set of clubs, taking as few strokes as possible

> **Did you know?**
>
> The word gobble is an onomatopoeic word and imitates the sound made by a turkey. It describes the act of eating food akin to how a turkey might hurriedly consume its food.

717. Goodies: (noun) things considered pleasant or desirable
718. Goose: (noun) any of numerous large, wild or domesticated waterfowl, with a stout body, long neck, webbed feet and a broad flat bill
719. Gossip: (noun) talk or writing about the private affairs of others; often in a spiteful and untrue manner
720. Gourd: (noun) a climbing plant that produces a large fruit with a hard woody outer shell

721. Grace: (noun) 1. elegance and beauty of form or movement, 2. politeness
722. Gradual: (noun) developing or happening slowly
723. Gramophone: (noun) a record player, especially an old-fashioned one
724. Grass: (noun) any of a family of plants that typically have long narrow leaves, a jointed upright hollow stem and flowers with no petals
725. Grate: (verb) to cut something into shreds by rubbing it against a rough or perforated surface
726. Grave: (noun) a trench dug in the ground for burying a dead body
727. Greasy: (adjective) Having an oily appearance or slippery texture
728. Green: (adjective) like the colour of leaves of most plants
729. Grey: (adjective) of a colour between black and white, the colour of ash
730. Grief: (noun) a great sorrow and unhappiness, especially at someone's death
731. Grieve: (verb) to feel grief, especially at a death, to mourn
732. Grin: (verb) to smile broadly, showing the teeth
733. Groin: (noun) the part of human body where the lower abdomen joins the upper thigh
734. Groom: 1. (noun) a bridegroom, 2. (verb) to clean, brush an animal, especially horse, 3. (verb) to train or prepare someone
735. Growl: (verb) of animals: to make a deep rough sound in the throat, showing hostility
736. Grudge: (noun) a long-standing feeling of resentment
737. Grumble: (verb) to complain in a bad-tempered way
738. Grumpy: (adjective) bad-tempered
739. Grunt: (verb) to make a low rough sound in the back of the throat
740. Guava: (noun) a small tropical tree or its edible yellow pear-shaped fruit
741. Guest: (noun) someone who receives hospitality in the home of or at the expense of, another

742. Guile: (noun) the ability to deceive or trick
743. Guineas: (noun) an old obsolete British gold coin
744. Gum: (noun) the firm fibrous flesh surrounding the roots of the teeth
745. Gush: (verb) of a liquid to flood out suddenly and violently
746. Gutter: (noun) a channel for carrying away rainwater, fixed to the edge of a roof or built between a pavement and a road
747. Gypsy: (noun) a member of a travelling people, originally from Northwest India, now scattered throughout Europe and North America
748. Habit: (noun) a tendency to behave, think, etc. in a specific way
749. Hailstones: (noun) grains of ice which fall from the clouds when there are strong rising air currents
750. Hair: (noun) a thread-like structure growing from the skin of animals
751. Halt: (noun) an interruption or stop to movement or growth
752. Ham: (noun) the top part of the back leg of a pig
753. Hammer: (noun) a tool with a heavy metal head on the end of a handle
754. Hamper: (verb) to hinder the progress or movement of someone or something
755. Hand: (noun) in humans: the extremity of the arm below the wrist
756. Happen: (verb) to take place or occur
757. Harden: (verb) to make or become hard or harder
758. Hardly: (adjective) barely, scarcely
759. Harm: (noun) physical, emotional injury or damage
760. Harsh: (adjective) 1. rough, grating, unpleasant to senses, 2. strict, cruel
761. Hatchet: (noun) a small axe that can be held in one hand
762. Hawk: (noun) a relatively small diurnal bird of prey with short, rounded wings
763. Hay: (noun) grass, clover, etc. that has been cut and dried in the field and stored for use as winter fodder for livestock.

764. Hazy: (adjective) misty, not clear
765. Head: 1. (noun) the uppermost or foremost part of an animal's body, containing the brain and the organs of sight, smell, hearing and taste, 2. (noun) the person with the most authority in an organization or group, 3. (verb) to move in a certain direction
766. Hear: (verb) to perceive sounds with the ear, to listen
767. Heart: (noun) a muscular organ that contracts and pumps blood around the body
768. Hearth: (noun) the floor of a fireplace or the area surrounding it
769. Heatwave: (noun) a prolonged period of unusually hot dry weather
770. Heaven: (noun) the place believed to be the abode of God, angels and the righteous, after death
771. Heel: (noun) the rounded back part of the foot below the ankle
772. Heir: (noun) someone who by law receives or is entitled to receive property, wealth, a title, etc. when the previous owner dies
773. Hell: (noun) the place or state of infinite punishment for the wicked after dead
774. Hen: (noun) a female bird of any kind
775. Hence: (adjective) for this reason or cause
776. Here: (adjective) at, in or to this place
777. Hermit: (noun) an ascetic who leads an isolated life for religious reasons
778. Heron: (noun) a large wading bird with a long neck and legs
779. Hibiscus: (noun) a tropical tree or shrub with large brightly coloured flowers
780. Hiccough: (noun) an involuntary spasm of the diaphragm and a burping sound caused by this.
781. Hide: (verb) to put, keep or conceal something from sight
782. Hind: (adjective) at the back
783. Hippopotamus: (noun) a hoofed mammal with a thick skin, large head and short legs

784. Hire: (verb) 1. to procure the temporary use of something in exchange for payment, 2. To employ or engage someone for wages
785. History: (noun) an account of past events and developments
786. Hoax: (noun) a deceptive trick either played humorously or maliciously
787. Hockey: (noun) a ball game played by two teams of eleven players with long clubs curved at one end, each team attempting to score goals
788. Hog: 1. (noun) a general name for a pig, 2. (verb) to take, use, occupy selfishly
789. Hold: (verb) to have or keep in one's hand or hands
790. Holes: (noun) hollow areas or cavities in something solid
791. Holy: (adjective) associated with God or gods; religious or sacred
792. Honest: (adjective) not inclined to steal, cheat or lie; truthful and trustworthy
793. Hood: (noun) a flexible covering for the whole head and the back of the neck, 2. A folding roof or cover on a car
794. Hoof: (noun) the horny structure that grows beneath and covers the ends of the digits on the feet of certain mammals
795. Hope: (noun) a desire for something, with some confidence or expectation of success
796. Horn: (noun) one of a pair of hard, hollow outgrowths, usually pointed, on the heads of many ruminant animals
797. Horror: (noun) intense fear, loathing or disgust
798. Horse: (noun) a large hoofed mammal, with a long neck a mane and long legs, used for riding or for pulling or carrying loads
799. Hound: (noun) a type of dog used in hunting
800. House: (noun) a building in which people, especially a single family, live
801. Hug: (verb) to hold tightly in one's arms, especially to show love
802. Huge: (adjective) very large or enormous
803. Human: (adjective) relating or belonging to people

804. Humble: (adjective) having a low opinion of oneself and one's abilities, etc.
805. Humid: (adjective) damp, moist
806. Hungry: (adjective) having a need or craving for food
807. Hunting: (noun) an act of chasing and killing wild birds or animals for food or sport
808. Hurt: (verb) to injure or to cause emotional or physical pain to
809. Husband: (noun) a man to whom a woman is married
810. Hut: (noun) a small and crudely built house, usually made of wood
811. Hyena: (noun) a dog-like mammal that feeds on carrion
812. Ideal: (adjective) best possible or conceivable
813. Identity (noun) who or what a person or a thing is
814. Idle: (adjective) not in use
815. Illegal: (adjective) not legal, not authorized by law
816. Impel: (verb) to push, drive or urge something forward
817. Imply: (verb) to suggest or express something indirectly
818. Import: (verb) to bring (goods, etc.) into a country from another country
819. Impress: (verb) to produce a strong and usually favourable impression on someone
820. Improve: (verb) to make or become better or of higher quality or value
821. Incessant: (adjective) going on without stopping
822. Incident: (noun) an event or occurrence
823. Incompetent: (adjective) lacking the necessary skill, ability or qualifications, especially for a job
824. Indeed: (adjective) without any question, in truth
825. Indicate: (verb) to point out or show
826. Indiscretion: (noun) an act of giving away too many secrets or too much information
827. Indivisible: (adjective) not able to be divided or separated
828. Indulging: (verb) to allow oneself or someone else pleasure or the pleasure of a specified thing

829. Infinity: (noun) space, time, distance or quantity that is without limit
830. Inflation: (noun) a general increase in the level of prices caused by an increase in the amount of money and credit available
831. Influence: (noun) the power that one person or thing has to affect another
832. Inhale: (verb) to draw (air, smoke, etc.) into lungs; to breathe in
833. Injured: (adjective) to be physically harmed or damaged by someone or something
834. Injustice: (noun) unfairness or lack of justice
835. Inquire: (verb) to seek or ask for information
836. Insect: (noun) an invertebrate animal, such as fly, beetle, ant or bee, typically with a segmented body and two pairs of wings
837. Inside: (noun) the inner side, surface or part of something
838. Insipid: (adjective) having little or no interest or liveliness
839. Insist: (verb) to maintain or assert something firmly
840. Install: (verb) to put something in place and make it ready to use
841. Instance: (noun) 1. an example, 2. a particular stage in a process
842. Instil: (verb) to impress, fix or plant (ideas, feelings, etc.) slowly or gradually in mind
843. Instinct: (noun) an unlearned and inherited response to a stimulus
844. Insult: (verb) to speak rudely or offensively to or about someone or something
845. Intention: (noun) an aim or purpose
846. Interpret: (verb) to explain the meaning of (something)
847. Intervene: (verb) to involve oneself in something which is happening in order to affect the outcome
848. Intestine: (noun) the muscular tube-like part of the alimentary canal between the stomach and the anus
849. Intimate: (adjective) marked by or sharing a close and affectionate relationship

850. Invade: (verb) 1. to enter (a country) by force with an army, 2. to interfere with (a person's privacy, rights, etc.)
851. Invest: (verb) 1. to put money into a company or business, 2. To devote (time, energy, effort, etc.) to something
852. Invisible: (adjective) not able to be seen
853. Involved: (adjective) concerned, implicated
854. Iron: 1. (noun) a strong hard greyish metallic element that is naturally magnetic, 2. (noun) a triangular flat-bottomed tool used for smoothing out creases and pressing clothes, 3. (verb) to smooth the creases out of or press (e.g., clothes) with an iron
855. Irresolute: (adjective) hesitating or doubtful, not able to take firm decisions
856. Irrigation: (noun) supply of water to a land
857. Jackal: (noun) a scavenging animal, closely related to the dog and wolf
858. Jar: (noun) a wide-mouthed cylindrical container usually made of glass
859. Javelin: (noun) a light spear for throwing, either as a weapon or in sport
860. Jaw: (noun) either of the two bony structures that form the framework of the mouth and in which the teeth are set
861. Jay: (noun) a bird of the crow family which has pinkish-brown plumage and blue, black and white bands on its wings
862. Jealous: (adjective) envious of someone else, their possessions, success, talents, etc.
863. Jibe: (verb) to mock, scoff or jeer
864. Join: (verb) to connect or unite
865. Joke: (noun) a humorous story
866. Jolly: (adjective) good-humoured, cheerful
867. Journalist: (noun) someone who is in the profession of writing for newspapers and magazines or for radio and television
868. Jug: (noun) a deep container for liquids, with a handle and a shaped lip for pouring
869. Jump: (verb) to spring off the ground, pushing off with the feet

870. Jungle: (noun) an area of dense vegetation, especially in a tropical region
871. Justice: (noun) the quality of being just; fairness
872. Jute: (noun) fibre from certain types of tropical bark
873. Kangaroo: (noun) a marsupial mammal with a thick tail and large powerful hind legs adapted for leaping
874. Kerosene: (noun) a combustible oily mixture of hydrocarbons obtained mainly by distillation of petroleum, used as a fuel
875. Kettle: (noun) a container with a spout, lid and handle, for boiling water
876. Kid: 1. (noun) a child, a young person, 2. (verb) to fool or deceive
877. Kidney: (noun) either of a pair of organs at the back of the abdomen whose function is to remove waste products from blood
878. Kiln: (noun) a heated oven or furnace used for drying timber, grain or hops or for firing bricks, pottery, etc.
879. Kind: 1. (adjective) friendly, helpful, generous or considerate, 2. (adjective) a group, class or type
880. Kindle: (verb) to start or make something start burning
881. King: (noun) a male ruler of a nation
882. Kite: (noun) 1. a bird of prey of the hawk family, 2. a light frame covered in paper with a long holding string attached to it, for flying in the air
883. Kitten: (noun) a young cat
884. Knee: (noun) the joint in the middle of the leg
885. Knife: (noun) a cutting instrument, typically in the form of a blade fitted into a handle or into machinery
886. Knot: (noun) a join or tie-in string made by looping the ends around each other and pulling tight
887. Know: (verb) to be aware of or be certain about something,
888. Lack: (verb) to be without or to have too little of something
889. Lad: (noun) (old-fashioned) a boy or youth
890. Ladle: (noun) a large spoon with a long handle and deep bowl
891. Laid: (verb) to have placed something on a surface, especially in a horizontal position

892. Lake: (noun) a large area of water, surrounded by land
893. Lamb: (noun) a young sheep
894. Lamp: (noun) a piece of equipment designed to give out light
895. Land: (noun) the solid part of earth as opposed to the area covered by water
896. Landlord: (noun) a man who rents property out to a tenant
897. Lantern: (noun) a lamp or light contained in a transparent case
898. Lap: (noun) the front part of the body from the waist to the knees, when in sitting position
899. Lark: (noun) a joke or piece of fun

After, afterwards, and later are all adverbs or conjunctions used to indicate time, but they differ in their usage slightly.

After: This word is usually used as a preposition or conjunction to indicate something that happens following a specific event or time. For example, 'We can go out after dinner.'

Afterwards: This word is used as an adverb to refer to a time following an event that has already been mentioned, often more formal than 'later.' For example, 'We went to the movie and had dinner afterwards.'

Later: This word is used as an adverb to indicate a time subsequent to the present or to a specific time that has been mentioned or is implied. It can be used more flexibly in informal contexts. For example, 'I'll see you later.'

900. Later: 1. (adjective) more late, 2. (adverb) at some time after or in the near future
901. Lauded: (verb) to have praised highly
902. Laugh: (verb) to make spontaneous sounds associated with happiness, amusement, scorn, etc.
903. Launch: (verb) 1. to send into (water, space), 2. to bring (a new product) on to the market
904. Lawyer: (noun) a person employed in the legal profession, especially a solicitor
905. Lay: (verb) to place something on a surface especially in a horizontal position

906. Lead: 1. (verb) to guide by going in front, 2. (noun) a highly toxic metallic element
907. Leader: (noun) someone or something that leads or guides others
908. Leaf: (noun) an expanded outgrowth, usually green and flattened, from the stem of a green plant
909. Least: (adverb) in the slightest or lowest degree
910. Leave: (verb) to go away from someone or somewhere
911. Leg: (noun) one of the limbs on which animals, birds and people walk and stand
912. Legend: (noun) 1. a traditional story which is popularly regarded as true, but not confirmed as such, 2. Someone famous about whom popularly believed stories are told
913. Leisure: (noun) free time, especially when a person can relax pursue a hobby, etc.
914. Lend: (verb) to allow someone to use something on the understanding that it (or its equivalent) will be returned
915. Length: (noun) the distance from one end of an object to the other, normally the longest dimension
916. Leopard: (noun) a large member of the cat family of Africa and Asia, with a black spotted tawny coat or a completely black coat
917. Letter: (noun) 1. a conventional written or printed mark, usually part of an alphabet, used to represent a speech sound or sounds, 2. A written or printed message normally sent by post in an envelope
918. Licence: (noun) an official document that allows someone to own something or that gives permission to do something
919. Lick: (verb) to pass the tongue over in order to moisten, taste or clean
920. Lid: (noun) a removable or hinged cover for a pot, box, etc.
921. Lifeless: (adjective) dead or unconscious
922. Lift: (verb) to raise or rise to a higher position
923. Lily: (noun) a plant with an underground bulb, narrow leaves, and white or brightly coloured flowers
924. Limbs: (noun) arms, legs or wings

925. Linen: (noun) cloth made from flax
926. Linger: (verb) to remain for a long time
927. Linguistics: (noun) the study of languages
928. Lion: (noun) a member of the cat family, found mainly in Africa, with a tawny coat, a tufted tail, and, in the male, a thick mane
929. Lip: (noun) either of the two fleshy parts which form the edge of the mouth
930. Liquor: (noun) strong alcoholic, especially distilled, drink
931. Listen: (verb) to try to hear, to pay attention
932. Literature: (noun) written material, such as novels, poems and plays, that is valued for its language, content, etc.
933. Litter: (noun) discarded paper, rubbish, etc. lying in a public space
934. Liver: (noun) a large dark red glandular organ whose main function is to regulate the chemical composition of blood
935. Loan: (noun) something lent, especially money lent at interest
936. Lock: 1. (noun) a mechanical device usually consisting of a sliding bolt moved by turning a key, dial, etc., 2. (verb) to fasten (a door, box, etc.) with a lock.
937. Lodging: (noun) a room or rooms rented in someone else's home; temporary accommodation
938. Loin: (noun) the area of the body in humans and some animals stretching from the bottom rib to the pelvis
939. Lonely: (adjective) of a person: sad because they have no companions or friends
940. Long: (adjective) measuring a great distance in space from one end to the other
941. Loom: (noun) a machine that weaves thread into fabric
942. Lord: (noun) a master or ruler
943. Lose: (verb) to fail to keep or obtain something, especially because of a mistake, carelessness, etc.
944. Lover: (noun) someone who loves someone else, especially in a romantic or sexual way
945. Lower: 1. (adjective) not as high in position, status, height, value, etc., 2. (verb) to pull down

946. Loyalty: (noun) the state or quality of being faithful and true
947. Lucky: (adjective) having good fortune
948. Lump: (noun) a small solid mass that has no definite shape
949. Lunch: (noun) a light meal eaten in the middle of the day
950. Lung: (noun) one of a pair of respiratory organs which remove carbon dioxide from the blood and replace it with oxygen
951. Lust: (noun) a strong sexual desire
952. Macaw: (noun) any of numerous large brilliantly-coloured parrots with long tails, found mainly in tropical Central and South America
953. Magic: (noun) the supposed act or practice of using the power of supernatural forces, spells, etc., to affect people, objects and events
954. Magistrate: (noun) any public official administering the law
955. Magpie: (noun) a black-and-white bird of the crow family. Known for its habit of collecting shiny objects
956. Mahogany: (noun) a tall evergreen tree of tropical Africa and America, grown commercially for timber
957. Maid: (noun) a female servant
958. Majestic: (adjective) stately, dignified or grand
959. Male: (adjective) belonging or relating to the sex that produces sperm and fertilizes the egg cell produced by the female
960. Mallet: (noun) a hammer with a large head, usually made of wood
961. Manager: (noun) someone who manages a commercial enterprise, organization, etc.
962. Manners: (noun) behaviour towards others
963. Manual: 1. (adjective) belonging or relating to the hand or hands, 2. (noun) a book of instructions
964. Marble: (noun) a hard, metamorphic rock
965. Mare: (noun) an adult female horse, ass, zebra, etc.
966. Marrow: (noun) the soft tissue that fills the internal cavities of bones
967. Mat: (noun) a flat piece of any carpet-like material, used as a decorative or protective floor-covering

968. Matchbox: (noun) a small cardboard box for holding matching
969. Mathematics: (noun) the science dealing with measurements, numbers, quantities and shapes usually expressed as symbol
970. Mattress: (noun) a large, flat, fabric-covered pad, usually made of cotton, foam rubber or springs, used for sleeping on
971. Meadow: (noun) a low-lying field of grass, used for grazing animals or making hay
972. Meagre: (adjective) lacking in quality or quantity
973. Measure: (verb) to determine the size, volume of, usually with a specially made instrument or by comparing it to something else
974. Meat: (noun) the flesh of any animal used as food
975. Medicated: (adjective) having added a healing or health-giving substance
976. Medicine: (noun) any substance used to treat or prevent disease or illness
977. Meditate: (verb) to spend time in deep religious or spiritual contemplation, often with the mind in a practised state of emptiness
978. Melody: (noun) the sequence of single musical notes forming the core of a tune
979. Melt: (verb) to make or become soft or liquid, especially through the action of heat
980. Memory: (noun) the ability of the mind to remember
981. Mental: (adjective) belonging or relating to or done by using, the mind or intelligence
982. Mention: (verb) to speak or to make reference to something or someone
983. Menu: (noun) 1. the range of dishes available in a restaurant, 2. A set of options on a computer screen
984. Mere: (adjective) nothing more than
985. Merits: (noun) worth, excellence or praiseworthiness
986. Merry: (adjective) cheerful and lively
987. Messy: (adjective) untidy, dirty

988. Metal: (noun) any of a class of chemical elements with certain shared characteristic properties, most being shiny, malleable, ductile and good conductors of heat and electricity
989. Midnight: (noun) twelve o' clock at night
990. Midst: (noun) among it or in the centre of it
991. Migrate: (verb) 1. of animals and birds: to travel from one region to another at certain times of the year, 2. of people: to leave one place and settle in another
992. Mild: (adjective) gentle in temperament or behaviour
993. Million: (noun) the cardinal number 106, meaning a thousand thousands
994. Mine: 1. (pronoun) something or someone belonging to or connected with me, 2. (noun) an opening or excavation in the ground, used to remove minerals, metal ores, coal, etc. from the earth's crust
995. Miner: (noun) someone who works in a mine
996. Mineral: (noun) a naturally occurring substance that is inorganic, and has characteristic physical and chemical properties by which it may be identified
997. Mingle: (verb) to become or make something become blended or mixed
998. Mint: (noun) 1. an aromatic plant with small, white or purple flowers, widely grown as a garden herb, 2. a place where coins are produced under government authority
999. Minute: 1. (noun) a unit of time equal to 1/60th of an hour; 60 seconds, 2. (adjective) very small, precise
1000. Miracle: (noun) an act or event that breaks the laws of nature, and is therefore thought to be caused by the intervention of God or another supernatural force
1001. Mirror: (noun) a smooth highly polished surface, such as glass, coated with thin layer of metal, that reflects an image of what is in front of it
1002. Mirth: (noun) laughter
1003. Mischief: (noun) behaviour that annoys or irritates people but does not mean or cause any serious harm

1004. Miserable: (adjective) very unhappy; habitually bad-tempered or depressed
1005. Misery: (noun) great unhappiness or suffering
1006. Mission: (noun) a purpose for which a person or group of people are sent
1007. Mistake: (noun) an error or a regrettable action
1008. Modern: (adjective) belonging to the present or to recent times
1009. Modesty: (noun) not having or showing pride
1010. Mole: (noun) 1. a small insectivorous burrowing mammal, 2. a dark permanent spot on the skin
1011. Moment: (noun) a short while; a particular point in time
1012. Monarch: (noun) a king, queen or other non-elected sovereign with a hereditary right to rule
1013. Mongoose: (noun) a small mammal that preys on snakes, etc. and has a long body, pointed nose and a bushy tail
1014. Monkey: (noun) any mammal belonging to the primates other than a human, ape, chimpanzee, gibbon, orangutan or lemur
1015. Mop: (noun) a tool for for washing or wiping floors, consisting of a large sponge or a set of thick threads fixed on to the end of a long handle
1016. Morning: (noun) the part of the day from sunrise to midday or from midnight to midday
1017. Morrow: (noun) the following day
1018. Mortal: (adjective) certain to die at some future time
1019. Mortar: (noun) a mixture of sand, water and cement or lime, used to bond bricks or stones
1020. Mother: (noun) a female parent
1021. Mount: (verb) to get up on to
1022. Mourn: (verb) to feel or show deep sorrow at the death or loss of them or it
1023. Mouse: (noun) a small rodent with a grey or brown coat, pointed muzzle, bright eyes and a long hairless tail
1024. Moustache: (noun) hair growing across the top of the upper lip

1025. Mouth: (noun) an opening in the head through which food is taken in and speech and sound is emitted.
1026. Move: (verb) to change position or make something change position or go from one place to another
1027. Mud: (noun) soft, wet earth
1028. Muggy: (adjective) unpleasantly warm and damp weather
1029. Mule: (noun) the offspring of a male donkey and a female horse
1030. Mum: 1. (noun) a mother, 2. (adjective) silent
1031. Muscle: (noun) an animal tissue composed of bundles of fibres that are capable of contracting to produce movement of part of the body
1032. Mushroom: (noun) a type of fungus which consists of a short white stem supporting an umbrella-shaped cap
1033. Music (noun) the art of making sound in a rhythmically organized, harmonious form
1034. Musician: (noun) someone who is skilled in music, especially in performing or composing it
1035. Mutton: (noun) the flesh of an adult sheep, used as food
1036. Mynah: (noun) a large bird of the starling family which can be taught to imitate human speech
1037. Mysterious: (adjective) difficult or impossible to understand or explain
1038. Mythology: (noun) a collection of myths; the study of myths
1039. Nail: (noun) the hard structure at the tip of a finger or toe

Lamb meat too is divided into different cuts:

1. **Shoulder:** The shoulder cut includes meats like shoulder roast, blade chops, and shoulder chops. This meat is usually good for slow roasting and is used in stews.
2. **Neck:** This cut has tender meat and is perfect for braising and used in stews. It is high in fat and had a deep rich flavor.
3. **Rack:** A rack of lamb is taken from the ribs of the animal perpendicular to the spine. It is known for its tenderness and flavour and is usually used to make rib roast, rib chops and crown roast.

1040. Native: (adjective) being in or belonging to the place of one's upbringing
1041. Natural: (adjective) 1. unsurprising, 2. relating to nature
1042. Nature: (noun) the physical world and the forces that have formed and control it
1043. Naught: (noun) nothing
1044. Navel: (noun) the small hollow or scar at the point where the umbilical cord was attached to the foetus
1045. Nay: (exclamation) no
1046. Nearby: (adjective) a short distance away
1047. Nearly: (adjective) almost
1048. Necessary: (adjective) needed; essential
1049. Necessity: (noun) something necessary or essential
1050. Neck: (noun) the part of the body between the head and the shoulders
1051. Necklace: (noun) a string of beads, chain, etc. work around the neck as jewellery
1052. Nectar: (noun) a sugary substance produced in flowers, collected by bees to make honey
1053. Need: (verb) 1. to lack, 2. to be required
1054. Needle: (noun) a slender pointed sewing instrument with a hole for a thread
1055. Negro: (noun) (often offensive) a person belonging to or descended from one of the dark-skinned races originally from Africa

Did you know?

'Negro' is derived from the Spanish and Portuguese word for 'black'. In the US, the word was used as a racial classification during the nineteenth and early twentieth centuries. During the Civil Rights Movement activists and leaders preferred to shift away from the word and used terms like 'Black' or 'African American' instead. The term has become controversial and many now consider it outdated and offensive.

1056. Neighbour: (noun) a person who lives near or next door
1057. Nephew: (noun) the son of one's brother or sister or of the brother or sister of one's wife or husband
1058. Nerve: (noun) a cord that carries instructions and information between the brain or spinal cord and other parts of the body

1059. Nest: (noun) a structure built by birds, rats, wasps, etc. in which they lay eggs or give birth to and look after young
1060. Newspaper: (noun) a daily or weekly publication composed of folded sheets, containing news, advertisements, topical articles, correspondence, etc.
1061. Nibble: (verb) to take very small bites of something
1062. Niece: (noun) the daughter of one's brother or sister or of the brother or sister of one's wife or husband
1063. Night: (noun) the time of darkness between sunset and sunrise
1064. Nightingale: (noun) a small, brown thrush known for its melodious song, heard especially at night
1065. Noise: (noun) 1. a sound, 2. a harsh disagreeable sound
1066. Nomad: (noun) a member of a people without a permanent home, who travel from place to place seeking food and pasture
1067. Normal: (adjective) usual, not extraordinary
1068. Nose: (noun) the projecting organ above the mouth, with which one smells and breathes
1069. Nostril: (noun) either of the two external openings in the nose, through which one breathes and smell, etc.
1070. Notice: (noun) an announcement displayed or delivered publicly
1071. Nuisance: (noun) an annoying or troublesome person, thing or circumstance
1072. Numerous: (adjective) many
1073. Oak: (noun) any tree which produces acorns
1074. Obey: (verb) to do what one is told to do by someone
1075. Obligation: (noun) a moral or legal duty or tie
1076. Observance: (noun) the fact or act of obeying rules or keeping customs, etc.
1077. Observe: (verb) to notice or become conscious of (something)
1078. Obstacle: (noun) someone or something that obstructs or hinders
1079. Obstinacy: (noun) the act of refusing to change one's opinion or course of action
1080. Obtain: (verb) to get something; to become the owner

1081. Obvious: (adjective) easily seen or understood
1082. Occasion: (noun) a particular event or happening or the time at which it occurs
1083. Occult: (adjective) involving, using or dealing with that which is magical, mystical or supernatural
1084. Occupy: (verb) to have possession of or live in (a house, etc.)
1085. Occurrence: (noun) anything that occurs; an event
1086. Ocean: (noun) the continuous expanse of saltwater that covers about 70% of earth's surface
1087. Offer: 1. (verb) to put forward (a gift, payment or suggestion, etc.) for acceptance, refusal or consideration, 2. (noun) an act of offering
1088. Official: 1. (adjective) relating or belonging to an office or position of authority, 2. (noun) someone with a position of authority in an organization
1089. Oil: (noun) any greasy, viscous and usually flammable substance, insoluble in water, that is derived from animals, plants or mineral deposits or manufactured artificially
1090. Oily: (adjective) like oil, greasy
1091. Olive: (noun) a small evergreen tree cultivated mainly in the mediterranean region
1092. Omen: (noun) a circumstance, phenomenon, etc. that is regarded as a sign of a future event, either good or evil
1093. Omit: (verb) to leave (something) out, either by mistake or on purpose
1094. Only: 1. (adverb) not more than; just, 2. (adjective) without any others of the same type
1095. Orbit: 1. (noun) the elliptical path of one celestial body around another or of an artificial satellite, spacecraft, etc. around a celestial body, 2. (verb) to circle in space
1096. Order: (noun) 1. a state in which everything is in its proper place, 2. an arrangement of objects, 3. A command, instruction or direction
1097. Origin: (noun) a beginning or a starting point
1098. Original: (adjective) 1. relating to an origin or beginning, 2. An idea or concept not thought of before
1099. Orphan: (noun) a child who has lost both parents

1100. Ostrich: (noun) the largest living bird, native bird to Africa, having an extremely long neck and legs and only two toes on each foot
1101. Outskirts: (noun) the outer parts of a town or city
1102. Oven: (noun) a closed compartment or arched cavity in which substances may be heated, used especially for baking or roasting food, drying clay, etc.
1103. Overjoyed: (adjective) very glad
1104. Owed: (verb) under an obligation to pay (money) to someone
1105. Owl: (noun) a nocturnal bird of prey with a flat face, large forward-facing eyes and short, hooded beak
1106. Owner: (noun) someone who has (something) as a possession or property
1107. Ox: (noun) an adult castrated bull, used for pulling loads or as a source of meat
1108. Pace: (noun) 1. a single step, 2. rate of walking or running
1109. Packed: (adjective) 1. tied into a bundle for carrying, 2. filled tightly or compactly
1110. Paddy (noun) a field filled with water in which rice is grown
1111. Padlock: (noun) a detachable lock with a U-shaped bar that pivots to one side so that it can be passed through a thing or chain and locked into position
1112. Pail: (noun) a bucket
1113. Palace: (noun) the official residence of a sovereign, bishop, archbishop or president
1114. Palanquin: (noun) a light covered litter used in the Orient
1115. Palate: (noun) 1. the roof of the mouth, 2. the sense of taste
1116. Pale: (adjective) having less colour than normal
1117. Palm: (noun) 1. the inner surface of the hand between the wrist and the fingers, 2. a topical tree with a woody unbranched trunk bearing the crown of large fan-shaped or feather-shaped leaves
1118. Palmistry: (noun) the art of telling someone's fortune by reading the lines on the palm of their hand

1119. Pan: (noun) a pot, usually made of metal, used for cooking
1120. Pangs: (noun) brief but painfully acute feeling of hunger, guilt, remorse, etc.
1121. Panther: (noun) a leopard, especially a black one
1122. Paper: (noun) a material manufactured in thin sheets from pulped wood, rags or other forms of cellulose, used for writing and printing on, wrapping things, etc.
1123. Paramour: (noun) a lover
1124. Parched: (adjective) very thirsty, very dry
1125. Pardon: (verb) to forgive or excuse someone for a fault or offence
1126. Parents: (noun) father and mother
1127. Parrot: (noun) a brightly coloured bird, native to the forests of warmer regions, with a large head and a strong, hooked bill
1128. Particle: (noun) a tiny piece, a minute piece of matter
1129. Particular: (adjective) single, individually known or referred to
1130. Parting: (noun) the act of taking leave; separation
1131. Partition: (noun) something that divides an object into two parts
1132. Pass: (verb) 1. to come alongside and progress beyond something or someone, 2. to run, flow, progress, etc.
1133. Passenger: (noun) a traveller in a vehicle, boat, aeroplane, etc. driven, sailed or piloted by someone else
1134. Past: (adjective) referring to an earlier time, of long ago
1135. Pastime: (noun) a hobby
1136. Pastures: (noun) an area of grassland suitable or used for the grazing of livestock.
1137. Pat: (verb) to strike (a person or animal) lightly or affectionately with the palm of one's hand
1138. Pathetic: (adjective) pitiful, hopelessly inadequate
1139. Patient: (adjective) having or showing patience; (noun) a person receiving or registered to receive medical treatment
1140. Pay: (verb) to give money to (someone) in exchange for goods, services, etc.

1141. Peacock: (noun) a large bird, the male of which has a train of green and gold feathers with large spots which it fans showily during courtship
1142. Peahen: (noun) female of peacock
1143. Peasantry: (noun) the peasant class (of farm worker or small farmer)
1144. Pebbles: (noun) a small fragment of rock especially one worn around and smoothened by the action of water
1145. Peeler: (noun) a small knife or device for peeling fruit and vegetables
1146. Pen: (noun) a writing instrument that uses ink
1147. Perform: (verb) to carry out a task, job, action, etc.; to do or accomplish
1148. Perhaps: (adverb) possibly
1149. Period: (noun) a portion of time
1150. Perish: (verb) to be destroyed or ruined
1151. Periwinkle: (noun) A climbing plant with slender trailing stems, oval shiny green leaves and single bluish-purple flowers
1152. Permanent: (adjective) lasting or intended to last, indefinitely; not temporary
1153. Permit: (verb) to consent to or give permission for something
1154. Persist: (verb) to continue with it in spite of resistance, difficulty, discouragement, etc.
1155. Personal: (adjective) coming from someone as an individual, not from group or organization
1156. Persuade: (verb) to urge successfully
1157. Petition: (noun) a formal written request to an authority to take some action, signed by a large number of people
1158. Pheasant: (noun) a ground-dwelling bird, the male of which is usually brightly coloured and has a long pointed tail
1159. Phlegm: (noun) a thick yellowish substance produced by the mucous membrane that lines the air passages, brought up by coughing
1160. Physical: (adjective) 1. relating to the body rather than the mind, 2. relating to objects that can be seen or felt
1161. Physique: (noun) the structure of the body with regard to size, shape, proportions and muscular development

1162. Pick: (verb) to choose or select
1163. Pickle: (noun) a preserve of vegetables in vinegar, salt water or tart sauce
1164. Picture: (noun) a representation of someone or something on a flat surface a drawing, painting or photograph
1165. Piece: (noun) a portion of some material; any of the sections into which something (e.g., a cake) is divided
1166. Pig: (noun) a hoofed mammal with a stout bristle-covered body and a protruding flattened stout, kept for its meat
1167. Pigeon: (noun) a medium-sized bird with a plump body a rounded tail and dense soft grey, brown or pinkish plumage
1168. Pile: (noun) a number of things lying on top of each other
1169. Pilgrim: (noun) someone who makes a journey to a holy place as an act of reverence
1170. Pillar: (noun) a vertical post of wood, stone, metal or concrete serving as a support to a main structure
1171. Pillow: (noun) a cushion for the head, especially a large rectangular one on a bed
1172. Pincers: (noun) a hinged tool with two claw-like jaws joined by a pivot, used for gripping objects, pulling nails, etc.
1173. Pine: (noun) an evergreen coniferous tree with narrow needle-like leaves
1174. Pitcher: (noun) 1. large earthenware jug with either one or two handles, 2. the baseball player who throws the ball to the person batting to hit
1175. Place: (noun) a portion of the earth's surface, particularly one considered as a unit
1176. Plain: (adjective) all of one colour; unpatterned; undecorated
1177. Plait: (verb) to arrange something (especially hair) by interweaving three or more lengths of it
1178. Plan: (noun) a thought-out arrangement or method for doing something
1179. Plane: (noun) 1. a flat surface, either real or imaginary, 2. an aeroplane
1180. Plate: (noun) a shallow dish, especially one made of earthenware or porcelain, for serving food on

1181. Play: 1. (verb) to spend time in recreation, e.g., dancing about, kicking a ball around, doing things in make-believe, generally having fun, 2. (verb) to perform on (an instrument), 3. (noun) a dramatic piece for the stage or the performance of it
1182. Plead: (verb) to appeal earnestly to somebody
1183. Pleasure: (noun) the feeling of enjoyment or satisfaction
1184. Plenty: (noun) a lot
1185. Plough: 1. (noun) a bladed farm instrument used to turn over the surface of the soil and bury stubble, weeds, etc. in preparation for the cultivation of the crop, 2. (verb) to till or turn over (soil, land, etc.) with a plough
1186. Plume: (noun) a conspicuous feather of a bird
1187. Plump: (adjective) full, rounded or chubby
1188. Plunge: (verb) to dive, throw oneself, fall or rush headlong into or onto it
1189. Pocket: (noun) a extra piece sewn into or onto a garment to form a pouch for carrying things
1190. Poet: (noun) a male or female writer of poems
1191. Poetry: (noun) 1. the art of composing poems, 2. poems collectively
1192. Police: (noun) the body of men and women employed by the government of a country to keep order, enforce the law, prevent crime
1193. Pollution: (noun) the contamination of something with harmful substances or impurities
1194. Polo: (noun) a game, similar to hockey, played on horseback by two teams of four players, using long-handled mallets to propel the ball along the ground
1195. Ponder: (verb) to consider or contemplate something deeply
1196. Pony: (noun) any of the several small hardy breeds of horse
1197. Pool: (noun) 1. a small area of still water, 2. a reserve of money, personnel, vehicles, etc. used as a communal resource
1198. Poor: (adjective) not having sufficient money or means to live comfortably
1199. Poppy: (noun) a plant with large, brightly coloured, bowl-

shaped flowers and a fruit in the form of a capsule

1200. Popular: (adjective) liked or enjoyed by most people; accepted by many people
1201. Porch: (noun) a structure that forms a covered entrance to the doorway of a building
1202. Porcupine: (noun) a large nocturnal rodent with long black-and-white spikes or quills on the back and sides of its body
1203. Pores: (noun) small, usually round opening in the surface of a living organism through which fluids, gases and other substances can pass
1204. Pork: (noun) the flesh of pigs used as food
1205. Pose: (noun) 1. a position or attitude of the body, 2. an artificial way of behaving, adopted for effect
1206. Possess: (verb) 1. to own, 2. to have something as a feature or quality
1207. Possible: (adjective) able to be done
1208. Posterity: (noun) future generations
1209. Pot: (noun) a container, usually a deep round one, used as a cooking or serving utensil or for storage
1210. Potato: (noun) a plant that produces edible tubers and is a staple crop of temperate regions worldwide
1211. Pour: (verb) to flow or cause something to flow in a downward stream
1212. Poverty: (noun) the condition of being poor
1213. Powder: (noun) any substance in the form of fine dust-like particles
1214. Powerful: (adjective) having great power, strength or vigour
1215. Practically: (adverb) 1. very nearly, 2. in a practical manner
1216. Praise: (verb) to express admiration or approval of someone or something
1217. Prayer: (noun) an address to one's god, making a request or giving thanks
1218. Precious: (adjective) 1. valuable, 2. dear, beloved
1219. Preference: (noun) the preferring of one person, thing, etc. to another
1220. Prejudice: (noun) a biased opinion, based on insufficient knowledge

1221. Prescribe: (verb) to advise (a medicine) as a remedy, especially by completing a prescription
1222. Present: 1. (adjective) being at the place or occasion in question, 2. (noun) the present time, 3. (verb) to give or award something; to introduce formally
1223. Preserve: (verb) to save something from loss, damage, decay or deterioration
1224. Presume: (verb) to suppose (something to be the case) without proof
1225. Pretend: (verb) to act as if or give the impressions that, something is the case when it is not
1226. Pretty: (adjective) facially attractive; charming to look at; decorative
1227. Prevent: (verb) to stop someone from doing something
1228. Prey: (noun) an animal or animals hunted as food by another
1229. Prick: (verb) to pierce slightly with a fine point; to make (a hole) by this means
1230. Pride: (noun) a feeling of pleasure and satisfaction at one's own or another's accomplishments, possessions, etc.
1231. Priest: (noun) an official who performs religious rites
1232. Primitive: (adjective) relating or belonging to earliest times or the earliest stages of development
1233. Prince: (noun) the son of the sovereign; a non-reigning male member of a royal or imperial family
1234. Print: 1. (verb) to reproduce (text or pictures) on paper with ink, using a printing press or other mechanical means, 2. (noun) a mark made on a surface by the pressure of something in contact with it
1235. Probe: (noun) 1. a long, slender and usually metal instrument used by doctors to examine a wound, locate a bullet, etc., 2. a comprehensive investigation
1236. Proceed: (verb) to make one's way; to go on
1237. Process: (noun) a series of stages which a product passes through, resulting in the development or transformation of it
1238. Prodding: (verb) 1. poking, jabbing something, 2. nudging, prompting or spurring into action
1239. Prodigal: (adjective) heedlessly extravagant or wasteful

1240. Produce: (verb) 1. to bring out or present something to view, 2. to yield (crops, fruit, etc.)
1241. Product: (noun) something produced, e.g., thorough manufacture or agriculture
1242. Profit: (noun) the money gained from selling something for more than it originally cost
1243. Progress: (noun) 1. movement while travelling in any direction, 2. advances or development
1244. Project: (noun) a plan, scheme or proposal; a research or study assignment
1245. Promise: (verb) to give an undertaking (to do or not do something)
1246. Promulgate: (verb) to make (a decree) effective by means of an official public announcement
1247. Proper: (adjective) genuine; able to be correctly described as (a specified thing); appropriate
1248. Property: (noun) something someone owns
1249. Propound: (verb) to put forward (an idea or theory, etc.) for consideration
1250. Prospect: (noun) an expectation of something due or likely to happen
1251. Protect: (verb) to shield someone or something from danger; to guard them or it against injury, destruction, etc.; to keep safe
1252. Proud: (adjective) feeling satisfaction, delight, etc. with one's own or another's accomplishments, possessions, etc.
1253. Prove: (verb) to show something to be true, correct or a fact
1254. Provide: (verb) to supply
1255. Provoke: (verb) to annoy or infuriate someone, especially deliberately
1256. Prowess: (noun) skill, ability
1257. Psychology: (noun) the scientific study of the mind and behaviour of humans and animals
1258. Public: (adjective) relating to or concerning all the people of a country or community
1259. Publish: (verb) to prepare, produce and distribute (printed material, computer software, etc.) for sale to the public

1260. Pudding: (noun) any of several sweet or savoury foods usually made with flour and eggs and cooked by steaming, boiling or baking
1261. Pulse: (noun) the rhythmic beat that can be detected in an artery, as the heart pumps blood around the body
1262. Pumpkin: (noun) a trailing or climbing plant which produces yellow flowers and large round fruits at ground level
1263. Punish: (verb) to cause (an offender) to suffer for an offence
1264. Pupil: (noun) someone who is being taught; a schoolchild or student
1265. Puppy: (noun) a young dog
1266. Purple: (noun) a colour that is a mixture of blue and red
1267. Purpose: (noun) the object or aim in doing something
1268. Pus: (noun) the thick, usually yellowish liquid that forms in abscesses or infected wounds
1269. Push: (verb) to exert pressure to force it away from one
1270. Puzzled: (adjective) perplexed, mystified, bewildered or baffled
1271. Quail: 1. (noun) a small migratory game bird of the partridge family, 2. (verb) to lose courage
1272. Quality: (noun) the degree or extent of excellence of something
1273. Quarrel: (noun) an angry disagreement or argument
1274. Quench: to satisfy (thirst, a desire, etc.)
1275. Quick: (adjective) taking little time; fast, speedy
1276. Quiet: (adjective) making little or no noise
1277. Quilt: (noun) a type of bedcover that is made by sewing together two layers of fabric, usually with some kind of soft padding in between them
1278. Quite: (adjective) 1. completely, entirely, 2. to a high degree
1279. Quota: (noun) the proportional or allocated share or part that is or that should be, done, paid, contributed out of a total amount
1280. Quote: (verb) 1. to cite or offer (someone else or the words, ideas, of someone else) to substantiate an argument, 2. to submit or suggest (a price) for doing specified job or for buying something

1281. Rabbit: (noun) a small burrowing herbivorous mammal with long ears and a small stubby tail
1282. Race: (noun) a contest of speed between runners, cars, etc.
1283. Race: (noun) any of the major divisions of humankind distinguished by a particular set of physical characteristics
1284. Rack: (noun) a framework with rails, shelves, hooks, etc. for holding things
1285. Radiant: (adjective) 1. emitting electromagnetic radiation, 2. shining; beaming with joy, love or health
1286. Radio: (noun) 1. the use of radio waves to transmit and receive information such as television or radio programmes, telecommunication and computer data, without connecting wires, 2. a wireless device that receives and may also transmit information in this manner
1287. Radish: (noun) a plant with pungent-tasting red-skinned white roots which are eaten raw in salads
1288. Rage: (noun) anger; a passionate outburst
1289. Ragged: (adjective) of clothes: old, worn and tattered
1290. Raid: (noun) a sudden unexpected attack or an incursion by police for the purpose of making arrests or searching for suspected criminals or illicit goods
1291. Rainfall: (noun) a shower of rain; the amount of rain that falls in a certain place over a certain period, measured by depth of water
1292. Raise: (verb) to move or lift to a higher position or level
1293. Raisin: (adjective) a dried grape
1294. Ram: (noun) an uncastrated male sheep
1295. Ram: (verb) to force something down or into position by pushing hard
1296. Range: (noun) an area between limits within which things may move or function, etc.
1297. Rapid: (adjective) moving, acting or happening quickly
1298. Rare: (adjective) not done, found or occurring very often
1299. Rash: 1. (adjective) overhasty, 2. (noun) an outbreak of red spots or patches on the skin
1300. Rat: (noun) a rodent, similar to a mouse but larger

1301. Rate: (noun) 1. the number of times something happens within a given period of time, 2. a price or charge; often measured per unit
1302. Raven: (noun) a large blue-black bird of the crow family
1303. Ray: (noun) a narrow beam of light or radioactive particles
1304. Razor: (noun) a sharp-edged instrument used for shaving
1305. Ready: (adjective) prepared and available for use or action
1306. Realize: (verb) to become aware of; to know or understand
1307. Really: (adjective) 1. in fact, 2. very
1308. Rear: (noun) the back part; the area at the back
1309. Reason: (noun) 1. a justification or motive for an action, belief, 2. the power to think, form opinions and judgments, etc.
1310. Recapture: (verb) to capture again
1311. Receive: (verb) to get, be given or accept (something offered, sent, etc.)
1312. Recent: (adjective) happening, done, having appeared not long ago
1313. Reception: (noun) the act of receiving or fact of being received
1314. Reckless: (adjective) without consideration of the consequences, danger, etc.
1315. Recognize: (verb) 1. to identify (a person or thing known or experienced before), 2. to show approval of and gratitude for
1316. Recommend: (verb) to suggest as being suitable, acceptable, etc.
1317. Record: (noun) a formal written complaint of facts, events or information
1318. Recount: (verb) to tell a (story) in detail
1319. Rectitude: (noun) correctness of behaviour or judgment
1320. Redeem: (verb) 1. to buy back, 2. to recover something by payment or service
1321. Reduce: (verb) to make or become less, smaller, etc.
1322. Refill: (noun) a new filling for something which has become empty through use
1323. Refine: (verb) to make pure by removing dirt, waste, etc.

1324. Reflect: (verb) of a surface: to send back light, heat, sound, etc.; to give an image of someone or something
1325. Reform: (verb) to improve or remove faults from (a person, behaviour, etc.)
1326. Refresh: (verb) to make fresh again
1327. Refuge: (noun) shelter or protection from danger or trouble
1328. Refuse: (verb) to indicate unwillingness to do something
1329. Regain: (verb) to get back again or recover
1330. Regard: (verb) to consider in a specified way
1331. Regime: (noun) a system of government
1332. Region: (noun) a area of the world or of a country
1333. Regulation: (noun) an act or instance or the process or state of regulating or being regulated
1334. Reign: (noun) the period of time when a king or queen rules
1335. Reindeer: (noun) a large deer antlered in both sexes, found in arctic and subarctic regions
1336. Rejoice: (verb) to feel, show or express great happiness or joy
1337. Rejoin: (verb) 1. to say in reply, especially abruptly or wittily, 2. to join again
1338. Related: (adjective) belonging to the same family by birth or marriage
1339. Relative: (noun) a person who is related to someone else by birth or marriage
1340. Relax: (verb) to make (part of the body, one's grip, etc.) less tense or stiff
1341. Release: (verb) to free (a prisoner) from captivity
1342. Relegate: (verb) to move down to a lower grade, position, status, etc.
1343. Relic: (noun) a fragment or part of the object left after the rest has decayed
1344. Relieve: (verb) to lessen or stop (pain, worry, boredom, etc.)
1345. Religious: (adjective) relating to religion; following the rules or forms of worship of a particular religion very closely
1346. Remain: (verb) to be left after others or other parts, have been used up, taken away, etc.
1347. Remark: (verb) to notice and comment on something

1348. Remedy: (noun) a drug or treatment which cures or controls a disease
1349. Remember: (verb) to bring something from the past to mind, 2. to keep (a fact, idea, etc.)
1350. Remind: (verb) to cause someone to remember something or to do something
1351. Remorse: (noun) a deep feeling of guilt, regret and bitterness for something wrong or bad
1352. Remote: (adjective) far away, distant in time or place
1353. Remove: (verb) to move to a different place
1354. Renew: (verb) to make fresh or like new again
1355. Rent: (noun) money paid periodically to the owner of a property by a tenant in return for the use or occupation of that property
1356. Repeat: (verb) to say, do, etc. again or several times
1357. Replace: (verb) 1. to put back in a previous or proper position, 2. to take the place of or be a substitute for
1358. Reply: (verb) to answer or respond in words, writing or action
1359. Report: (noun) a detailed statement, description or account, especially one made after some form of investigation
1360. Repute: (verb) to consider (a having some specified quality, etc.)
1361. Requisite: (adjective) required or necessary
1362. Rescue: (verb) to save or set free from danger, captivity, etc.
1363. Research: (noun) detailed and careful investigation into some subject with the aim of discovering and applying new facts
1364. Resemble: (verb) to be like or similar to (someone or something else)
1365. Resident: (noun) someone who lives permanently in a particular place
1366. Resign: (verb) to give up a job
1367. Resolute: (adjective) determined with a fixed purpose or belief
1368. Resolve: (verb) to decide firmly or make up one's mind
1369. Resource: (noun) someone or something that provides a source of help, support, etc.; something helpful

1370. Respect: (noun) a good opinion; the state of being honoured, admired or well thought of
1371. Rest: (noun) a period of relaxation or freedom from work, activity, etc.
1372. Restore: (verb) to return (a building, painting, etc.) to a former condition by repairing, cleaning, etc.
1373. Restrain: (verb) to prevent (someone, oneself, etc.) from doing something
1374. Resume: (verb) to return to or begin again after an interruption
1375. Retaliate: (verb) to repay an injury, wrong, etc. in kind
1376. Return: (verb) to come or go back again to a former place, state, owner
1377. Revenge: (noun) malicious injury, harm or wrong done in return for injury, harm or wrong received
1378. Reverie: (noun) A state of dreamy and absent-minded thought
1379. Revive: (verb) to come or bring back to consciousness, strength, health, etc.
1380. Revolt: (verb) To rebel or rise up against the government, authority, etc.
1381. Revolver: (noun) a pistol with a revolving cylinder holding several bullets
1382. Reward: (noun) something given or received in return for work done, good behaviour, etc.
1383. Rhinoceros: (noun) a large herbivorous mammal with very thick skin and either one or two horns on its snout
1384. Rib: (noun) in vertebrates: any of the curved paired bones that articulate with the spine and form the chest wall
1385. Rich: (adjective) having a lot of money, property or possessions
1386. Rider: (noun) someone who rides
1387. Ridicule: (noun) contemptuous mockery or derision
1388. Right: 1. (adjective) indicating, relating to or on the side facing east from the point of view of someone or something facing north, 2. (noun) a power, privilege, title, etc.

1389. Rigor: (noun) the quality of being extremely thorough, accurate or strict; severity of strictness, often in relation to rules or discipline
1390. Ring: (noun) a small circle of gold, silver, etc., worn on the finger
1391. Ripe: (adjective) of fruit, grain, etc.: fully matured and ready to be eaten
1392. Rise: (verb) to get or stand up, from a sitting or lying position; to move upwards
1393. Risk: (noun) the chance or possibility of suffering loss, injury, damage, etc.
1394. Rites: (noun) a formal ceremony or observance, especially a religious one
1395. Ritual: (noun) a set order or words used in a religious ceremony
1396. Roar: (verb) to give a loud, growling cry
1397. Roast: (verb) to cook (meat, potatoes, etc.) by exposure to dry heat, especially in an oven
1398. Rob: (verb) to steal from (a person or place)
1399. Rock: a mass of one or more minerals that forms part of the Earth's crust e.g., granite, limestone, etc.
1400. Roll: 1. (noun) a cylinder or tube formed by rolling up anything flat, 2. (verb) to move or make something move by turning over and over
1401. Roof: (noun) the top outside covering of a building
1402. Root: (noun) 1. a structure in a plant which anchors the plant in the soil and absorbs water and nutrients, 2. a basic cause, source or origin of something
1403. Rope: (noun) a strong thick cord made by twisting fibres together
1404. Rose: (noun) a thorny shrub that produces large, often fragrant, flowers
1405. Rosy: (adjective) 1. pink, 2. hopeful or optimistic, often overly so
1406. Rotate: (verb) to turn or cause to turn about an axis like a wheel

1407. Round: 1. (adjective) shaped like or approximately like, a circle or a ball, 2. (noun) one of a recurring series of events, actions, etc.
1408. Routine: (noun) a regular or unvarying series of actions or way of doing things
1409. Row: (noun) a number of people or things arranged in a line
1410. Royal: (adjective) relating to or suitable for a king or queen
1411. Rub: (verb) to apply pressure and friction to something by moving one's hand or an object backwards and forwards
1412. Rude: (adjective) impolite or discourteous
1413. Ruffian: (noun) a coarse, violent, brutal or lawless person
1414. Ruin: (noun) a broken, destroyed, decayed or collapsed state
1415. Rule: (noun) a governing or controlling principle, regulation, etc.
1416. Rumble: (verb) to make a deep, low grumbling sound
1417. Run: (verb) to move so quickly that both or all feet are off the ground together for an instant during part of each step
1418. Rural: (adjective) relating to or suggestive of the countryside
1419. Rush: (verb) to move forward or go quickly
1420. Rustle: (verb) to make a soft whispering sound like that of dry leaves
1421. Sack: (noun) a large bag, especially one made of coarse cloth or paper
1422. Sacred: (adjective) devoted to a deity, saint, etc.; connected with religion or worship
1423. Saddle: (noun) a leather seat for horse riding, which fits on the horse's back and is secured under its belly
1424. Safe: (adjective) free from danger or harm
1425. Saffron: (noun) 1. a crocus which has lilac flowers with large bright orange stigmas; 2. a bright orange-yellow colour
1426. Sage: (noun) 1. a shrub with greyish green aromatic leaves, 2. someone of great wisdom and knowledge, especially an ancient philosopher
1427. Sailor: (noun) any member of a ship's crew, especially one who is not an officer

1428. Saliva: (noun) a clear liquid produced by the salivary glands of the mouth, which moistens and softens food and begins the process of digestion
1429. Saloon: (noun) a large public cabin or dining room on a passenger ship
1430. Salt: (noun) Sodium chloride, especially as used to season and preserve food
1431. Salutation: (noun) a word, act or gesture of greeting
1432. Salvation: (noun) the act of saving someone or something from harm
1433. Sanctuary: (noun) a holy or sacred place, e.g., a church or temple
1434. Sandal: (noun) a type of lightweight shoe consisting of a sole attached to the foot by straps
1435. Sanitation: (noun) standards of public hygiene
1436. Sanskrit: (noun) the ancient Indo-European religious and literary language of India
1437. Satchel: (noun) a small briefcase-like bag for school books, often leather and usually with shoulder straps.
1438. Satisfied: (adjective) having fulfilled the needs, desires or expectations of someone
1439. Saucer: (noun) a shallow, round dish especially one for placing under a cup
1440. Save: (verb) to rescue, protect or preserve someone or something from danger, evil, loss or failure
1441. Saw: 1. (verb) past tense of see, 2. (noun) any of various toothed cutting tools, either hand-operated or power-driven, used especially for cutting wood
1442. Scarcely: (adjective) not often found; in short supply
1443. Scented: (adjective) having a smell; fragrant or perfumed
1444. Schedule: (noun) a list of events or activities planned to take place at certain times
1445. Scholar: (noun) a learned person, especially an academic
1446. Science: (noun) the systematic observation and classification of natural phenomena in order to learn about them and bring them under general principles and laws

1447. Scissors: (noun) a one-handed cutting device with two long blades pivoted in the middle so the cutting edges close and overlap
1448. Scoff: (verb) to express scorn or contempt for them
1449. Scold: (verb) 1. to reprimand or rebuke, 2. to use strong or offensive language
1450. Scope: (noun) the size or range of a subject or topic covered
1451. Scorching: (adjective) very hot
1452. Scorn: (noun) extreme or mocking contempt
1453. Scramble: (verb) to crawl or climb using hands and feet especially hurriedly or frantically
1454. Scratch: (verb) to draw a sharp or pointed object across (a surface), causing damage or making marks
1455. Scream: (verb) to cry out in a loud high-pitched voice as in fear, pain or anger
1456. Scruffy: (noun) shabby and untidy
1457. Scruple: (noun) a sense of moral responsibility making one reluctant or unwilling to do wrong
1458. Sculpture: (noun) the art or act of carving or modelling with clay, wood, stone, plaster, etc.
1459. Sea: (noun) the large expanse of saltwater covering the greater part of the Earth's surface
1460. Search: (verb) to explore something thoroughly in order to try to find someone or something
1461. Season: (noun) any of the four major periods (spring, summer, autumn, and winter) into which the year is divided according to changes in weather patterns and other natural phenomena; (verb) to add salt, herbs, spices or other flavourings to food
1462. Seat: (noun) anything designed or intended for sitting on, e.g., a chair, bench, saddle, etc.
1463. Second: (noun) 1. someone or something next in sequence after the first, 2. a unit of time equal to 1/60th of a minute
1464. Secret: (adjective) kept hidden or away from the knowledge of others

1465. Section: (noun) the act or process of cutting or the cut or division made, 2. any of the parts into which something is or can be divided or of which it may be composed
1466. Sector: (noun) 1. a portion of a circle bounded by two radii and an arc, 2. a division or section of a nation's economic operations
1467. Security: (noun) the state of being secure
1468. Seed: (noun) in flowering and cone-bearing plants: the structure that develops from the ovule after fertilization, and is capable of developing into a new plant
1469. Seek: (verb) to look for someone or something
1470. Seep: (verb) of a liquid: to escape slowly or ooze through or as if through, a narrow opening
1471. Seize: (verb) to take or grab suddenly, eagerly or forcibly
1472. Selfless: (adjective) tending to consider the welfare of others before one's own
1473. Sensible: (adjective) having or showing reasonableness or good judgment
1474. Sensitive: (adjective) 1. feeling or responding readily strongly or painfully, 2. easily upset or offended, 3. secret or confidential
1475. Sentence: (noun) 1. a sequence of words forming a meaningful grammatical structure that can stand alone as a complete utterance, and which in written English usually begins with a capital letter, and ends with a full stop or exclamation mark, 2. a punishment pronounced by a court or judge
1476. Serious: (adjective) grave or solemn, not inclined to flippancy or lightness of mood
1477. Servant: (noun) a person employed by another to do household or menial work for them
1478. Servant: (noun) a person who acts for the good of others in any capacity
1479. Serve: (verb) to be in the service of someone
1480. Service: (noun) 1. the condition or occupation of being a servant or someone who serves, 2. work carried out for or on behalf of others

1481. Session: (noun) 1. a meeting of a court, council or parliament or the period during which such meetings are regularly held, 2. a period of time spent engaged in any particular activity
1482. Settle: (verb) to make or become securely, comfortably or satisfactorily positioned or established
1483. Settling: (verb) to come to an agreement about something
1484. Several: (adjective) more than a few but not a great number
1485. Severely: (adverb) extremely and with difficult to endure
1486. Sewage: (noun) any liquid-borne waste matter, especially human excrement carrying, in drains
1487. Shade: (noun) the blocking or partial blocking out of sunlight or the relative darkness caused by this
1488. Shake: (verb) to move with quick, often forceful to-and-fro and up-and-down movements
1489. Share: (noun) a part allotted, contributed or owned by each of several people or groups; a portion, section or division
1490. Sharp: (adjective) having a thin edge or point that cuts or pierces
1491. Shatter: (verb) to break into tiny fragments, usually suddenly or with force
1492. Sheath: (verb) a case or covering for the blade of a sword
1493. Shed: a wooden or metal outbuilding, usually small small, sometimes open-fronted, for working in or storage or for shelter
1494. Sheep: a herbivorous mammal, with a stocky body covered with a thick woolly fleece, kept as a farm animal for its meat and wool
1495. Shelf: (noun) a usually narrow, flat board fixed to a wall or part of a cupboard, bookcase, etc.
1496. Shield: (noun) a piece of armour consisting of a broad plate, carried to deflect weapons
1497. Shine: (verb) to give out or reflect light; to beam with a steady radiance
1498. Shiver: (verb) to quiver or tremble, e.g., with fear; (verb) to make an involuntary muscular movement in response to the cold

1499. Shock: (noun) a strong emotional disturbance
1500. Shortage: (noun) a lack or deficiency
1501. Shot: (verb) the act of shooting or firing a gun
1502. Shoulder: (noun) in humans and animals: the part on either side of the body, just below the neck, where the arm or front limb joins the trunk
1503. Shout: (noun) a loud cry or call
1504. Shovel: (noun) a tool with a deep-sided spade like blade and a handle, for lifting and carrying loose material
1505. Show: 1. (verb) to make or become visible, known or noticeable, 2. (verb) to prove, indicate or reveal, 3. (noun) any form of entertainment or spectacle
1506. Shower: (noun) 1. a device that produces a spray of water for bathing under, usually while standing, 2. a sudden but short and usually light fall of rain, snow or hail
1507. Shrewd: (adjective) possessing or showing keen judgment gained from practical experience
1508. Shriek: (verb) to cry out with a piercing scream
1509. Shrill: (adjective) of a voice, sound, etc.: high-pitched and piercing
1510. Shrub: (noun) a woody plant or bush, without any main trunk, which branches into several main stems at or just below ground level
1511. Shrug: (verb) to raise up and drop the shoulders briefly as an indication of doubt, indifference, etc.
1512. Shun: (verb) to intentionally avoid someone or something
1513. Shut: (verb) to place or move so as to close an opening
1514. Shuttle: (noun) an aircraft, train or bus that runs a frequent service between two places, usually at a relatively short distance from one another
1515. Shy: (adjective) of a person: embarrassed or unnerved by the company or attention of others
1516. Sick: (adjective) ill; feeling the need to vomit
1517. Sickle: (noun) a tool with a short handle and curved blade for cutting grain crops

1518. Sigh: (verb) to release a long deep audible breath, expressive of sadness, longing, tiredness or relief
1519. Sight: (noun) the power or faculty of seeing; a thing or object seen
1520. Sign: (noun) 1. a printed mark with a meaning, 2. an indication
1521. Significant: (adjective) worth noting or considering
1522. Silence: (noun) absence of sound or speech

> **Did you know?**
>
> Within youth culture the word 'sick' is used colloquially to express admiration, excitement or approval. It is used to describe something impressive, excellent or cool. This sort of shift in language is a form of semantic change where words that have negative connotations are repurposed to convey positive sentiments or vice versa.

1523. Silent: (adjective) free from noise; unaccompanied by sound
1524. Silken: (adjective) made of silk
1525. Silly: (adjective) not sensible; trivial or frivolous
1526. Simple: (adjective) not difficult; not complex or complicated
1527. Sin: (noun) an act that breaches a moral and especially a religious law or teaching
1528. Since: (conjugate) from the time that; seeing that
1529. Sincerity: (noun) honesty, truthfulness
1530. Single: (adjective) 1. comprising only one part, 2. having no partner; unmarried, especially never having been married
1531. Sink: 1. (verb) to fall or cause to fall and remain below the surface of water, either partially or completely, 2. (noun) a basin with built-in water supply and drainage for washing dishes, etc.
1532. Sire: (noun) 1. the father of a horse or other animal, 2. a term of respect used in addressing a king
1533. Sister: (noun) 1. a female child of the same parents as another, 2. a nun, 3. a senior female nurse
1534. Situate: (verb) to place in a certain position, context or set of circumstances
1535. Sizzle: (verb) to make a hissing sound when or as if when, frying in hot fat

1536. Skill: (noun) 1. dexterity, 2. a talent, craft or accomplishment, naturally acquired or developed through training
1537. Skin: (noun) the tough flexible waterproof covering of the human or animal body
1538. Skull: (noun) the hard cartilaginous or bony framework of the head
1539. Slack: (adjective) 1. not pulled or stretched tight, 2. not careful or diligent
1540. Slave: (noun) someone owned by and acting as servant to another, with no personal freedom
1541. Slay: (verb) to kill
1542. Sleep: (noun) a readily reversible state of natural unconsciousness during which the body's functional powers are restored, and physical movements are minimal
1543. Sleet: (noun) rain mixed with snow and/or hail
1544. Slid: (verb) to move or cause to move or run smoothly along a surface
1545. Slip: (verb) 1. to lose one's footing and slide accidently, 2. to make a slight mistake inadvertently rather than due to ignorance
1546. Slogan: (noun) a phrase used to identify a group or organization or to advertise a product
1547. Slope: (noun) a slanting surface
1548. Slough: (noun) a mud-filled hollow
1549. Slum: (noun) a run-down, dirty and usually overcrowded house and/or an area or neighbourhood containing such housing
1550. Slush: (noun) half-melted snow
1551. Small: (adjective) little in size or quantity
1552. Smash: (verb) to break voluntarily into pieces to destroy or be destroyed in this way
1553. Smoke: (noun) a visible cloud given off by a burning substance
1554. Snail: (noun) a mollusc with a coiled or conical shell on its back
1555. Sneer: (verb) to show scorn or contempt, especially by drawing the top lip up at one side

1556. Sneeze: (verb) to blow air out through the nose suddenly, violently and involuntarily, especially because of irritation in the nostrils
1557. Snooze: (verb) to sleep lightly
1558. Snore: (verb) to breathe heavily and with a snorting sound while sleeping
1559. Snout: (noun) the projecting nose and mouth parts of certain animals, e.g., the pig
1560. Soap: (noun) a cleansing agent consisting of a fatty acid that is soluble in water, in the form of solid block, liquid or powder
1561. Sob: (verb) to cry uncontrollably with gulps for breath
1562. Sofa: (noun) an upholstered seat with a back and arms, for two or more people
1563. Soil: (noun) the mixture of fragmented rock, plant and animal debris that lies on the surface of the earth
1564. Soldier: (noun) a member of a fighting force, especially a national army
1565. Sole: 1. (noun) the underside of the foot, 2. (adjective) alone; only
1566. Solve: (verb) to discover the answer to (a puzzle) or a way out of (a problem)
1567. Sombre: (adjective) sad and serious
1568. Sort: (noun) 1. a kind, type or class, 2. (verb) to arrange into different groups according to some specified criterion, 3. (verb) to fix something or put it back into working order
1569. Soul: (noun) the spiritual part of someone, which is often regarded as the source of personality, will, emotions and intellect, and which is believed by some people to survive after death
1570. Sour: (adjective) having an acid taste or smell, similar to that of lemon juice or vinegar
1571. Source: (noun) the place, thing, person, circumstance, etc., that something begins or develops from
1572. Sow: (verb) to scatter or place (plant seeds, a crop, etc.) on or in the earth, in a plant pot, etc.; (noun) an adult female pig

1573. Spade: (noun) 1. a long-handled digging tool with a broad blade which is pushed into the ground with the foot, 2. one of the four suits of playing-card, with a black spade-shaped symbol
1574. Span: (noun) the distance, interval, length, etc. between two points in space or time
1575. Spaniel: (noun) a dog with a wavy coat and long silky ears
1576. Spare: (adjective) kept for occasional use or as a replacement
1577. Sparkle: (verb) to give off sparks
1578. Sparrow: (noun) a small grey or brown bird with a short conical beak
1579. Speak: (verb) to utter words in an ordinary voice, as opposed to shouting, singing, screaming, etc.
1580. Spear: (noun) a weapon that consists of a long pole with a hard sharp point, which is thrown from the shoulder
1581. Special: (adjective) distinct from, and usually better than, others of the same kind
1582. Speed: (noun) the rate of movement or action
1583. Spend: (verb) 1. to pay money for something, 2. to use or devote (time, energy, effort, etc.)
1584. Spices: (noun) aromatic or pungent substances that are derived from plants and used for flavouring food
1585. Spicy: (adjective) flavoured with or tasting or smelling of spices
1586. Spider: (noun) any of numerous species of invertebrate animals, with eight legs and two main body parts, many of which produce silk and spin webs to trap their prey
1587. Spinach: (noun) a dark green leafy vegetable
1588. Spine: (noun) in vertebrates: the flexible bony structure that surrounds and protects the spinal cord
1589. Spirit: (noun) 1. the animating force that motivates, invigorates or energises someone or something, 2. a distilled alcoholic drink
1590. Spittle: (noun) saliva, especially when it has been spat from the mouth
1591. Spittoon: (noun) a container for spitting into

1592. Splash: (verb) to make (a liquid or semi-liquid substance) fly around or land in drops
1593. Spleen: (noun) a delicate organ, located beneath the diaphragm on the left side, which destroys red blood cells that are no longer functional
1594. Splinter: (noun) a small thin sharp piece that has broken off a hard substance e.g., wood or a glass
1595. Splutter: (verb) to put or throw out drops of liquid, bits of food, sparks, etc. with spitting sounds
1596. Spoon: (noun) a metal, wooden or plastic utensil that has a handle with a shallow bowl-like part at one end, and which is used for eating, serving or stirring food
1597. Sport: (noun) an activity, competition, etc. that usually involves a degree of physical exertion and which people take part in for exercise and/or pleasure
1598. Spot: (noun) a small mark or stain
1599. Spotted: (verb) to have seen
1600. Sprawl: (verb) to sit or lie lazily with arms and legs spread out wide
1601. Spray: (noun) a fine mist of small flying drops of liquid
1602. Spread: (verb) to apply or be capable of being applied, in a smooth coating over a surface
1603. Spring: 1. (verb) to leap with a sudden quick launching action, 2. (noun) a metal coil that can be scratched or compressed and which will return to its original shape when the pool or pressure is released
1604. Sprinkle: (verb) to scatter in or cover with a scattering of, tiny drops or particles
1605. Squash: (verb) to crush or flatten by pressing or squeezing
1606. Squirrel: (noun) a rodent that has a bushy tail, beady eyes and tufty ears, and usually lives in trees
1607. Stack: (noun) a large pile
1608. Stag: (noun) an adult male deer
1609. Stamen: (noun) in flowering plants: the male reproductive structure where the pollen grains are produced
1610. Starch: (noun) a carbohydrate that occurs in all green plants, where it serves as an energy store

1611. Start: (verb) to begin; to bring or come into being
1612. Starve: (verb) to die or cause to die because of a lack of food
1613. State: (noun) 1. the condition, e.g., of health, appearance, etc., that someone or something is in at a particular time, 2. a territory governed by a single political body
1614. Statue: (noun) a sculpted, moulded or cast figure, especially of a person or animal, usually life-size or larger
1615. Status: (noun) rank or position in relation to others within society
1616. Stay: (verb) to remain in the same place or condition, without moving or changing
1617. Steady: (adjective) firmly fixed or balanced; not wobbling
1618. Steal: (verb) to take away (another person's property) without permission or legal right
1619. Steam: (noun) the colourless gas formed by vaporizing water at 100 degree Celsius
1620. Steer: (verb) to guide or control the direction of (a vehicle or vessel) using a steering wheel, rudder, etc.
1621. Stick: 1. (noun) a twig or thin branch of a tree, 2. (verb) to fix or be or stay fixed, with an adhesive
1622. Stifling: (adjective) unpleasantly hot or airless
1623. Still: (adjective) motionless; inactive
1624. Sting: (noun) a defensive puncturing organ that is found in certain animals and plants, which can inject poison or venom
1625. Stint: 1. (noun) an allotted amount of work or a fixed time for it, 2. (verb) to be mean or grudging in giving or supplying something
1626. Stocks: (noun) goods or raw material that a shop, factory, warehouse, etc., has on the premises at a given time
1627. Stocky: (adjective) of a person or animal: broad, strong-looking, and usually not very tall
1628. Stodgy: (adjective) of food: heavy and filling but usually fairly tasteless
1629. Stomach: (noun) in the alimentary canal of vertebrates: a large sack-like organ where food is temporarily stored until it is partially digested

1630. Stool: 1. (noun) a simple seat without a back, 2. faeces
1631. Stop: (verb) to bring or come to rest, a standstill for an end; to seize or cause to seize moving, operating or progressing
1632. Storey: (noun) a level, floor or tier of a building
1633. Stork: (noun) a large wading bird that has long legs, a long bill, and usually black and white plumage
1634. Storm: (noun) an outbreak of violent weather, with severe winds and heavy falls of rain, hail or snow, often accompanied by thunder and lightning
1635. Stove: (noun) any cooking or heating apparatus
1636. Straight: (adjective) 1. not curved, bent, curly or wavy, 2. without deviations or detours
1637. Strange: (adjective) not known or experienced before
1638. Stream: (noun) a very narrow river; any constant flow of liquid
1639. Street: (noun) a public road with pavements and buildings at the side or sides, especially one in a town
1640. Strength: (noun) the quality or degree of being physically or mentally strong
1641. Stress: (noun) physical or mental overexertion
1642. Stretch: (verb) to make or become temporarily or permanently longer or wider by pulling or drawing out
1643. Strict: (adjective) demanding obedience or close observance of rules
1644. Strike: (verb) to hit someone or something
1645. String: (noun) thin cord or a piece of this
1646. Stripe: (noun) a band of colour
1647. Strive: (verb) to try extremely hard
1648. Stroke: (noun) 1. any act or way of striking, 2. a sudden interruption to the supply of blood to the brain that results in loss of consciousness, often with paralysis and loss of speech, caused by bleeding from or rupture of an artery
1649. Strut: (verb) to walk in a proud way
1650. Student: (noun) someone who is following a formal course of study, especially in higher or further education
1651. Stuff: 1. (noun) any material or substance, 2. (verb) to cram or thrust

1652. Stumble: (verb) to lose one's balance and trip forwards after accidentally catching or misplacing one's foot
1653. Stump: 1. (noun) the part of a felled or fallen tree that is left in the ground, 2. (verb) to baffle or perplex
1654. Stunned: (adjective) unable to speak or think clearly, e.g., through shock
1655. Stupid: (adjective) having or showing a lack of common sense, comprehension, perception, etc.
1656. Submerge: (verb) to plunge or sink or cause to plunge or sink under the surface of water or other liquid
1657. Submit: (verb) to surrender; to give in, especially to the wishes or control of another person
1658. Substance: (noun) the matter or material that a thing is made of
1659. Succeed: (verb) to achieve an aim or purpose
1660. Suck: (verb) to draw (liquid) into the mouth
1661. Sudden: (adjective) happening or done quickly, without warning or unexpectedly
1662. Suffer: (verb) to undergo or endure (pain or other unpleasantness)
1663. Sugary: (adjective) like sugar in taste or appearance
1664. Suitable: (adjective) appropriate, proper
1665. Sum: (noun) the total that is arrived at when two or more numbers, quantities, etc. are added together
1666. Summer: (noun) the warmest season of the year between spring and autumn
1667. Summit: (noun) the highest point of a mountain or hill
1668. Summon: (verb) to order someone to come or appear, e.g., in a court of law as a witness, defendant, etc.
1669. Sunflower: (noun) a tall plant which produces large yellow flower heads with closely-packed seeds in the middle
1670. Supply: (verb) to provide or furnish (something believed to be necessary)
1671. Support: (verb) 1. to keep something upright or in place, 2. to keep from falling

1672. Suppose: (verb) to consider something likely even when there is a lack of tangible evidence for it to be so
1673. Supreme: (adjective) highest in rank, power, importance, etc.
1674. Sure: (adjective) confident beyond doubt in one's belief or knowledge
1675. Surface: (noun) the upper or outer side of anything, often with regard to texture or appearance
1676. Surplus: (noun) an amount that exceeds the amount required or used; an amount that is leftover after requirements have been met
1677. Surprise: (noun) a sudden, unexpected or amazing event, gift, etc.
1678. Survival: (noun) the fact of continuing to live, especially after some risk that might have prevented this
1679. Suspect: (verb) to consider or believe likely
1680. Swagger: (verb) to walk with a self-important air
1681. Swallow: (verb) to perform a muscular movement to make (food or drink) go from the mouth, down the oesophagus and into the stomach
1682. Swan: (noun) a large, generally white, graceful aquatic bird with a long, slender elegant neck, powerful wings, and webbed feet
1683. Swear: (verb) 1. to use indecent or blasphemous language, 2. to assert something solemnly, sometimes with an oath
1684. Sweat: (noun) the salty liquid produced by glands and given out through the pores of the skin, especially in response to heat, physical exertion, nervousness or fear
1685. Sweep: (verb) to clean (a room, a floor, etc.) with a brush or broom
1686. Swell: (verb) to make or become bigger or fatter through injury or infection or by filling with liquid or air
1687. Swift: (adjective) fast-moving, able to move fast
1688. Swimming: (verb) propelling oneself through water by moving the arms and legs or (in fish) the tail and fins
1689. Swine: (noun) 1. a pig, 2. a despicable person

1690. Swing: (verb) to move in a curving motion, pivoting from a fixed point
1691. Switch: (noun) 1. a manually operated or automatic device that is used to open or close an electric circuit, 2. an exchange or changeover
1692. Sword: (noun) a weapon like a large long knife, with a sharp blade usually ending in a point
1693. Symbol: (noun) a thing that represents another, usually something concrete representing an idea or emotion
1694. Symptom: (noun) an indication of the presence of a disease or disorder
1695. Table: (noun) a piece of furniture consisting of a flat horizontal surface supported by one or more legs
1696. Tackle: (verb) an act of trying to get the ball away from an opposing player
1697. Tale: (noun) a story or narrative
1698. Tamarind: (noun) The fruit of a tropical evergreen tree, the acidic pulp of which is used medicinally and as a flavouring
1699. Tame: (adjective) of animals: living or working with people
1700. Tangible: (adjective) able to be felt by touch
1701. Tap: (noun) 1. a quick or light touch, knock or blow or the sound made by this, 2. a device attached to a pipe, barrel, etc. for controlling the flow of liquid or gas
1702. Task: (noun) a piece of work to be done
1703. Tawny: (noun) a yellowish brown colour
1704. Teak: (noun) the heavy yellowish-brown durable wood of a large tropical deciduous tree, used in furniture making, etc.
1705. Tears: (noun) drops of clear saline liquid from the eye, especially when crying
1706. Tease: (verb) to annoy or irritate deliberately or unkindly
1707. Technique: (noun) proficiency or skill in the practical or formal aspects of something, e.g., painting, music, etc.
1708. Telephone: (noun) an instrument for transmitting speech in the form of electrical signals or radio waves
1709. Temper: (noun) a characteristic state of mind, mood or humour

1710. Temple: (noun) 1. a building in which people worship, 2. the flat part at either side of the head in front of the ears
1711. Tempt: (verb) to seek or persuade (someone) to do something wrong, foolish, etc.
1712. Tend: (verb) to take care of or look after
1713. Tennis: (noun) a game in which two players or two pairs of players use rackets to hit a ball across a net on a rectangular grass, clay or cement court
1714. Tense: (adjective) suffering emotional, nervous or mental strain; (noun) a grammatical category that expresses time of action or state (past, present, future) in relation to the moment of speaking
1715. Term: (noun) 1. a word or expression, especially one with a precise meaning in a specialized field, 2. a limited or clearly defined period of time
1716. Terrible: (adjective) very bad
1717. Territory: (noun) a stretch of land; a region
1718. Thaw: (verb) of snow, ice, frozen, food, etc.: to melt
1719. Thigh: (noun) the part of the leg between the knee and hip in humans or the corresponding part in animals
1720. Thimble: (noun) a cap worn on the finger to protect it and push the needle when sewing
1721. Thin: (adjective) having a relatively short distance between opposite sides
1722. Think: (verb) to have or form ideas in the mind
1723. Thought: (noun) an idea, concept or opinion
1724. Thread: (noun) a strand of silk, cotton, wool, etc., for sewing
1725. Thrift: (noun) careful spending, use or management of resources, especially money
1726. Thrifty: (adjective) showing thrift
1727. Throat: (noun) the top part of the windpipe or gullet
1728. Throne: (noun) a ceremonial chair of a monarch, bishop, etc.
1729. Throw: (verb) to propel or hurl through the air with force
1730. Thud: (noun) a dull sound like something heavy falling to the ground
1731. Thunder: (noun) a deep rumbling or loud cracking sound heard soon after a flash of lightning

1732. Thus: (adverb) in the way or manner shown or mentioned
1733. Tide: (noun) the twice-daily rise and fall of the water level in the oceans and seas
1734. Tiger: (noun) a large carnivorous Asian member of the cat family with a fawn or reddish coat, with black or brownish-black transverse stripes
1735. Tight: (adjective) fitting very or too closely
1736. Timber: (noun) wood, especially for building or carpentry
1737. Time: (noun) the continuous passing and succession of minutes, days, years, etc.
1738. Tinkle: (verb) to make or cause to make a succession of jingling sounds
1739. Tiny: (adjective) very small
1740. Tire: (verb) to make or become physically or mentally weary
1741. Title: (noun) the distinguishing name of a book, play, work of art, piece of music, etc.
1742. Toe: (noun) one of the five digits at the end of the human foot
1743. Toil: (verb) to work long and hard
1744. Tomato: (noun) a round fleshy red, orange or yellow fruit, eaten raw or uncooked
1745. Tongs: (noun) a tool consisting of two joined arms, used for holding and lifting
1746. Tongue: (noun) a fleshy, muscular organ in the mouth, used for tasting, licking and swallowing and, in humans, speech
1747. Tonight: (noun) the night of this present day
1748. Tonsil: (noun) either of two lumps of lymphoid tissue at the back of the mouth
1749. Tool: (noun) an implement, especially one used by hand, for cutting, digging, etc., such as a spade or hammer
1750. Tooth: (noun) in vertebrates: any of the hard structures, usually embedded in the upper and lower jaw bones, used for biting and chewing food
1751. Toothbrush: (noun) a brush for cleaning the teeth
1752. Top: (noun) the highest part, point or level of anything
1753. Torment: (noun) great pain, suffering or anxiety

1754. Torture: (noun) the infliction of severe pain or mental suffering, especially as a punishment or as a means of persuasion
1755. Tourist: (noun) someone who travels for pleasure and relaxation
1756. Trace: (noun) a mark or sign that some person, animal or thing has been in a particular place
1757. Track: (noun) a mark or series of marks or footprints, etc., left behind
1758. Tradition: (noun) a belief, custom, story, etc., passed on from generation to generation
1759. Traffic: (noun) the vehicles that are moving along a route
1760. Train: (noun) a string of railway carriages or wagons with a locomotive
1761. Tramp: (verb) to walk with firm heavy footsteps
1762. Trample: (verb) to tread heavily; to crush underfoot
1763. Transfer: (verb) to move from one place, person, group, team, etc., to another
1764. Translate: (verb) to express a word, speech, written text, etc., in another language
1765. Transparent: (adjective) able to be seen through
1766. Travel: (verb) to go from place to place; to make a journey
1767. Traveller: (noun) someone who travels
1768. Tray: (noun) a flat piece of wood, metal, plastic, etc., usually with a small raised edge used for carrying dishes, etc.
1769. Tread: (verb) to walk or step
1770. Treasure: (noun) wealth and riches, in the form of gold silver, jewels, etc., especially accumulated over a period of time and hoarded
1771. Treat: (verb) to deal with or behave towards (someone or something) in a specified manner
1772. Treatise: (noun) a formal piece of writing that deals systematically and in depth with a subject
1773. Treaty: (noun) a formal agreement between states or governments
1774. Tremble: (verb) to shake or shudder involuntarily, e.g., with cold, fear, weakness, etc.

1775. Trial: (noun) a legal process in which someone who stands accused of crime is judged in a court of law
1776. Trick: (noun) 1. something done or said to cheat, deceive, fool or humiliate someone, 2. a deceptive appearance; an illusion
1777. Trifle: (noun) something of little or no value
1778. Trip: 1. (verb) to stumble or cause to stumble, 2. (noun) a short journey or excursion, especially for pleasure
1779. Triumph: (noun) a great or notable victory, success, achievement, etc.
1780. Trivial: (adjective) of very little importance or value
1781. Trouble: (noun) a distress, worry or concern
1782. Trousers: (noun) an outer garment for the lower part of the body, reaching from the waist and covering each leg separately, usually down to the ankle
1783. Trumpet: (noun) a brass instrument with a narrow tube, flared bell and a set of valves
1784. Trunk: (noun) the long nose of the elephant
1785. Trust: (noun) a belief or confidence in the truth, goodness, power, ability, etc., of someone or something
1786. Try: (verb) to attempt, to seek, to attain or achieve
1787. Tumble: (verb) to fall or cause to fall headlong
1788. Tumbler: (noun) a flat-bottomed drinking cup without a stem or handle, usually of glass
1789. Turban: (noun) a headdress worn especially by Muslim and Sikh men, and formed by wrapping a length of cloth around the head
1790. Turbulent: (adjective) violently disturbed or unruly
1791. Turnip: (noun) a plant of the cabbage family
1792. Twice: (adjective) two times
1793. Twine: (noun) strong string or cord of twisted cotton, hemp, etc.
1794. Twinkle: (verb) of a star, etc.: to shine with a bright flickering light
1795. Twinkle: (noun) a gleam or sparkle in the eyes

1796. Typical: (adjective) having or showing the usual features, traits, etc., or being a characteristic or representative example
1797. Ugly: (adjective) Unpleasant to look at extremely unattractive
1798. Umbrella: (noun) a device carried to give shelter from rain, etc., consisting of a rounded fabric canopy supported on a lightweight collapsible framework of ribs fitted around a central stick
1799. Unbelievable: (adjective) too unusual or unexpected to be believed
1800. Uncanny: (adjective) weird, strange or mysterious, especially in an unsettling or uneasy way
1801. Uncle: (noun) the brother or brother-in-law of father or mother
1802. Unconscious: (adjective) of a person or animal: in a state of insensibility, characterized by loss of awareness of the external environment, and inability to respond to sensory stimuli
1803. Undergo: (verb) to endure, experience or be subjected to something
1804. Unexpected: (adjective) not expected; surprising; unforeseen
1805. Uniform: 1. (noun) distinctive clothing, always of the same colour, cut, etc., worn by all members of a particular organization or profession, e.g., by schoolchildren or soldiers, 2. (adjective) unchanging or unvarying in form, nature or appearance; always the same regardless of changes in circumstances
1806. Union: (noun) the action or an act of uniting two or more things
1807. Unity: (noun) the state or quality of being one; oneness
1808. Universe: (noun) (the universe) all existing space energy and matter
1809. Unless: (conjugate) if not; except when; except if
1810. Unlucky: (adjective) bringing, resulting from or constituting bad luck
1811. Unreasonable: (adjective) not based on reason or good sense
1812. Untidy: (adjective) not tidy; messy or disordered
1813. Unusual: (adjective) not usual; uncommon

1814. Upstairs: (adjective) up the stairs; to or on an upper floor or floors of house, etc.
1815. Urdu: (noun) an Indo-Aryan language, the official language of Pakistan, also spoken in Bangladesh and among Muslims in India
1816. Urge: (verb) to persuade someone forcefully or incite them (to do something)
1817. Useful: (adjective) able to be used advantageously; serving a helpful purpose; able to be put to various purposes
1818. Usual: (adjective) done, happening most often
1819. Utter: (verb) to give audible vocal expression to (an emotion etc.); to emit (a sound) with the voice
1820. Vacancy: (noun) the state of being vacant; emptiness
1821. Vacation: (noun) a holiday
1822. Vain: (adjective) having too much pride in one's appearance, achievements or possessions
1823. Valley: (noun) a long flat area of land, usually containing a river or stream, flanked on both sides by higher land
1824. Vanish: (verb) to disappear suddenly
1825. Vapour: (noun) the substance in the form of a mist, fume or smoke, especially one coming off from a solid or liquid
1826. Variety: (noun) any of various types of the same thing
1827. Various: (adjective) several different; disparate, diverse
1828. Vase: (noun) an ornamental glass or pottery container, especially one for holding cut flowers
1829. Veil: (noun) a fabric covering for a woman's head or face, forming part of traditional dress in some societies
1830. Vein: (noun) a blood vessel that carries deoxygenated blood back towards the heart
1831. Velvet: (noun) a fabric with a very short, soft, closely woven pile on one side
1832. Vermillion: (noun) a bright scarlet colour
1833. Vermin: (noun) a collective name for wild animals that spread disease or generally cause a nuisance, especially rats and other rodents

1834. Vessel: (noun) 1. a container, especially for liquid, 2. a ship or large boat
1835. Vexed: (adjective) annoyed; angry; troubled
1836. Vice: (noun) a habit or activity considered immoral, evil or depraved, especially involving prostitution and drugs
1837. Victim: (noun) a person or animal subjected to death, suffering, ill treatment or trickery
1838. Vigour: (noun) great strength and energy of body or mind
1839. Violet: (noun) a bluish-purple colour
1840. Virtue: (noun) a quality regarded as morally good
1841. Visitor: (noun) someone who visits a person or place
1842. Visualize: (verb) to form a clear mental image of someone or something
1843. Voice: (noun) a sound produced by the vocal organs and uttered through the mouth, especially by humans in speech or song
1844. Volume: (noun) 1. the amount of three-dimensional space occupied by an object, gas or liquid, 2. loudness of sound
1845. Vouch: (verb) to give a firm assurance or guarantee of their authenticity, trustworthiness
1846. Vulture: (noun) a large bird, with a bare head and a strong curved beak, which feeds on carrion
1847. Wages: (noun) a regular, especially weekly, payment from an employer to an employee
1848. Wail: (noun) a prolonged and high-pitched mournful or complaining cry
1849. Wake: (verb) to rouse (somebody) or be roused from sleep
1850. Wall: a solid vertical brick or stone construction serving as a barrier, division, protection, etc.
1851. Wallet: a flat folding case, often of leather, for holding banknotes, credit cards, etc.
1852. Wander: (verb) to walk or travel about, with no particular destination
1853. Warn: (verb) to make (somebody) aware of (possible or approaching danger or difficulty)

1854. Warrior: (noun) a skilled fighter
1855. Wastage: (noun) the process of wasting; loss through wasting
1856. Waste: 1. (verb) to use or spend purposelessly or extravagantly, 2. (noun) refuse, rubbish
1857. Watch: 1. (verb) to look at or focus one's attention on (someone or something) that is moving or doing something, etc., 2. (noun) a small timepiece, usually strapped to the wrist or on a chain in the waistcoat pocket or attached to clothing
1858. Wave: 1. (verb) to move one's hand to and fro in greeting, farewell or as a signal, 2. (noun) any of a series of moving ridges on the surface of the sea or some other body of water
1859. Wavy: (adjective) full of waves
1860. Way: (noun) a route, entrance or exit, etc. that provides passage or access somewhere
1861. Wealth: (noun) riches, valuables and property or the possession of them
1862. Weapon: (noun) an instrument or device used to kill or injure people, usually in a war or fight
1863. Wear: (verb) to be dressed in (something) or have (it) on one's body
1864. Weary: (adjective) tired out; exhausted
1865. Weed: (noun) any plant growing where it is not wanted, especially when hindering the growth of cultivated plants
1866. Weights: (noun) a piece of metal of a standard weight, against which to measure the weight of other objects
1867. Weird: (adjective) eerie or supernatural; uncanny; strange or bizarre
1868. Welfare: (noun) the health, comfort, happiness and general well-being of a person or group, etc.
1869. Wheeze: (verb) to breathe in a laboured way with a gasping noise
1870. Whimsical: (adjective) delicately fanciful or playful; odd, weird or fantastic
1871. Whip: (noun) a lash with a handle for driving animals or punishing people
1872. Whirling: (verb) to spin or revolve rapidly

1873. Whirr: (noun) a rapid drawn-out whirling, humming or vibratory sound
1874. Whisper: (verb) to speak or say (something) quietly, breathing rather than voicing the words
1875. Whistle: (noun) a shrill sound produced through pursed lips or through the teeth, used to signal or to express surprise, etc.
1876. Whole: (noun) all the constituents or components of something
1877. Wick: (noun) the twisted string running up through a candle or lamp, that burns and draws the fuel to the flame
1878. Wicked: (adjective) evil or sinful; immoral
1879. Wide: (adjective) large in extent from side to side
1880. Wife: (noun) the woman to whom a man is married; a married woman
1881. Wild: (adjective) of animals: not dependent on humans; of plants: growing in a natural and cultivated state

Did you know?

The word 'husband' was derived from the word 'wife'?
The origins of the word 'wife' can be traced back to the Old English word 'wif' which meant 'woman' or 'female'. The word 'wif' referred to a woman of any age, and not just a married one. Over time the word denoted a married woman, and the word 'hus', which meant house, was added to create 'huswif'. This word eventually became 'husband' for the male partner in a marriage.

1882. Will: (noun) the power of conscious decision and deliberate choice of action
1883. Wind: (noun) the movement of air across the Earth's surface as a result of differences in atmospheric pressure between one location and another
1884. Window: (noun) an opening in a wall to look through or let in light and air, consisting of a wooden or metal frame fitted with panes of glass
1885. Wine: (noun) an alcoholic drink made from fermented grape juice

1886. Wink: (verb) to shut an eye briefly, as an informal or cheeky gesture or greeting
1887. Wire: (noun) metal drawn out into a narrow flexible strand
1888. Wired: (adjective) highly strung; stressed out
1889. Wisdom: (noun) the quality of being wise; the ability to make sensible judgments and decisions
1890. Wish: (verb) to want; to have a desire
1891. Withdraw: (verb) 1. to leave, to go away, 2. to take (money) from a bank account for use
1892. Wolf: (noun) a wild carnivorous mammal of the dog family which hunts in packs
1893. Wonder: 1. (noun) the state of mind produced by something extraordinary, new or unexpected, 2. (verb) to be curious
1894. Wool: (noun) the soft wavy hair of sheep and certain other animals
1895. Work: (noun) physical or mental effort to achieve or make something, e.g., labour, study, research, etc.
1896. Worker: (noun) someone employed in manual work
1897. Worm: (noun) a small soft-bodied limbless invertebrate that is characteristically long and slender
1898. Worry: (verb) to be anxious; to fret
1899. Worst: (adjective) most bad, awful or unpleasant, etc.
1900. Worth: (noun) 1. importance or usefulness, 2. financial value
1901. Wrap: (verb) to fold or wind (something) round (someone or something)
1902. Wrestling: (noun) the sport or exercise governed by certain fixed rules, in which two people wrestle
1903. Wrinkle: (noun) a crease or line in the skin, especially of the face, appearing with advancing age
1904. Wrist: (noun) the joint between the forearm and the hand
1905. Wrong: (adjective) not correct; mistaken; not appropriate or suitable
1906. Yam: (noun) a climbing plant cultivated in tropical regions for its edible tubers
1907. Yankee: (noun) a person from the US

1908. Yard: (noun) 1. an area of enclosed ground associated with the building, 2. a unit of length equal to 3 feet
1909. Yell: (noun) a loud shout or cry
1910. Yellow: (adjective) of the colour of gold, butter, egg yolk, lemon, etc.
1911. Yield: (verb) to produce (an animal product such as meat or milk or a crop, interest, etc.)
1912. Yoke: (noun) a wooden frame placed over the necks of oxen to hold them together when they are pulling a plough, cart, etc.
1913. Zebra: (noun) a stocky black-and-white striped African mammal with a stubby mane, related to the horse
1914. Zest: (noun) keen enjoyment; enthusiasm
1915. Zoo: (noun) a garden or park where wild animals are kept for the purpose of study, breeding of rare species for conservation, etc., and where they are usually on show to the public
1916. Zoology: (noun) the scientific study of animals, including their structure, function, behaviour, ecology, evolution, and classification

LIST OF WORDS THAT HAVE UNDERGONE SEMANTIC CHANGE OR REVERSAL

This sort of semantic change or reversal involves words taking on meanings opposite to their original intent. This concept is applied when people say one thing but mean another usually to emphasize, for humour or to express sarcasm. Some of the words that have undergone this change are:

1. Beast: Originally, the word refers to a large, four-legged animal or one that is wild and dangerous. It was also used to describe someone who is extremely aggressive, cruel or tough. Now, it means someone who is talented or skilled.
2. Bomb: The word originally refers to an explosive device. Now it means someone that is fantastic or is used when something has failed.
3. Bust: The word traditionally refers to a sculpture of a person's head, shoulders and chest. Over time it also referred to an arrest made by the police. Now it is also used when something breaks or damages.
4. Chill: The word used to mean something that is kept cool. Now it means to relax or take it easy.
5. Crazy: It originally meant something that was cracked or flawed, but over time the meaning has evolved to describe someone who was mentally unbalanced or insane. Today it means something that exciting or intense.
6. Dumb: The word used to refer to someone who was unable to speak, and over time it was used to describe someone perceived as lacking intelligence. In modern usage the word can also be used to mean awesome or impressive.
7. Fat (Phat): Originally, the word meant someone who was overweight or big-boned. Today, it means excellent or impressive.
8. Fire: The word originally referred to the combustion or burning of material producing heat and light. Today, it also refers to something that is excellent.

9. Fly: The word traditionally meant to move through air, typically with wings. Today, it also refers to something that is attractive or stylish.
10. Fresh: Traditionally, this word was related to the idea that something was recently made or obtained and has not yet become stale or old. Today, the word is also used to refer to something that is original.
11. Hype: The word originally is derived from the term 'hyperbole', which means exaggerated statements or claims that are not mean to be taken literally. Today, it also refers to something that causes excitement or anticipation.
12. Jacked: The word originally meant to lift or raise something with a jack. Today, it also refers to someone who is strong and muscular.
13. Legit: The word is a shortform of legitimate which historically means conforming to the law or to rules. Today it means something that is genuine or authentic.
14. Literally: The original meaning of 'literally' refers to the precise or exact meaning of words, as opposed to the figurative or metaphorical interpretations. However, over time it is now used to mean things figuratively (often used for emphasis ironically).
15. Savage:, The word originally meant someone that's uncivilized or barbaric or action that is extremely violent, brutal and cruel. Today, it also means something or someone that is awesome and fierce.
16. Shady: Originally, it described something that provided shade, such as a tree ora a place out of direct sunlight. Over time, the term has evolved to describe something or someone that is dubious or untrustworthy.
17. Sick: The word originally used to describe something or someone that was unwell. Today, it also refers to something or someone that is impressive and cool.
18. Swag: It originally meant to move unsteadily and to refer to a drooping or sagging appearance. Today, it also refers to someone's style or confidence.

19. Thick: It originally referred to something that had a large distance between opposite surfaces. Now it also means someone that is dense or stupid.
20. Sweet: It originally means something that is pleasant to taste. But now it also means something that is excellent or good.

'Each' and 'every' are both used to refer to individual items in a group, but they have different nuances and uses.

'Each' emphasizes individuality within a group and focuses on individual items or people. 'Every' emphasizes the group as a while, considering all members collectively but focusing on them individually.

For example: 'Each student in the class has a textbook.' Here we are considering the students one by one, emphasizing their individual possession of the textbook.

'Every student in the class has a textbook.' Here we are considering all students together but affirming that each one has a textbook.

Most of the time, 'each' is used when talking about a smaller and more manageable number of items or people. 'Every' is used when talking about a larger number of items or people, suggesting comprehensiveness.

For example: 'Each book on this shelf has been read.' We are referring to a shelf with a relatively small number of books.

'Every book in the library has been catalogued.' We are referring to a large number of books emphasizing the entirety of the collection.

'Each' and 'Every' can also have similar meanings. For example: Each/Every car in the lot is new.

Here both sentences mean that all cars are new, but 'each' focuses on the cars individually, while 'every' considers them collectively.

Write a descriptive passage using at least seven of the phrasal verbs given below:

(draw in, got away with, help out, lash out, meet up, nurse along, pass away, put forward, ramp up, take out, bear with, brought about, watch out, yield to, zone out)

Dialogue for a job interview between interviewer and candidate

Interviewer: Good morning. How are you?

Candidate: Good morning. Um, I'm well thanks. How about you? Thanks for having me.

Interviewer: I'm doing absolutely fine. Good, good. Then, how about we start with you telling me a little about yourself and your background?

Candidate: Okay. So I graduated from XYZ University with a degree in Marketing and um, over the past five years, I've worked at ABC Corporation. Basically, I started as a marketing assistant and then they promoted me to marketing manager, which was pretty cool. I managed a team of five and was responsible for all the digital marketing campaigns.

Interviewer: That is cool. Tell me about a particular successful campaign you led at ABC.

Candidate: Um, let me think. Okay, so of our most successful campaigns was the 'Summer Splash' campaign. We wanted to increase our social media presence and drive sales for our new summer product line. I developed the strategy, coordinated with the design team for visuals, and collaborated with influencers, and well, the campaign resulted in a 35% increase in online sales and a 50% growth in social media followers.

Interviewer: That sounds great. So do you handle deadlines and pressure well?

Candidate: I try to, I guess. See, I prioritize tasks based on their urgency and importance, and try my best to maintain open communication with my team. I try to stay focused during high-pressure situations through planning and breaking down tasks. This approach has helped me so far to stay organized.

Interviewer: That's good. I try and do the same. Tell me something, why are you interested in this position with our company?

Candidate: Oh, I've wanted to work here for long. I admire your company's innovative approach to marketing and its very strong emphasis on customer satisfaction. My skills and experiences align well with the goals of your team, and I would love to be part of it.

Interviewer: Thank you so much. I think this should do it for now. By the way, do you have any questions for us?

Candidate: Yes, yes. Can you tell me more about the team I would be working with and the main projects you'll be focusing on in the next few months?

Interviewer: Oh sure, yes. You would be working with a dynamic team of six marketing professionals, and all of them are quite cool. You won't have to worry. And, let's see, our main projects for the upcoming months include launching a new product line and expanding our digital marketing initiatives.

Candidate: Exciting stuff then! I'm interested in being a part of these projects. Thanks so much for the opportunity to interview.

Interviewer: Of course, thank you for coming in. We'll keep in touch with you and call you soon.

Candidate: Thank you. Have a great day.

Interviewer: You too. Goodbye.

Candidate: Goodbye.

The word 'do' is a versatile word in English with several distinct uses.

1. Auxiliary Verb: Used to form questions, negatives and emphatic statements in the simple present and simple past tenses.
   For example: Do you like coffee?/I do not understand/I do want to see that movie.
2. Main Verb: Used to indicate the performance of an action, task or activity.
   For example: I do my homework every evening/She did the dishes after dinner/They are doing a great job.
3. Substitute Verb: Used to avoid repetition of a previously mentioned verb or action.
   For example: I want to relax, and so does he.
4. Idiomatic Expressions: Used in various idiomatic phrases and expressions to convey specific meanings.
   For example: Do away with it/Do without/Make do/Do me a favour

PHOBIAS:

Phobias are an extreme or irrational fear or aversion to something. They are of different types. There are phobias of flying, of heights, of weather, of illnesses and many other kinds. Below listed are some common types of phobias and their meanings.

1. Agoraphobia: Fear of open or crowded spaces.
2. Nomenophobia: Fear of names.
3. Senecophobia: Fear of old age.
4. Cadophobia: Fear of corpses.
5. Doxophobia: Fear of expressing opinions or receiving praise.
6. Zoophobia: Fear of animals.
7. Mysophobia: Fear of germs or dirt.
8. Haematophobia: Fear of blood.
9. Necrophobia: Fear of death or dead things.
10. Xenophobia: Fear of strangers or foreigners.
11. Chronophobia: Fear of time or the passage of time.
12. Thermophobia: Fear of heat.
13. Cynophobia: Fear of dogs.
14. Iatrophobia: Fear of doctors or medical treatment.
15. Ophidiophobia: Fear of snakes.
16. Acrophobia: Fear of heights.
17. Gynophobia: Fear of women.
18. Graphophobia: Fear of writing or handwriting.
19. Gamophobia: Fear of marriage or commitment.
20. Anthrophobia: Fear of flowers.
21. Arachnophobia: Fear of spiders.
22. Catoptrophobia: Fear of mirrors.
23. Daemonophobia: Fear of demons or evil supernatural beings.
24. Glossophobia: Fear of public speaking.
25. Hydrophobia: Fear of water.
26. Hypochondria: Fear of having a serious illness.
27. Nyctophobia: Fear of the dark or night.
28. Thalassophobia: Fear of the sea or deep water.
29. Trypophobia: Fear of holes or patterns of holes.
30. Verminophobia: Fear of germs or being infested by parasites.

Some English words taken from Indian languages:

1. Avatar: A person who embodies, represents or is a manifestation of a concept or quality.
   Taken from the Sanskrit word *avatara*, which refers to the incarnation of a deity, particularly Vishnu, in Hinduism.
2. Bandana: A piece of cloth worn around the head or neck.
   Taken from the Hindi word *bandhana*, which means to tie or bind.
3. Bungalow: A type of single-story house, typically with a large porch, common in India.
   Taken from the Hindi word *bangla*, meaning the same.
4. Cheetah: A spotted big cat known for its speed.
   Taken from the Hindi word that is pronounced and means the same.
5. Cot: A light, portable bed or a small child's bed with high sides.
   Taken from the Hindi word *khat*, meaning the same.
6. Curry: A spiced sauce or stew, popular worldwide.
   Taken from the Tamil word *kari*, which means the same.
7. Dinghy: A small boat.
   Taken from the Hindi word *dingi*.
8. Juggernaut: A huge, powerful and overwhelming force or institution.
   Taken from the Sanskrit word Jagannatha, which refers to a form of the Hindu god Vishnu.
9. Jungle: Forest or wilderness.
   Taken from the Hindi word *jangal*.
10. Loot: Stolen good or plunder.
    Taken from the Hindi word *lut*.
11. Nirvana: A state of perfect happiness of peace.
    Taken from the Sanskrit word *nirvana* referring to the transcendent state free from suffering and individual existence.
12. Pajamas: Loose-fitting trousers, typically word for sleeping
    Taken from the Hindi word *pajama*.

13. Shampoo: Refers to the act of washing hair.
    Taken from the Hindi word *champi*, which refers to massage or kneading.
14. Thug: Swindler or deceiver.
    Taken from the Hindi word *thag*, which refers to the members of a historical Indian criminal organization.
15. Veranda: A roofed platform along the outside of a house similar to a porch.
    Taken from the Hindi word *baramada*.

Political terms:

1. Racist: A person who believes that one race is superior to others and discriminates against people based on their race.
2. Fascist: A person who supports or believes in a political system characterized by authoritarianism, nationalism and suppression of opposition.
3. Oppression: The systematic and pervasive exercise of power in a cruel, unjust or harmful way over a group or individual.
4. Activist: A person who campaigns for social or political change.
5. Anarchy: A state of society without government or law, often resulting in disorder and chaos.
6. Antisocial Behaviour: Actions that harm or lack consideration for the well-being of others, often violating social norms or laws.
7. 'Big Brother': A term used to describe an overly controlling and intrusive government or authority, often referencing George Orwell's novel *1984*.
8. Capitalism: An economic system where trade, industry, and the means of production are largely or entirely privately owned and operated for profit.
9. Communism: A political and economic ideology advocating for a classless society in which all property and resources are communally owned.
10. Centrist: A person who holds moderate political views, avoiding extremes of left-wing or right-wing ideologies.
11. Right-wing: Political beliefs that favour free-market capitalism, a strong national defence, and traditional social values, often emphasizing individualism.
12. Left-wing: Political beliefs that advocate for social equality, government intervention in the economy and progressive social policies.
13. Liberal: A person who supports political and social reform, individual freedoms, and government intervention in the economy to address social inequalities.

14. Conservative: A person who advocates for preserving traditional institutions, values and practices, and is generally resistant to rapid change.
15. Despot: A ruler who holds absolute power and often exercises it in a cruel or oppressive manner.
16. Ideology: A system of ideas and ideals that form the basis of economic or political theory and policy.
17. Pacifism: The belief in and commitment to peace, often rejecting the use of violence to resolve conflicts.
18. Partisan: A strong supporter of a specific party, cause or ideology, often showing biased loyalty.
19. Socialism: An economic and political system advocating for collective or governmental ownership and administration of the means of production and distribution of goods.
20. Whistle-blower: A person who exposes wrongdoing or illegal activities within an organization to the public or authorities.
21. Sedition: Conduct or speech inciting people to rebel against the authority of a state.

PHRASAL VERBS:

Phrasal verbs are expressions formed by a verb followed by one or more particles, typically prepositions or adverbs. They often have idiomatic meanings that can be different from the meanings of their individual parts. For example, 'turn off' means to the stop the operation of something, not to turn something in an off direction.

1. Act up: Misbehave or not function properly.
   Example: 'The kids started to act up when they got bored.'
2. Add up: Make sense; be consistent or logical.
   Example: 'Her story just doesn't add up.'
3. Aim at: Direct something toward a target.
   Example: 'The policy is aimed at reducing unemployment.'
4. Answer back: Reply rudely.
   Example: 'Don't answer back to your parents.'
5. As far as it goes: To a limited extent; within certain limits.
   Example: 'It's a good plan, as far as it goes, but it needs more detail.'
6. Ask around: Inquire about something by questioning multiple people.
   Example: 'I'll ask around and see if anyone knows where she is.'
7. Ask out: Invite someone to go on a date.
   Example: 'He asked her out to dinner.'
8. Back away: Retreat or move backwards.
   Example: 'The dog growled, so I backed away slowly.'
9. Bail out: Help someone out of a difficult situation, especially financial.
   Example: 'The government bailed out the failing banks.'
10. Be brought into force: To come into effect.
    Example: 'The new law will be brought into force next year.'
11. Bear out: Confirm or support.
    Example: 'The evidence bears out her story.'

12. Bear up: Endure or withstand.
    Example: 'He's bearing up well under the pressure.'
13. Bear with: Be patient with.
    Example: 'Please bear with me while I find your file.'
14. Beat down: Bargain to reduce the price of something.
    Example: 'I managed to beat him down to $50.'
15. Blow up: Explode or cause to explode; suddenly become very angry.
    Example: 'The bomb blew up in the city center.'
16. Break away: Leave or escape suddenly.
    Example: 'The horse broke away from its handler.'
17. Break down: Stop functioning; have an emotional collapse.
    Example: 'The car broke down on the way home.'
18. Break into: Enter by force or illegally.
    Example: 'Someone tried to break into the house last night.'
19. Break out: Start suddenly, especially something unwelcome (like a war or disease).
    Example: 'War broke out in the country.'
20. Break up: End a relationship; disband.
    Example: 'They decided to break up after five years together.'
21. Bring about: Cause to happen.
    Example: 'The new manager brought about significant changes.'
22. Bring along: Take someone or something with you.
    Example: 'Can I bring a friend along to the party?'
23. Bring back: Return something or someone to a place.
    Example: 'Can you bring back my book tomorrow?'
24. Bring down: Cause to fall or collapse.
    Example: 'The scandal may bring down the government.'
25. Bring forth: Produce or give rise to.
    Example: 'The plan will bring forth positive results.'
26. Bring in: Introduce or implement.
    Example: 'They are planning to bring in new regulations.'
27. Bring on: Cause something to happen or appear.
    Example: 'Stress can bring on illness.'

28. Bring out: Make something more noticeable; publish or release.
    Example: 'The new dress really brings out the color of your eyes.'
29. Bring round: Restore to consciousness; persuade.
    Example: 'We used smelling salts to bring him round.'
30. Bring up: Raise a child; mention a topic.
    Example: 'She was brought up in a small village.'
31. Bringing out: Highlight or emphasize; publish or release.
    Example: 'He has a way of bringing out the best in people.'
32. Broke her heart: Cause emotional pain or sorrow.
    Example: 'When he left, it broke her heart.'
33. Broke the record: Surpass a previous achievement.
    Example: 'She broke the record for the 100 meters.'
34. Brought about: Caused to happen.
    Example: 'The invention of the internet brought about a revolution in communication.'
35. Brought into the open: Made public.
    Example: 'The scandal was brought into the open by the media.'
36. Brought to a head: Brought to a point of crisis or resolution.
    Example: 'The conflict was brought to a head by the latest incident.'
37. Brought to light: Revealed or disclosed.
    Example: 'The investigation brought to light new evidence.'
38. Brought up: Mentioned a topic; raised a child.
    Example: 'She brought up the issue at the meeting.'
39. Brush up: Improve knowledge or skill in something.
    Example: 'I need to brush up on my French before the trip.'
40. Build up: Increase gradually.
    Example: 'She built up a successful business from scratch.'
41. Call off: Cancel something that was planned.
    Example: 'They decided to call off the wedding.'
42. Came across: Find or meet by chance.
    Example: 'I came across an old friend at the market.'

43. Came at: Attack or move towards someone aggressively.
    Example: 'The dog came at me suddenly.'
44. Came up: Occur or become noticeable; be mentioned.
    Example: 'The question of funding came up during the meeting.'
45. Carry on: Continue doing something.
    Example: 'Despite the interruptions, she carried on with her speech.'
46. Carry out: Perform or complete a task.
    Example: 'The scientists carried out an important experiment.'
47. Catch up: Reach the same standard or level as others.
    Example: 'She needs to catch up on her homework.'
48. Check in: Register upon arrival at a hotel or airport.
    Example: 'We need to check in at least two hours before the flight.'
49. Check out: Pay the bill and leave a hotel; investigate.
    Example: 'We will check out of the hotel at noon.'
50. Cheer up: Become happier or make someone happier.
    Example: 'She tried to cheer him up with a joke.'
51. Clean up: Tidy or clear a space.
    Example: 'We need to clean up the kitchen after cooking.'
52. Clear up: Make something clean or tidy; explain or solve.
    Example: 'Can you clear up this mess?'
53. Come across: Find or meet by chance (same as #42).
    Example: 'She came across her old diary in the attic.'
54. Come along: Accompany someone; progress.
    Example: 'Would you like to come along to the movies?'
55. Come around: Regain consciousness; change one's opinion.
    Example: 'She finally came around and agreed with us.'
56. Come between: Cause a disagreement or separation between people.
    Example: 'Don't let misunderstandings come between friends.'
57. Come by: Obtain or visit.
    Example: 'Good jobs are hard to come by these days.'

58. Come into: Inherit something.
Example: 'She came into a large sum of money after her aunt passed away.'
59. Come off: Happen successfully or as planned.
Example: 'The party came off without a hitch.'
60. Come out: Be published or become known.
Example: 'The new book will come out next month.'
61. Come round: Regain consciousness; visit casually (same as #55).
Example: 'He came round after fainting.'
62. Come up: Occur or appear unexpectedly (same as #44).
Example: 'Something urgent has come up, and I need to leave.'
63. Comes before: Precede in importance or order.
Example: 'Your health comes before anything else.'
64. Count on: Rely or depend on.
Example: 'You can count on me for support.'
65. Cross out: Draw a line through something written.
Example: 'Please cross out the wrong answers.'
66. Cut down: Reduce in size or amount.
Example: 'You need to cut down on sugar.'
67. Cut off: Stop the supply of something; interrupt.
Example: 'The electricity was cut off due to non-payment.'
68. Cut out: Stop doing something; remove.
Example: 'He was advised to cut out fatty foods.'
69. Deal with: Handle or manage a situation or problem.
Example: 'He has to deal with a lot of stress at work.'
70. Die away: Gradually diminish or fade.
Example: 'The sound of the train died away.'
71. Die down: Become less intense.
Example: 'The storm finally died down after midnight.'
72. Dig in: Start eating enthusiastically; adopt a firm position.
Example: 'The food is ready, so dig in!'
73. Do away with: Get rid of; abolish.
Example: 'They decided to do away with the old rules.'

74. Do out of: Deprive someone of something in an unfair way.
    Example: 'She was done out of her rightful inheritance.'
75. Do over: Repeat or redo something.
    Example: 'You will need to do the assignment over.'
76. Do without: Manage without something.
    Example: 'We'll have to do without a car for a while.'
77. Double up: Share or use something together.
    Example: 'We had to double up in the hotel room due to a shortage of rooms.'
78. Draw in: Become night; attract.
    Example: 'The days are drawing in as winter approaches.'
79. Draw up: Prepare a document; come to a stop.
    Example: 'They drew up a new contract.'
80. Dress down: Scold; dress casually.
    Example: 'She was dressed down by her boss for being late.'
81. Dress up: Put on formal or fancy clothes.
    Example: 'We need to dress up for the party.'
82. Drive away: Cause to leave.
    Example: 'His rude behaviour drove away all his friends.'
83. Drive off: Leave in a vehicle.
    Example: 'They drove off without saying goodbye.'
84. Drive up: Increase something.
    Example: 'Demand is driving up prices.'
85. Drop by: Visit casually.
    Example: 'I'll drop by your house later.'
86. Drop in: Visit casually (same as #86).
    Example: 'Feel free to drop in any time.'
87. Drop off: Decrease; fall asleep; deliver.
    Example: 'I'll drop off the package on my way home.'
88. Drop out: Withdraw from something, especially school.
    Example: 'He decided to drop out of college.'
89. Dry out: Become dry, especially after being wet.
    Example: 'The clothes need to dry out before you can wear them.'
90. Dry up: Stop being available; cease talking.
    Example: 'The river has dried up after the drought.'

`91. Dust off: Remove dust; prepare to use something after a long period.
Example: 'He dusted off his old guitar and started playing again.'
92. Ease up: Become less severe; relax effort.
Example: 'You can ease up now; the hardest part is over.'
93. End up: Finally be in a particular place or situation.
Example: 'She ended up working as a teacher.'
94. Engage in: Participate in.
Example: 'They engaged in a heated debate.'
95. Enter into: Begin something, especially an agreement.
Example: 'They entered into a partnership.'
96. Even out: Make level or equal.
Example: 'We need to even out the workload.'
97. Expose to: Subject to.
Example: 'Don't expose the plant to too much sunlight.'
98. Extend to: Include or cover.
Example: 'The invitation extends to your family as well.'
99. Eye up: Look at someone with interest or desire.
Example: 'He was eyeing up the new car.'
100. Face up to: Confront or accept something difficult.
Example: 'You need to face up to your responsibilities.'
101. Fall apart: Break into pieces; become emotionally upset.
Example: 'The chair fell apart when I sat on it.'
102. Fall back on: Use something as a backup plan.
Example: 'He had his savings to fall back on after losing his job.'
103. Figure out: Understand or solve something.
Example: 'I can't figure out this math problem.'
104. Fill in: Complete a form or document; substitute for someone.
Example: 'Please fill in this form.'
105. Find out: Discover information.
Example: 'I found out the truth about her.'
106. Finish off: Complete or use the last part of something.
Example: 'Let's finish off this cake.'

107. Fix up: Repair or arrange something.
Example: 'We need to fix up the house before we sell it.'
108. Follow up: Continue or pursue something.
Example: 'You should follow up on that job application.'
109. Fool around: Behave playfully or aimlessly.
Example: 'Stop fooling around and get to work.'
110. Forge ahead: Make strong progress.
Example: 'She is forging ahead with her plans.'
111. Freak out: Become very anxious, upset or afraid.
Example: 'He freaked out when he saw the spider.'
112. Free up: Make something available
Example: 'By delegating some of her tasks to her assistant, she was able to free up more time for strategic planning.'
113. Get across: Successfully communicate an idea or message.
Example: 'She managed to get her point across during the meeting.'
114. Get along: Have a good relationship.
Example: 'They get along well with each other.'
115. Get around: Move from place to place or avoid an obstacle.
Example: 'She uses a wheelchair to get around.'
116. Get at: Imply or suggest something indirectly.
Example: 'What exactly are you getting at?'
117. Get away with: Avoid punishment for something.
Example: 'He always manages to get away with cheating on his taxes.'
118. Get behind: Fall behind schedule or in progress.
Example: 'If you get behind in your work, you'll need to catch up quickly.'
119. Get by: Manage to survive or cope.
Example: 'She gets by on a small pension.'
120. Get down: Depress or discourage someone.
Example: 'Don't let the bad news get you down.'
121. Get down to: Start focusing on or dealing with something seriously.
Example: 'Let's get down to business.'

122. Get my own back: Take revenge.
Example: 'He was determined to get his own back on those who had wronged him.'

123. Get on: Continue doing something or make progress; board a vehicle.
Example: 'It's getting late; we should get on with the project.'

124. Get out of: Avoid doing something or escape a situation.
Example: 'He tried to get out of doing his homework.'

125. Get over: Recover from something, such as an illness or a difficult situation.
Example: 'It took her months to get over the breakup.'

126. Get round: Persuade someone to do something.
Example: 'She knew how to get round her parents to get what she wanted.'

127. Get through: Successfully deal with a difficult situation or make contact by phone.
Example: 'He helped her get through the tough times.'

128. Get up to: Be involved in, typically something mischievous or surprising.
Example: 'What did you get up to at the weekend?'

129. Get-together: A casual meeting or gathering.
Example: 'We had a small get-together with friends.'

130. Give away: Reveal something, usually unintentionally; donate something.
Example: 'She gave away the surprise by mistake.'

131. Give back: Return something to its owner.
Example: 'Make sure you give back the book you borrowed.'

132. Give in: Yield or surrender to demands.
Example: 'She finally gave in to her kids' requests for a pet.'

133. Give off: Emit or release something, like a smell or light.
Example: 'The fire was giving off a lot of smoke.'

134. Give up: Stop trying or quit.
Example: 'He gave up smoking last year.'

135. Go ahead: Proceed with something.
Example: 'You can go ahead and start without me.'
136. Go far: Be very successful or make significant progress.
Example: 'With his talents, he'll go far in life.'
137. Go for: Choose or select; attempt to achieve something.
Example: 'I'm going to go for the job in New York.'
138. Go over: Review or examine something carefully.
Example: 'Let's go over the report before the meeting.'
139. Go through: Experience or endure something difficult or unpleasant.
Example: 'She went through a lot of pain after the accident.'
140. Goes against: Contradict or be in opposition to something.
Example: 'Cheating goes against my principles.'
141. Goes for: Applies to; is true for.
Example: 'What I said goes for you too.'
142. Going on: Happening or occurring.
Example: 'What's going on here?'
143. Gone bankrupt: Become insolvent or unable to pay debts.
Example: 'The company has gone bankrupt.'
144. Got rid of: Eliminated or disposed of.
Example: 'I finally got rid of my old clothes.'
145. Grow into: Gradually develop into a particular role or condition.
Example: 'He has grown into a confident young man.'
146. Grow out of: Become too large for something; stop doing something as one matures.
Example: 'She has grown out of her old clothes.'
147. Hand in: Submit something, such as a document or assignment.
Example: 'Please hand in your reports by Friday.'
148. Hand out: Distribute to a group of people.
Example: 'They handed out flyers to promote the event.'
149. Hang around: Spend time idly or without a specific purpose.
Example: 'We used to hang around the mall after school.'
150. Hang on: Wait for a short time; hold tightly.
Example: 'Hang on a minute, I'll be right back.'

151. Hang out: Spend time relaxing or socializing.
Example: 'Do you want to hang out at my place tonight?'
152. Hang up: End a phone call; hang something, such as clothes.
Example: 'She hung up the phone abruptly.'
153. Head off: Prevent something from happening; leave to go somewhere.
Example: 'We should head off any potential problems early.'
154. Help out: Assist someone.
Example: 'Can you help out with the preparations for the party?'
155. Hit on: Make a pass at someone; discover or think of something.
Example: 'He hit on a great idea for a new project.'
156. Hold back: Restrain or prevent from advancing.
Example: 'Don't hold back your emotions.'
157. Hold on: Wait for a moment; maintain a grip.
Example: 'Hold on, I need to grab my coat.'
158. Hold over: Postpone or extend the duration of something.
Example: 'The decision was held over until the next meeting.'
159. Hold up: Delay; rob someone with a threat of violence.
Example: 'The traffic held us up for an hour.'
160. Hunt down: Search for and capture someone or something.
Example: 'The police hunted down the escaped prisoner.'
161. Hurry up: Move or act quickly.
Example: 'Hurry up, we're going to be late!'
162. Hush up: Suppress or conceal something.
Example: 'They tried to hush up the scandal.'
163. Identify with: Associate oneself closely with a person or group.
Example: 'She identifies with the main character in the book.'
164. Immerse in: Become completely involved in something.
Example: 'He immersed himself in his studies.'
165. Inquire about: Ask for information regarding something.
Example: 'I called to inquire about the job opening.'

166. Insist on: Demand something firmly or persistently.
Example: 'She insisted on paying for the meal.'
167. Intend to: Have a plan or purpose to do something.
Example: 'I intend to finish my project by next week.'
168. Invest in: Put money, effort or time into something for future benefits.
Example: 'She decided to invest in a new business venture.'
169. Invite over: Ask someone to come to your home.
Example: 'Let's invite them over for dinner.'
170. Iron into: Press with an iron to make smooth.
Example: 'He ironed his shirt into perfect form.'
171. Iron out: Resolve or clear up difficulties or disagreements.
Example: 'We need to iron out the details of the contract.'
172. Itch for: Strongly desire or be eager for something.
Example: 'She was itching for a fight.'
173. Jack up: Increase sharply; raise using a jack.
Example: 'They jacked up the prices during the holiday season.'
174. Jam out: Play music enthusiastically.
Example: 'The band jammed out at the party.'
175. Jazz up: Make something more interesting or lively.
Example: 'She jazzed up her outfit with a bright scarf.'
176. Jerk around: Treat someone inconsiderately or unfairly.
Example: 'Stop jerking me around and tell me the truth.'
177. Jet off: Leave quickly, especially by airplane.
Example: 'They're jetting off to Paris for the weekend.'
178. Jiggle around: Move or shake something in quick, small movements.
Example: 'She jiggled the keys around in the lock.'
179. Join in: Participate in an activity with others.
Example: 'Would you like to join in the game?'
180. Jot down: Write something quickly.
Example: 'He jotted down her phone number on a napkin.'
181. Jump at: Eagerly accept an opportunity.
Example: 'She jumped at the chance to work abroad.'

182. Jump in: Enter a conversation or activity abruptly.
Example: 'Feel free to jump in with your thoughts.'
183. Keep away: Stay at a distance.
Example: 'Keep away from the construction site.'
184. Keep on: Continue doing something.
Example: 'She kept on talking despite the interruptions.'
185. Keep to: Stick to or adhere to something.
Example: 'We should keep to the original plan.'
186. Keep up: Maintain the same level or pace.
Example: 'Keep up the good work!'
187. Key into: Enter or input data into a system.
Example: 'Key your password into the login screen.'
188. Kick back: Relax or take it easy.
Example: 'After a long day, I like to kick back with a book.'
189. Kick up: Cause a disturbance or commotion.
Example: 'The kids kicked up a fuss when they couldn't have dessert.'
190. Knock out: Defeat or render unconscious.
Example: 'The boxer knocked out his opponent in the third round.'
191. Know about: Have knowledge of something.
Example: 'Do you know about the changes to the schedule?'
192. Knuckle down: Start working hard, especially after a period of inactivity.
Example: 'It's time to knuckle down and finish this project.'
193. Lace up: Tighten or fasten with laces.
Example: 'He laced up his shoes before the run.'
194. Lash out: Suddenly attack someone verbally or physically.
Example: 'He lashed out at his critics during the interview.'
195. Lay off: Dismiss employees from their jobs due to lack of work.
Example: 'The company had to lay off workers during the recession.'
196. Lead to: Result in or cause something to happen.
Example: 'His efforts led to significant improvements.'

197. Leak out: Become known or escape, usually of confidential information.
Example: 'News of the merger leaked out before the official announcement.'
198. Leave out: Exclude or omit.
Example: 'Please don't leave out any details.'
199. Let down: Disappoint someone.
Example: 'She felt let down by her friend's actions.'
200. Let go of: Release or relinquish something.
Example: 'It's time to let go of past mistakes.'
201. Let it slip: Reveal something unintentionally.
Example: 'She let it slip that he was planning a surprise party.'
202. Let me be: Leave someone alone.
Example: 'I need some time to myself; just let me be.'
203. Let out: Allow to leave; make something known.
Example: 'The teacher let the students out early.'
204. Light up: Illuminate or become brighter; show a sudden expression of happiness.
Example: 'Her face lit up when she saw the gift.'
205. Look after: Take care of someone or something.
Example: 'Can you look after the kids while I'm out?'
206. Look into: Investigate or examine.
Example: 'The police are looking into the case.'
207. Look on the bright side: Find the positive aspects in a negative situation.
Example: 'Even though you lost the game, look on the bright side; you played well.'
208. Look out: Be vigilant or careful.
Example: 'Look out for traffic when crossing the street.'
209. Look up: Search for information; improve.
Example: 'Things are looking up for the new business.'
210. Looks down her nose at: Consider someone or something inferior.
Example: 'She looks down her nose at anyone who doesn't have a college degree.'

211. Make do: Manage with what is available.
Example: 'We don't have all the ingredients, but we'll have to make do.'

212. Make for: Move towards or head in the direction of.
Example: 'They made for the exit as soon as the show ended.'

213. Make for: Contribute to or result in.
Example: 'This will make for a much better working environment.'

214. Make of: Understand or interpret something.
Example: 'What do you make of this news?'

215. Make off: Leave quickly, usually to avoid trouble or after committing a crime.
Example: 'The thieves made off with the stolen goods.'

216. Make out: Discern or understand something with difficulty.
Example: 'I can't make out what he's saying.'

217. Make over: Change or improve the appearance of someone or something.
Example: 'They made over the old house into a modern home.'

218. Make up: Invent a story or excuse; reconcile after a disagreement.
Example: 'She made up an excuse for being late. They had a fight but later made up.'

219. Make up for: Compensate for something.
Example: 'He bought flowers to make up for missing her birthday.'

220. Make up to: Try to win favour with someone by being nice.
Example: 'He made up to the boss to get a promotion.'

221. Mark down: Reduce the price of something.
Example: 'The store has marked down many items for the sale.'

222. Mark up: Increase the price of something.
Example: 'They marked up the prices before the holiday season.'

223. Measure up: Meet a particular standard.
Example: 'She didn't measure up to the company's expectations.'
224. Meet up: Gather or come together with someone.
Example: 'Let's meet up for coffee tomorrow.'
225. Melt down: Collapse emotionally or lose control; change from solid to liquid.
Example: 'She had a melt down after the stressful week.'
226. Mess around: Spend time doing unimportant things; engage in playful or aimless activity.
Example: 'Stop messing around and start working.'
227. Mess around: Be involved romantically or sexually in an informal or casual way.
Example: 'He's been messing around with a lot of different people.'
228. Mess up: Make a mistake or cause a problem.
Example: 'I messed up the presentation by forgetting my notes.'
229. Mix up: Confuse two or more things or people.
Example: 'I always mix up their names.'
230. Move in: Start living in a new home.
Example: 'They decided to move in together.'
231. Move out: Leave your home to live somewhere else.
Example: 'She's moving out at the end of the month.'
232. Nail down: Understand or identify something precisely.
Example: 'We need to nail down the exact time for the meeting.'
233. Name after: Give someone the same name as another person.
Example: 'He was named after his grandfather.'
234. Name for: Give a place or thing a name in honour of someone.
Example: 'The park is named for a famous local hero.'
235. Narrow down: Reduce the number of options or choices.
Example: 'We need to narrow down the list of candidates.'
236. Nip in: Enter a place briefly.
Example: 'I need to nip in the store to buy some milk.'

237. Nod at: Signal approval or acknowledgment with a nod.
Example: 'He nodded at me as he walked past.'
238. Nod off: Fall asleep, usually unintentionally.
Example: 'He nodded off during the lecture.'
239. Nod to: Give a sign of approval or acknowledgment/refer to or acknowledge subtly.
Example: 'The director nodded to the new changes.'/'The film nods to classic Hollywood movies.'
240. Note down: Write something down to remember it.
Example: 'She noted down the address quickly.'
241. Note on: Comment or give an opinion about something.
Example: 'He noted on the progress of the project.'
242. Note with: Observe with a particular feeling.
Example: 'She noted with surprise how much he had changed.'
243. Nudge out: Displace someone or something slightly.
Example: 'He nudged out his competitor for the top spot.'
244. Number among: Be part of a group.
Example: 'She is numbered among the top scientists in her field.'
245. Nurse along: Help or encourage the progress of someone or something.
Example: 'They nursed the injured bird along until it could fly.'
246. Observe on: Comment or remark on something.
Example: 'He observed on the changes in the landscape.'
247. Offer up: Present or give something, often in a formal or religious context.
Example: 'They offered up prayers for the victims.'
248. Open up: Become more accessible or allow more access; start to talk more freely.
Example: 'New opportunities are opening up in the field./ She opened up about her feelings.'
249. Opt for: Choose or decide in favour of something.
Example: 'They opted for a more practical car.'

250. Opt out: Choose not to participate.
Example: 'He opted out of the company health plan.'

251. Outdo oneself: Perform exceptionally well, surpassing one's own previous efforts.
Example: 'She really outdid herself with this project.'

252. Overcome with: Be strongly affected by an emotion.
Example: 'She was overcome with joy when she heard the news.'

253. Own up: Admit to doing something wrong.
Example: 'He owned up to breaking the window.'

254. Pass away: Die.
Example: 'Her grandfather passed away last year.'

255. Pass out: Faint or lose consciousness.
Example: 'He passed out from the heat.'

256. Pass up: Decline an opportunity.
Example: 'Don't pass up the chance to see the show.'

257. Passed away: Died.
Example: 'She passed away peacefully in her sleep.'

258. Pay off: Pay all of a debt; result in success.
Example: 'He finally paid off his student loans./His hard work paid off.'

259. Pick on: Bully or harass someone.
Example: 'The other kids used to pick on him at school.'

260. Pick out: Choose or select.
Example: 'She picked out a new dress for the party.'

261. Pick up: Lift something; learn something new; start again; increase.
Example: 'He picked up the book./She picked up Spanish quickly./Business is picking up.'

262. Play along: Pretend to agree or cooperate.
Example: 'He decided to play along with the prank.'

263. Play up: Emphasize or highlight; behave badly.
Example: 'The media played up the scandal./The kids are playing up again.'

264. Point out: Draw attention to something.
Example: 'She pointed out the mistake in the report.'

265. Point to: Indicate or suggest something.
Example: 'All evidence points to him being the culprit.'

266. Pull off: Succeed in doing something difficult.
Example: 'She pulled off a brilliant performance.'

267. Pulls in: Attract or bring in.
Example: 'The new store pulls in a lot of customers.'

268. Put away: Store or tidy something; save money.
Example: 'He put away his toys./She's putting away money for a new car.'

269. Put forward: Suggest or propose.
Example: 'He put forward a new plan.'

270. Put in: Install something; contribute effort or time.
Example: 'They put in a new heating system./She put in a lot of work on the project.'

271. Put off: Postpone something; discourage someone.
Example: 'They put off the meeting until next week./The smell put him off his food.'

272. Put on: Wear clothing; organize an event; gain weight.
Example: 'She put on her coat./They're putting on a play./He put on weight over the holidays.'

273. Put out: Extinguish a fire; inconvenience someone.
Example: 'The firefighters put out the blaze./I hope I'm not putting you out.'

274. Put up: Provide accommodation; raise something.
Example: 'Can you put me up for the night?/They put up a new sign.'

275. Putting across: Communicate or explain clearly.
Example: 'He put his ideas across well in the presentation.'

276. Putting down: Criticize someone; euthanize an animal.
Example: 'She was always putting him down./They had to put down the old dog.'

277. Queue up: Form or join a line.
Example: 'We had to queue up for tickets.'

278. Quicken up: Increase speed.
Example: 'The runners quickened up as they neared the finish line.'

279. Quiet down: Become quieter or make something quieter.
Example: 'The teacher asked the students to quiet down.'
280. Rack up: Accumulate or gather.
Example: 'He racked up a lot of frequent flyer miles.'
281. Raise up: Lift to a higher position; inspire to a better state.
Example: 'The coach raised up the team's spirits.'
282. Rake in: Earn a lot of money.
Example: 'They're raking in the profits.'
283. Ramp up: Increase or enhance.
Example: 'The company is ramping up production.'
284. Rat out: Inform on someone.
Example: 'He ratted out his accomplices to the police.'
285. Read up: Study or research by reading.
Example: 'She read up on the subject before the interview.'
286. Reap off: Cheat or defraud.
Example: 'They reaped off customers with their overpriced products.'
287. Rearrange: Change the position or order of something.
Example: 'We need to rearrange the furniture.'
288. Reason out: Think through and resolve logically.
Example: 'Let's reason out the solution to this problem.'
289. Rely on: Depend on or trust.
Example: 'You can rely on her to keep a secret.'
290. Run out: Exhaust the supply of something.
Example: 'We've run out of milk.'
291. Run over: Hit with a vehicle; exceed time limit; practice quickly.
Example: 'The car ran over a squirrel./The meeting ran over by 30 minutes./Let's run over the script one more time.'
292. Sack out: Go to sleep.
Example: 'I'm exhausted, I think I'll sack out early tonight.'
293. Sand down: Smooth a surface using sandpaper.
Example: 'We need to sand down the rough edges before painting the table.'
294. Save up: Accumulate money for a specific purpose.
Example: 'I'm saving up for a new car.'

295. Scale back: Reduce in size or scope.
Example: 'Due to budget cuts, we need to scale back our project.'
296. Scatter about: Distribute or spread things in different directions.
Example: 'She scattered her toys about the room.'
297. Scramble up: Climb or move quickly using hands and feet.
Example: 'They scrambled up the rocky hill.'
298. Screw up: Make a mistake or cause a problem.
Example: 'I really screwed up my presentation.'
299. Set fire to: Ignite something so that it burns.
Example: 'Someone set fire to the abandoned building.'
300. Set foot in: Enter or visit a place.
Example: 'I have never set foot in that store.'
301. Set in her ways: Be stubborn or inflexible in one's habits.
Example: 'She's set in her ways and refuses to try new things.'
302. Set on fire: Ignite something to burn.
Example: 'They set the logs on fire to start the campfire.'
303. Settle down: Become stable or start living a quieter life.
Example: 'He decided to settle down and start a family.'
304. Shape up: Improve or develop properly.
Example: 'He needs to shape up if he wants to keep his job.'
305. Shell out: Spend money, often reluctantly.
Example: 'I had to shell out a lot of money for repairs.'
306. Shoe up: Put on shoes (less commonly used).
Example: 'Make sure to shoe up before going outside.'
307. Shut up: Stop talking or be quiet.
Example: 'He told them to shut up during the movie.'
308. Sign in: Register or log in.
Example: 'Please sign in at the front desk.'
309. Sing along: Join in singing with someone else.
Example: 'Everyone started to sing along with the band.'
310. Sit back: Relax and do nothing.
Example: 'Just sit back and enjoy the show.'

311. Skim off: Remove a substance from the surface.
Example: 'She skimmed off the fat from the soup.'
312. Sleep in: Stay in bed later than usual.
Example: 'I love to sleep in on weekends.'
313. Slip up: Make a mistake.
Example: 'I slipped up and called him by the wrong name.'
314. Slow down: Reduce speed or activity.
Example: 'You need to slow down, you're working too hard.'
315. Sort through: Organize or look through items.
Example: 'I need to sort through these papers.'
316. Speak out: Express one's opinions publicly.
Example: 'She decided to speak out against injustice.'
317. Spin off: Create something new based on something existing.
Example: 'The company decided to spin off a new division.'
318. Stand up: Rise to a standing position; confront or defend.
Example: 'Please stand up when the judge enters./Stand up for your rights.'
319. Stick around: Stay in a place for a period of time.
Example: 'You can stick around for dinner if you like.'
320. Take advantage of: Exploit for one's own benefit.
Example: 'He took advantage of the sale to buy a new TV.'
321. Take after: Resemble in appearance or behaviour.
Example: 'She takes after her mother in looks and personality.'
322. Take apart: Disassemble or dismantle.
Example: 'He took the engine apart to fix it.'
323. Take back: Retract a statement; return something.
Example: 'He had to take back his hurtful comments./I need to take back this shirt to the store.'
324. Take back: Regain possession of something.
Example: 'I wish I could take back my old job.'
325. Take down: Remove something from a higher position; write down.
Example: 'Please take down the decorations./She took down his address.'

326. Take for granted: Fail to appreciate something.
Example: 'Don't take your health for granted.'
327. Take in: Absorb or understand; give shelter.
Example: 'She took in all the information quickly./They took in a stray cat.'
328. Take in: Visit or experience something.
Example: 'They took in the sights of the city.'
329. Take in her stride: Deal with something difficult calmly.
Example: 'She took the criticism in her stride.'
330. Take off: Leave the ground (for planes); become successful quickly; remove something.
Example: 'The plane will take off soon./Her career took off after the movie./Take off your shoes.'
331. Take on: Accept a challenge or responsibility; hire someone.
Example: 'I'll take on the project./They're taking on new staff.'
332. Take on: Compete against or fight.
Example: 'He's willing to take on anyone in a game of chess.'
333. Take out: Remove something; take someone on a date; kill or destroy.
Example: 'Take out the trash./He took her out to dinner./The sniper took out the target.'
334. Take over: Assume control or responsibility.
Example: 'She will take over the project next week.'
335. Take pride in: Be proud of something.
Example: 'He takes pride in his work.'
336. Take up: Start a new activity; fill space or time.
Example: 'She decided to take up painting./The table takes up too much space.'
337. Take up: Discuss or deal with an issue.
Example: 'We'll take up this matter in the next meeting.'
338. Taken in: Deceived or tricked.
Example: 'She was taken in by the scam.'
339. Taken off: Become successful quickly; leave quickly.
Example: 'His business has really taken off./He took off without saying goodbye.'

340. Taking care: Looking after someone or something.
Example: 'She's taking care of her elderly parents.'
341. Taking off: Leaving the ground (for aircraft) or becoming successful quickly.
Example: 'The plane is taking off./His career is taking off.'
342. Talk down to: Speak to someone in a condescending manner.
Example: 'She hates it when people talk down to her.'
343. Talk over: Discuss something thoroughly.
Example: 'We need to talk over the details of the contract.'
344. Tear apart: Destroy or criticize something or someone severely.
Example: 'The critics tore apart the new play.'
345. Tear down: Demolish or take apart a structure.
Example: 'They decided to tear down the old building.'
346. Tear up: Rip into pieces or start crying.
Example: 'She tore up the letter./The sad movie made him tear up.'
347. Think over: Consider something carefully.
Example: 'I'll think over your proposal.'
348. Think up: Invent or create something in one's mind.
Example: 'She thought up a brilliant marketing strategy.'
349. Throw away: Dispose of something.
Example: 'Don't throw away those old magazines.'
350. Throw out: Dispose of something or expel someone.
Example: 'They had to throw out the spoiled food./He was thrown out of the club.'
351. Throw up: Vomit.
Example: 'The ride made him throw up.'
352. Tie up: Bind or secure with a rope; be busy.
Example: 'They tied up the boat./I'm tied up with work right now.'
353. To put someone's back up: Annoy or irritate someone.
Example: 'His constant criticism puts my back up.'
354. Took my breath away: Impress or amaze someone greatly.
Example: 'The view from the mountain took my breath away.'

355. Took off: Left the ground or became successful quickly.
Example: 'The plane took off./Her career took off after the promotion.'
356. Took part in: Participated in an activity.
Example: 'She took part in the charity run.'
357. Took to: Began to like someone or something.
Example: 'He took to his new job right away.'
358. Try on: Put on clothing to see if it fits.
Example: 'She tried on several dresses before choosing one.'
359. Try out: Test something to see if it works.
Example: 'He tried out the new software.'
360. Tune in: Watch or listen to a broadcast.
Example: 'Tune in to the news at 6 PM.'
361. Turn down: Reject an offer or reduce the volume.
Example: 'She turned down the job offer./Turn down the music.'
362. Turn into: Change or transform into something.
Example: 'The caterpillar turned into a butterfly.'
363. Turn off: Stop a machine or make someone lose interest.
Example: 'Turn off the lights./His rude comments really turned me off.'
364. Turn on: Start a machine or attract someone.
Example: 'Turn on the TV./He knows how to turn me on.'
365. Turn out: Result in a particular way or attend an event.
Example: 'It turned out to be a great day./A lot of people turned out for the concert.'
366. Turn up: Increase the volume or appear suddenly.
Example: 'Turn up the heat./He turned up late to the meeting.'
367. Turned down: Rejected or reduced in volume.
Example: 'She turned down the proposal./The music was turned down.'
368. Undertake: Begin or attempt something.
Example: 'She undertook the challenging task.'
369. Upset about: Disturbed or distressed by something.
Example: 'He was upset about the news.'

370. Urge on: Encourage someone to continue.
Example: 'The coach urged the team on.'
371. Use in: Incorporate or utilize in a process.
Example: 'They used high-quality materials in the construction.'
372. Use out: Fully utilize or exhaust.
Example: 'He used out all the supplies.'
373. Use up: Consume entirely.
Example: 'She used up all the paper in the printer.'
374. Vamp up: Enhance or improve something.
Example: 'They vamped up the old car to look brand new.'
375. Vary from: Differ from something.
Example: 'Opinions vary from person to person.'
376. Vent out: Express feelings openly.
Example: 'She needed to vent out her frustrations.'
377. Venture forth: Go out or travel, often into unfamiliar or dangerous areas.
Example: 'They decided to venture forth into the wilderness.'
378. Venture out: Same as above.
Example: 'Despite the storm, they ventured out to find help.'
379. Vie for: Compete eagerly for something.
Example: 'Several candidates are vying for the position.'
380. Visit around: Travel to various places or see multiple people.
Example: 'She spent the weekend visiting around the city.'
381. Visit with: Spend time with someone socially.
Example: 'We visited with old friends over the holidays.'
382. Voice out: Express opinions or feelings.
Example: 'He voiced out his concerns at the meeting.'
383. Volunteer for: Offer to do something willingly.
Example: 'She volunteered for the community project.'
384. Volunteer to: Offer to do something willingly.
Example: 'He volunteered to lead the team.'
385. Vote down: Reject something by voting against it.
Example: 'The proposal was voted down by the committee.'

386. Vote in: Elect someone to office.
Example: 'He was voted in as the new president.'
387. Vote out: Remove someone from office by voting.
Example: 'The mayor was voted out in the last election.'
388. Vote with: Show agreement or support through voting.
Example: 'She voted with the majority on the issue.'
389. Vouch for: Guarantee or affirm something.
Example: 'I can vouch for his honesty.'
390. Vow to: Make a solemn promise to do something.
Example: 'She vowed to complete the project on time.'
391. Wake up: Stop sleeping.
Example: 'She wakes up at 7 a.m. every day.'
392. Walk away: Leave a situation or place.
Example: 'He decided to walk away from the argument.'
393. Wash up: Clean oneself, especially hands and face.
Example: 'Make sure to wash up before dinner.'
394. Watch out: Be careful or alert.
Example: 'Watch out for that slippery floor!'
395. Wear out: Become unusable through use.
Example: 'These shoes are worn out and need to be replaced.'
396. Weigh down: Burden or oppress.
Example: 'She felt weighed down by her responsibilities.'
397. Went off: Made a sudden loud noise; exploded; left a place.
Example: 'The alarm went off at midnight./The bomb went off./He went off to college.'
398. Went on: Continued; happened.
Example: 'The meeting went on for hours./What went on here?'
399. Went through: Experienced or endured.
Example: 'She went through a difficult time.'
400. Went to great lengths: Made a lot of effort.
Example: 'He went to great lengths to ensure the event was perfect.'
401. Whip up: Prepare quickly; excite emotions.
Example: 'She whipped up a quick meal./He whipped up the crowd with his speech.'

402. Wind up: End up in a particular state; conclude.
Example: 'He wound up in debt./Let's wind up this meeting.'
403. Work out: Exercise; find a solution.
Example: 'She works out at the gym every day./We need to work out this problem.'
404. Yank off: Pull something off forcefully.
Example: 'He yanked off the bandage.'
405. Yap at: Talk noisily and at length.
Example: 'The dog yapped at the mailman.'
406. Yearn for: Long for something.
Example: 'She yearned for a simpler life.'
407. Yell out: Shout loudly.
Example: 'He yelled out for help.'
408. Yield to: Give way to something; submit.
Example: 'He yielded to temptation.'
409. Yield up: Surrender or relinquish.
Example: 'They yielded up their weapons to the authorities.'
410. Yoke up: Join or link together.
Example: 'The farmers yoked up the oxen.'
411. Zero in: Focus closely on something.
Example: 'She zeroed in on the main issue.'
412. Zip up: Close something with a zipper.
Example: 'Zip up your jacket, it's cold outside.'
413. Zone out: Stop paying attention.
Example: 'He zoned out during the lecture.'
414. Zoom in: Focus closely with a camera or concentrate on details.

Dialogue between a customer and salesman at a shoe shop. Can you spot any phrasal verbs?

Customer: Good morning. I'm looking for a pair of running shoes.

Salesman: Good morning! You've come to the right place. Do you have a specific brand or style in mind?

Customer: I usually go for the Nike Air series, but I noticed online that you might have run out of stock.

Salesman: Let me check our inventory. We often restock quickly. Please hold on for a moment.

Salesman: It appears we did run out of the Nike Air series earlier this week, but we have a new shipment coming in tomorrow.

Customer: That's good to hear. In the meantime, can you suggest any similar alternatives?

Salesman: Absolutely. We have a new line from Adidas that's quite popular. Would you like to try them on to see if they suit you?

Customer: Sure, I'll give them a shot.

Salesman: Here you go. Let's get you shoed up with these and see how they feel.

Customer: Thanks. They feel pretty comfortable. How do they hold up in terms of durability?

Salesman: They hold up very well, especially for long-distance running. We also put up detailed reviews from other customers on our website if you'd like to check them out.

Customer: That sounds great. I think I'll go with these. Thank you for your help.

Salesman: My pleasure! I'll ring these up for you. If you need any further assistance, feel free to ask.

EXERCISES:

Fill in the blanks with the appropriate word from the list:

(bedecked, censor, amass, bereft, omen, paramour, scrupulous, meagre, incessant, rectitude, guile, yoke, sheath, relegate)

1. He managed to __________ a small fortune through careful saving and investment.
2. The hall was __________ with beautiful decorations for the wedding.
3. Feeling __________ after the loss of her pet, she sought comfort in her friends.
4. The editor had to __________ parts of the article that were deemed inappropriate.
5. His __________ plan to deceive the investors ultimately failed.
6. The __________ noise from the construction site made it hard to concentrate.
7. Despite his __________ income, he always found a way to save a little each month.
8. The dark clouds were a/an __________ of the impending storm.
9. She was known to be his __________, even though they kept their relationship private.
10. The manager decided to __________ the underperforming employee to a less critical role.
11. His __________ prevented him from participating in the dubious scheme.
12. The knight drew his sword from its __________ and prepared for battle.
13. She used her charm and ______________ to outwit her competitors in the business deal.
14. The farmer used a __________ to secure the oxen together while plowing.

SOLVE THE CROSSWORD

Across

3. someone new in anything
4. to breathe in a laboured way with a gasping noise
6. to persuade using flattery, promises, etc.
8. causing death
10. keen enjoyment; enthusiasm

Down

1. of a liquid, e.g., blood: to thicken or coagulate, especially through cooling
2. to mock, scoff or jeer
5. an act of trying to get the ball away from an opposing player
7. a person or a thing that announces or predicts something to come
9. someone sent to preach about Christ in the early Church, especially one of the twelve disciples

Choose the correct word from the list given:

1. The judge decided to __________ the meeting until the following week.
   a) adjourn b) conduct c) prepone
2. The desert was so __________ that hardly any vegetation could grow.
   a) dark b) arid c) blue
3. The horse began to __________ at the unfamiliar obstacle on the path.
   a) stalk b) strut c) balk
4. The scandal threatened to __________ the politician's reputation.
   a) besmirch b) revive c) relieve
5. The new evidence helped to __________ their argument.
   a) besmirch b) bolster c) gobble
6. She tried to __________ her friend into going to the party.
   a) preserve b) warn c) cajole
7. The birds began to __________ as the sun rose.
   a) chirp b) cry c) muse
8. The __________ of the crowd grew louder as the band took the stage.
   a) shriek b) clamour c) decorum
9. The students were expected to maintain __________ during the ceremony.
   a) quarrel b) scorn c) decorum
10. She decided to __________ herself to her studies to achieve her goals.
    a) devote b) derive c) discomfort
11. The medicine was __________ from a rare plant found in the rainforest.
    a) injected b) derived c) discomforted
12. He experienced __________ after sitting in the uncomfortable chair for hours.
    a) joy b) nuisance c) discomfort

13. The bride's family gave a large __________ as part of the marriage arrangement.
   a) dowry b) effigy c) heron
14. The protestors burned an __________ of the unpopular leader.
   a) statue b) effigy c) boat
15. The cat was __________, always disappearing just when you thought you found it.
   a) small b) nimble c) elusive
16. The invention of the steam engine marked the beginning of a new __________.
   a) epoch b) year c) day
17. The bus __________ had increased since last year.
   a) rate b) fare c) pace
18. The crowd's __________ for the cause was evident in their passionate chants.
   a) chant b) shake c) fervor
19. She showed great __________ in facing the difficult situation.
   a) fortitude b) shrug c) fervour
20. The __________ blew fiercely, making it difficult to walk outside.
   a) rage b) gale c) sister
21. The ancient warrior wore a __________ around his waist.
   a) slogan b) sombre c) girdle
22. She continued to __________ over the loss of her beloved pet.
   a) grieve b) tinkle c) grin
23. The lumberjack used a __________ to chop down the tree.
   a) broom b) hatchet c) heron
24. The __________ stood still by the edge of the pond, waiting for a fish.
   a) lark b) gypsy c) heron
25. His strong beliefs __________ him to take action.
   a) impel b) growl c) clatter
26. The soup was __________ and lacked flavour.
   a) tasty b) insipid c) spicy

27. The sack was made from __________, a natural fiber.
    a) banana b) fenugreek c) jute
28. She couldn't untangle the __________ in the string.
    a) knot b) cheek c) streak
29. The actor was __________ for his outstanding performance.
    a) blamed b) lauded c) bored
30. He found a __________ of clay in the middle of the garden.
    a) mountain b) stone c) lump
31. The carpenter used a __________ to drive the chisel into the wood.
    a) mallet b) nail c) drill
32. The __________ moved from place to place, never settling in one location.
    a) gypsy b) nomad c) bird
33. The buzzing fly was a __________ during the picnic.
    a) sound b) nomad c) nuisance
34. The __________ practices of the cult were hidden from the public.
    a) occult b) funny c) holy
35. The peacock displayed its colourful __________ to attract a mate.
    a) hoof b) plume c) horn
36. The athlete's __________ on the field was admired by all.
    a) jaw b) foot c) prowess
37. The siblings often __________ over trivial matters.
    a) quarrel b) hug c) jump
38. The __________ was known for its beautiful landscapes and diverse wildlife.
    a) house b) region c) joke
39. She was lost in a __________, daydreaming about her future.
    a) clash b) region c) reverie
40. He felt __________ when his suggestion was ignored.
    a) scorn b) long c) share
41. The police managed to __________ the stolen goods from the thieves.
    a) lose b) seize c) share

42. They decided to __________ the profits equally among all members of the team.
    a) scorn b) seize c) share
43. The __________ businessman made a very profitable deal.
    a) shrewd b) magic c) majestic
44. She used a __________ to protect her finger while sewing.
    a) horn b) thimble c) mallet
45. The __________ weather made flying very difficult.
    a) popular b) silken c) turbulent
46. The patient had to __________ several painful procedures during treatment.
    a) undergo b) slack c) sneeze
47. His __________ attempt to win her love was met with disappointment.
    a) lover b) vain c) sole
48. She tried to __________ her goals by creating a detailed vision board.
    a) force b) attest c) visualize
49. The __________ artwork in the gallery drew the attention of all visitors.
    a) whimsical b) lazy c) sure
50. The farmer's fields were expected to __________ a large harvest this year.
    a) gather b) yield c) support

Write a descriptive passage using at least twenty of the adjectives given below:

(amenable, ardent, bare, calm, concerned, domestic, dusky, faint, fatal, gifted, harsh, insipid, irresolute, lifeless, majestic, nearby, normal, occult, original, parched, plump, quite, ragged, remote, sacred, savage, significant, tangible, unexpected, vexed, wavy)

LEVEL 2

LIST OF WORDS

1. Abattoir: (noun) a slaughterhouse
2. Abbot: (noun) the man in charge of a group of nuns living in an abbey
3. Abbreviation: (noun) shortening, especially to represent (a long word) by a shortened form
4. Abdicate: (verb) to give up one's right to (the throne)
5. Ablution: (noun) the washing of the body, the hands or ritual vessels as part of religious ceremony
6. Aborigines: (noun) members of any people who were the first to live in a country or region
7. Abridge: (verb) to make (a book) shorter
8. Accelerate: (verb) to increase the speed of something
9. Accentuate: (verb) to emphasise, stress or make something more evident or prominent
10. Accomplice: (noun) someone who helps another commit a crime
11. Acoustics: (noun) the characteristics of a room, theatre, etc. that determine the nature and quality of sounds heard within it
12. Acronym: (noun) a word made from the first letters or syllables of other words, and usually pronounced as a word in its own right
13. Acumen: (noun) the ability to judge quickly and well
14. Addict: (noun) someone who is dependent on the habitual intake of a drug
15. Adolescence: (adjective) of a young person: between the beginning of puberty and adulthood
16. Adulation: (noun) excessive praise or flattery

17. Advertisement: (noun) a public notice, announcement or short television film which advertises something
18. Aerial: (adjective) relating to the air or aircraft
19. Aesthetic: (adjective) able to appreciate beauty; artistic, tasteful
20. Affinity: (noun) a strong natural liking for or feeling of attraction or closeness towards someone or something
21. Affluent: (adjective) having more than enough money; rich
22. Afforestation: (noun) to establish a forest on bare or cultivated land
23. Agenda: (noun) a list of things to be done or discussed
24. Aggression: (noun) the act of attacking another person or country without being provoked
25. Agnosticism: (noun) the belief that one can know only about material things, and that nothing can be known about the existence of God
26. Agoraphobia: (noun) an irrational fear of open spaces or public places
27. Alien: (noun) 1. a foreign-born resident of a country who has not adopted that country's nationality, 2. an inhabitant of another planet
28. Alimony: (noun) money for support paid by a man to his ex-wife or by a woman to her ex-husband, when they are legally separated or divorced
29. Allegory: (noun) a story, play, poem, picture in which the characters represent moral or spiritual ideas or messages
30. Alleviate: (verb) to make (pain, a problem, suffering, etc.) less severe
31. Alliteration: (noun) the repetition of the same sound at the beginning of each word or each stressed word in a phrase
32. Allopathy: a system of conventional medicine that treats diseases with remedies such as drugs or surgery, aiming to produce effects different from those caused by the disease
33. Altimeter: (noun) a device used in aircraft for measuring height above sea or ground level
34. Altitude: (noun) height, especially above sea level, of a mountain, aircraft, etc.

35. Altruist: (noun) someone with an unselfish concern for the welfare of others
36. Amateur: (noun) someone who takes part in a sport, pastime, etc. as a hobby and without being paid for it
37. Ambidextrous: (adjective) able to use both hands equally well
38. Ambiguous: (adjective) having more than one possible meaning
39. Ammunition: (noun) bullets, shells, bombs, etc. made to be fired from a weapon

> Alliteration, rooted in ancient literature like 'Beowulf,' remains a versatile literary device used for rhythm and emphasis, famously found in tongue twisters like 'She sells seashells.' Beyond literature, it's a staple in advertising (think Coca-Cola) and education, aiding phonetic understanding. Its mnemonic value and catchy quality make it ideal for memorable brand names and slogans, showcasing its enduring relevance and multifaceted role in language and culture.

40. Amnesia: (noun) the loss or impairment of memory
41. Amnesty: (noun) a general pardon, especially for people convicted or accused of political crimes
42. Amphibian: (noun) a cold-blooded animal, e.g., a frog, toad or newt, which lives partly or entirely on land but returns to water to lay its eggs
43. Anaesthetist: (noun) someone who has been specifically trained in the administration of anaesthetics to patients
44. Anarchist: (noun) someone who believes that governments and laws are unnecessary and should be abolished
45. Anecdote: (noun) a short entertaining account of an incident
46. Anglophile: (noun) someone who admires England and the English
47. Animosity: (noun) a strong dislike or hatred
48. Anniversary: (noun) a date on which some event took place in a previous year
49. Annuity: (noun) a yearly grant or allowance
50. Anodyne: (noun) a medicine or drug that relieves or alleviates pain

51. Anomaly: (noun) something that is unusual or different from what is expected
52. Antagonist: (noun) an opponent or enemy
53. Anthropology: (noun) the study and analysis of the origins and characteristics of human beings and their societies, customs and beliefs
54. Antibiotics: (noun) a substance that can selectively destroy or inhibit bacteria or fungi
55. Antimony: (noun) a brittle bluish-white metallic element used to increase the hardness of lead alloys
56. Antipathy: (noun) a feeling of strong dislike or hostility
57. Antiquarian: (adjective) referring or relating to or dealing in, antiques and/or rare books
58. Apartheid: (noun) an official state policy, especially that operating in South Africa until 1992, of racial segregation
59. Apathy: (noun) lack of interest or enthusiasm
60. Aphasia: (noun) loss or impairment of the ability to speak or write or to understand the meaning of spoken or written language
61. Aphelion: (noun) the point in the planet's orbit when it is farthest from the Sun
62. Apiary: (noun) a place where honey bees are kept
63. Apostasy: (noun) the rejection of one's religion or principals or of one's affiliation to a political party, etc.
64. Apostate: (noun) someone who rejects a religion, belief, political affiliation, etc. that they previously held
65. Appalling: (adjective) causing feelings of shock or horror
66. Apprentice: (noun) someone, usually a young person, who works with a senior for an agreed period of time in order to learn a craft or trade
67. Aquarium: (noun) a glass tank that fish, other water animals or water plants are kept in so that they can be observed or displayed
68. Aquatic: (adjective) living or growing in, on or near water
69. Arbitrary: (adjective) based on subjective factors or random choice and not on objective principles
70. Arboreal: (adjective) relating to or resembling a tree

71. Archaeology: (noun) the study of the physical remains of earlier civilizations, especially buildings and artefacts
72. Archipelago: (noun) a group or chain of islands separated from each other by narrow bodies of water
73. Archive: (noun) a collection of old public documents, records, etc.
74. Arena: (noun) an area surrounded by seats for public shows, sports contests, etc.
75. Aristocracy: (noun) the highest social class
76. Armistice: (noun) an agreement between warring factions to suspend all fighting so that they can discuss peace terms; a truce
77. Arsenal: (noun) a store for weapons, explosives, etc.
78. Articulate: (verb) to pronounce (words) or speak clearly and distinctly
79. Artiste: (noun) a professional performer, especially a singer or dancer in a theatre, circus, etc.
80. Ascetic: (noun) someone who abstains from all physical comfort and pleasure, especially in solitude and for religious reasons
81. Ascribe: (verb) to attribute, assign
82. Assailant: a person who attacks another person, usually physically
83. Astrology: (noun) the study of the movements of the stars and planets, and of how they are thought to exert influences on people's lives, character traits, etc.
84. Astronaut: (noun) someone who is trained to travel in space
85. Asylum: (noun) 1. a place of safety or protection, 2. a mental hospital
86. Atheist: (noun) someone who believes that there is no god
87. Audience: (noun) a group of people watching a performance, e.g., of a play, concert, etc.
88. Auditor: (noun) a person who is professionally qualified to audit accounts
89. Authentic: (adjective) genuine; true to the original
90. Autonomy: (noun) the power or right of self-government

91. Avarice: (noun) excessive desire for money, possessions, etc.
92. Aviary: (noun) a large enclosed area where birds are kept
93. Axiom: (noun) a proposition, fact, principle, etc., which, because it is long-established, is generally accepted as true
94. Ayurvedic: a traditional system of medicine from India that uses natural remedies and holistic practices to promote health and treat illnesses
95. Balderdash: (noun) nonsense
96. Bankrupt: (noun) someone who is legally recognized as not being able to pay their debts
97. Barbarian: (noun) someone who is cruel and wild in behaviour
98. Barometer: (noun) an instrument which measures atmospheric pressure, especially in order to predict changes in the weather or to estimate height above sea level
99. Barracks: (noun) a building or a group of buildings for housing soldiers
100. Barrel: (noun) a large round container with a flat top and bottom and curving out in the middle, usually made of planks of wood held together with metal bands
101. Barricade: (noun) a barrier, especially one erected hastily
102. Barrister: (noun) in England and Wales: a lawyer qualified to act for someone in the higher law courts
103. Bellicose: (adjective) likely to or seeking to, cause an argument or war; aggressive; warlike
104. Belligerent: (adjective) aggressive and unfriendly; ready to argue
105. Belligerent: (noun) a person, faction or country fighting a war
106. Benefactor: (noun) a person who gives help, especially financial help, to an institution, cause or person
107. Beneficiary: (noun) a person who benefits from something
108. Bevy: (noun) alcoholic drink
109. Bibliography: (noun) a list of books by one author or one subject
110. Biennial: (adjective) of an event: occurring once in every two years

111. Bigamy: (noun) the crime of being married to two wives or husbands at the same time
112. Bilingual: (adjective) 1. written or spoken in two languages, 2. of a person: able to speak two languages
113. Biodegradable: (adjective) of a substance or waste product: capable of being broken down by bacteria, fungi or other living organisms
114. Biography: (noun) an account of a person's life, written by someone else and published or intended for publication
115. Bitumen: (noun) any of various black solid or tarry flammable substances composed of an impure mixture of hydrocarbons and which is used for surfacing roads and pavements, etc.
116. Blacksmith: (noun) a person who makes and repairs by hand things made of iron, such as horseshoes
117. Blasphemy: (noun) speaking about God or sacred matters in a disrespectful or rude way
118. Bleat: (verb) to cry like a sheep, goat or calf
119. Bliss: (noun) the special happiness of heaven
120. Bodice: (noun) the close-fitting upper part of a woman's dress, from shoulder to waist
121. Bohemian: (noun) someone who lives in a way which ignores standards customs and rules of social behaviour
122. Bombard: (verb) to attack (a place, target, etc.) with large heavy guns or bombs
123. Boomerang: (noun) a piece of flat curved wood used by Australian Aborigines for hunting, often so balanced that, when thrown to a distance, it returns towards the person who threw it

> Bohemian is a term rich in cultural connotations. Originating from the unconventional lifestyle of Bohemia in the Czech Republic, it evolved into a descriptor for individuals who prioritize artistic expression and free-spirited living over societal norms. This term gained prominence during the nineteenth century, associated with artists, writers and intellectuals who rejected traditional values in favour of creative exploration and personal liberation. Today, being Bohemian is synonymous with nonconformity, creativity, and a passion for individuality, influencing fashion, music and lifestyle choices worldwide.

124. Boorish: rude, insensitive behaviour and manner
125. Botany: (noun) the branch of biology concerned with the scientific study of plants
126. Bouquet: (noun) a bunch of flowers arranged in an artistic way
127. Bovine: (adjective) belonging or relating to or characteristic of, cattle
128. Bower: (noun) a place in a garden which is enclosed and shaded from the sun by plants and trees
129. Brevity: (noun) the use of few words
130. Brigand: (noun) a member of a band of robbers, especially one operating in a mountain area
131. Brittle: (adjective) of a substance: hard but easily broken or likely to break
132. Broaden: (verb) to become or make something broad or broader
133. Brocade: (noun) a heavy silk fabric with a raised design on it, often one using gold or silver threads
134. Brood: (verb) to think anxiously or resentfully about something for a period of time
135. Brunette: (noun) a woman or girl with brown or dark hair
136. Bungle: (verb) to do something carelessly or badly
137. Bureaucracy: (noun) a system of government by officials who are responsible to their department heads and are not elected
138. Burglar: (noun) a person who commits the crime of entering a building illegally in order to steal or to commit another crime
139. Burrow: a hole in the ground, especially one dug by a rabbit or other small animal for shelter
140. Byre: (noun) a cowshed
141. Cacophony: (noun) a disagreeable combination of loud noises
142. Callous: (adjective) unconcerned for the feelings of others; deliberately cruel
143. Campaign: (noun) an organized series of actions intended to gain support for or build up opposition to a particular practice, group, etc.

144. Cannibal: (noun) someone who eats human flesh
145. Capsize: (verb) usually of a boat: to tip over completely
146. Caravan: (noun) a vehicle fitted for living in, designed for towing by a motor vehicle
147. Carcass: (noun) the dead body of an animal
148. Caricature: (noun) a representation, especially a drawing, of someone with their most noticeable and distinctive features exaggerated for comic effect
149. Carnage: (noun) great slaughter
150. Carnival: (noun) a period of public festivity with e.g., street processions, colourful costumes, singing and dancing
151. Carnivorous: (adjective) feeding mainly on the flesh of other animals
152. Cartography: the science and practice of map-making
153. Cashmere: (noun) a type of very fine soft wool from a long-haired Asian coat
154. Casino: (noun) a public building or room for gambling
155. Catalogue: (noun) a list of items arranged in a systematic order especially alphabetically
156. Catastrophe: (noun) a terrible blow, calamity or disaster
157. Cauldron: (noun) a very large metal pot, often with handles for boiling or heating liquids especially over a fire
158. Caustics: (adjective) of a chemical substance e.g., sodium hydroxide: strongly alkaline and corrosive to living tissue
159. Cavalry: (noun) the part of an army consisting of soldiers on horseback
160. Ceasefire: (noun) a break in the fighting during a war, agreed to by all sides
161. Celibacy: (noun) having no sexual relations with anyone
162. Celibate: (adjective) 1. unmarried, especially in obedience to a religious vow, 2. having no sexual relations with anyone
163. Cemetery: (noun) a burial ground
164. Centenary: (noun) the one-hundredth anniversary of some event
165. Chafe: (verb) to make or become sore or worn by rubbing
166. Chagrin: (noun) acute annoyance or disappointment

167. Chandelier: (noun) an ornamental light-fitting hanging from the ceiling, with branching holders for candles or light bulbs
168. Changeling: (noun) a child substituted by the fairies for an unbaptized human baby
169. Chapel: (noun) a recess within a church or cathedral with its own altar
170. Charlatan: (noun) someone posing as an expert in some profession, especially medicine
171. Chassis: (noun) the structural framework of a motor vehicle, to which the body and movable working parts are attached
172. Chauffeur: (noun) someone employed to drive a car for someone else
173. Choir: (noun) an organized group of trained singers, especially one that performs in church
174. Choreography: the study of designing and arranging dance movements and sequences
175. Chronology: (noun) the study or science of determining the correct order of historical events
176. Churlish: (adjective) ill-mannered or rude
177. Circumlocution: (noun) an unnecessarily long or indirect way of saying something
178. Clamp: (noun) a tool with adjustable jaws for gripping things firmly or pressing parts together
179. Claustrophobia: (noun) an irrational fear of being in confined spaces
180. Coagulate: (verb) of a liquid: to become clotted or curdled or to form a soft semi-solid mass
181. Coast: (noun) the land that borders the sea
182. Cockpit: (noun) in an aircraft: the compartment for the pilot and crew
183. Codicil: (noun) a supplement to a will
184. Coerce: (verb) to force or compel somebody to do something
185. Coercion: the act of forcing someone to act against their will, usually through threats
186. Coffer: (noun) a large chest for holding valuables
187. Cognate: (adjective) descended from or related to a common ancestor

188. Colleague: (noun) a fellow-worker, especially in a profession
189. Colloquy: (noun) a conversation
190. Collusion: (noun) secret co-operation for the purpose of fraud or other criminal activity
191. Colossus: (noun) a gigantic statue; an overwhelmingly powerful person or organization
192. Combustible: (adjective) liable to catch fire and burn readily
193. Comedian: (noun) a male or female entertainer who tells jokes and performs comic sketches
194. Commemorate: (verb) to honour the memory of (a person or event) with a ceremony
195. Commodious: (noun) comfortably spacious
196. Compass: (noun) any device for finding direction, especially one consisting of a magnetized needle that points to the magnetic north, from which true north can be calculated
197. Compatriot: (noun) someone from one's own country
198. Compere: (noun) someone who hosts a radio or television show, introduces performers
199. Complacent: (adjective) too easily satisfied; disinclined to worry
200. Complement: (noun) something that completes; something that provides a needed balance or contrast
201. Complexion: (noun) the colour or appearance of the skin, especially of the face
202. Compositor: (noun) someone who sets or arranges pages of type ready for printing
203. Compulsory: (adjective) required by the rules, law, etc.
204. Conceited: (adjective) having too good an opinion of oneself
205. Condominium: (noun) a building, e.g., an apartment block in which each apartment is individually owned and any common areas are commonly owned
206. Condone: (verb) to pardon or overlook (an offence or wrong)
207. Conductor: (noun) 1. the person who conducts a choir or an orchestra, 2. a material that conducts heat or electricity, 3. someone who collects fares from passengers on a bus, etc.
208. Confectioner: (noun) someone who makes or sells sweets or cakes

209. Confiscate: (verb) to take away something from someone, usually as a penalty
210. Conflagrant: burning or blazing intensely
211. Confluence: (noun) 1. the point where two rivers flow into one another, 2. an act of meeting together
212. Congenital: (adjective) of a disease or deformity: present at or before birth but not inherited
213. Conglomerate: (noun) 1. a miscellaneous collection or mass, 2. a business group composed of a large number of firms with diverse and often unrelated interests
214. Congruent: (adjective) of two or more figures: identical in size and shape
215. Conjecture: (noun) an opinion based on incomplete evidence
216. Connoisseur: (noun) someone who is knowledgeable about and a good judge of a particular subject, e.g., the arts, wine, food, etc.
217. Conscience: (noun) the moral sense of right and wrong that determines someone's thoughts and behaviour
218. Conscript: (verb) to enlist for compulsory military service
219. Consortium: (noun) an association of several banks, businesses, etc.
220. Constable: (noun) a police officer of the most junior rank
221. Constellation: (noun) a named group of stars seen as forming a recognizable pattern in the night sky
222. Consternation: (noun) anxiety, dismay or confusion
223. Constrained: (adjective) awkward; embarrassed
224. Consummate: (verb) to finish, perfect or complete something
225. Contagious: (adjective) of a disease: only able to be transmitted by direct contact with or close proximity to an infected individual, e.g., the common cold
226. Contemporary: (adjective) belonging to the same period of time as something
227. Contented: feeling satisfied and at ease
228. Contiguous: (adjective) touching
229. Contractor: (noun) a person or firm that undertakes work on contract

230. Contrite: (adjective) sorry for something one has done
231. Convalescence: (noun) the gradual recovery of health and strength
232. Convent: (noun) a community of nuns
233. Conventicle: (noun) a secret, especially unlawful, religious meeting
234. Convention: (noun) a large and formal conference or assembly
235. Coronation: (noun) the ceremony of crowning a monarch or consort
236. Corroborate: (verb) to confirm (e.g., someone's statement) especially by providing evidence
237. Cosmography: the study or description of the universe, including its structure, features and phenomena.
238. Cosmopolitan: (adjective) belonging to or representative of all parts of the world
239. Couplet: (noun) a pair of consecutive lines of verse, especially ones which rhyme and have the same metre
240. Credible: (adjective) capable of being believed
241. Credulous: (adjective) apt to be too ready to believe something, without sufficient evidence
242. Creed: (noun) 1. a statement of the main points of Christian belief, 2. any set of beliefs or principles either personal or religious
243. Crematorium: (noun) a place where corpses are cremated
244. Crepe: (noun) 1. a thin finely wrinkled silk fabric, 2. a thin pancake often containing a filling
245. Criterion: (noun) a standard or principle on which to base a judgment
246. Critic: (noun) 1. a professional reviewer of literature, art, drama, music, etc., 2. Someone who finds fault with or disapproves of something
247. Cruise: (verb) to sail about for pleasure, calling at a succession of places
248. Crumble: (verb) to break into crumbs for powdery fragments
249. Crusade: (noun) a strenuous campaign in aid of a cause

250. Cryptography: the practice and study of techniques for secure communication in the presence of third parties. It involves creating and deciphering codes and ciphers to transmit information securely
251. Culpable: (adjective) deserving blame
252. Cultivator: (noun) a tool for breaking up the surface of the ground
253. Curator: (noun) the custodian of a museum or other collection
254. Curfew: (noun) an official order restricting people's movements, especially after a certain hour at night
255. Curiosity: (noun) eagerness to know
256. Currency: (noun) the system of money or the coins and notes, in use in a country
257. Cygnet: (noun) a young swan
258. Cynic: (noun) someone who takes a pessimistic view of human goodness or sincerity
259. Dagger: (noun) a pointed knife for stabbing
260. Damask: (noun) a patterned silk or linen cloth, used for tablecloth, curtains, etc.
261. Deadlock: (noun) a situation in which no further progress towards an agreement is possible
262. Debacle: (noun) total disorder, defeat, collapse of organization, etc.
263. Deepened: (adjective) made deeper, greater, more intense, etc.
264. Defamation: the act of damaging someone's reputation through false statements or actions, either spoken (slander) or written (libel)
265. Defiance: (noun) open disobedience or opposition
266. Delegate: (verb) to give (part of one's work, power, etc.) to someone else
267. Deliberation: (noun) careful thought
268. Delinquent: (noun) someone, especially a young person, guilty of a minor crime
269. Demagogue: (noun) someone who tries to win power or support by appealing to people's emotions and prejudices

270. Democracy: (noun) a form of government in which the people govern themselves or elect representatives to govern them
271. Denature: (verb) to change the structure or composition of (something)
272. Denigrate: (verb) to attack or belittle someone's reputation, character or worth
273. Denizen: (noun) 1. an inhabitant, 2. a species of animal or plant which has become well established in a place to which it is not native
274. Depict: (verb) 1. to paint or draw something, 2. to describe something
275. Deponent: (noun) someone who makes a deposition, especially under oath
276. Deprecate: (verb) to express or feel disapproval of something
277. Depreciate: (verb) to fall or make something fall, in value
278. Deranged: mentally disturbed or insane; exhibiting irrational or abnormal behaviour
279. Derelict: (adjective) abandoned
280. Deride: (verb) to laugh at or make fun of someone
281. Despondent: (adjective) feeling extremely discouraged, hopeless or disheartened
282. Destitute: (adjective) extremely poor; lacking basic necessities such as food, shelter and resources
283. Detective: (noun) a police officer whose job is to solve crime by observation and gathering evidence
284. Deterrence: (noun) the act of discouraging an action or behaviour through the threat of consequences and punishment
285. Detrimental: (adjective) harmful; damaging
286. Devious: (adjective) not totally open or honest
287. Dexterous: (adjective) having, showing or done with dexterity
288. Diagnose: (verb) to identify a medical disorder on the basis of its symptoms
289. Diatribe: (noun) a bitter or abusive critical attack
290. Dibble: (noun) a short, pointed hand tool used for making holes in the ground for seeds, young plants, etc.

291. Dictator: (noun) a ruler with total power
292. Diffuse: (verb) to spread or send out in all directions
293. Dilemma: (noun) a situation in which one must choose between two or more courses of action, both/all equally undesirable
294. Dilettante: (noun) someone interested in a subject but who does not study it in depth
295. Diligent: (adjective) hard-working and careful
296. Diplomacy: (noun) the art or profession of making agreements, treaties, etc. between countries or of representing and looking after the affairs of one's own country in a foreign country
297. Dirge: (noun) a funeral song or hymn
298. Disability: (noun) the state of being disabled; a physical or mental handicap
299. Disaster: (noun) an event causing great damage, injury or loss of life
300. Discrepancy: (noun) a failure (e.g., of sets of information) to correspond or be the same
301. Discus: (noun) 1. a heavy disc thrown in athletic competitions, 2. the competition itself
302. Disguise: (verb) to hide the identity of someone or something by a change of appearance
303. Disintegrate: (verb) to break into tiny pieces
304. Dismal: (adjective) not cheerful, causing or suggesting sadness
305. Disrupt: (verb) to disturb the order or peaceful progress of (an activity, process, etc.)
306. Dividend: (noun) a portion of a company's profits paid to a shareholder
307. Domicile: (noun) a legally recognized place of permanent residence
308. Dominion: (noun) rule; power
309. Dormant: (adjective) temporarily quiet, inactive or out of use
310. Dorsal: (adjective) belonging or relating to the back
311. Draper: (noun) someone who sells fabric

312. Draw: (verb) 1. to make a picture of something or someone especially with a pencil, 2. To pull out or take out something
313. Drey: (noun) a squirrel's nest
314. Drove: (noun) a moving heard of animals, especially cattle
315. Drudgery: (noun) tedious, menial or unpleasant work that requires a lot of effort and yields little satisfaction
316. Druggist: (noun) a pharmacist
317. Ductile: (adjective) denoting metals that can be drawn out into a thin wire without breaking
318. Duel: (noun) a pre-arranged fight between two people to settle a matter of honour
319. Dwarf: 1. (noun) an abnormally small person, 2. (adjective) very small
320. Dyke: (noun) a wall or embankment built to prevent flooding
321. Eavesdrop: (verb) to listen secretly to a private conversation
322. Ebullient: (adjective) very high-spirited
323. Eccentric: (adjective) of a person or behaviour, etc.: odd or unconventional
324. Ecology: (noun) the relationship between living things and their surroundings
325. Economical: (adjective) not wasting money or resources
326. Edible: (adjective) fit to be eaten; suitable to eat
327. Edify: (verb) to improve the mind or morals of someone
328. Efface: (verb) to rub or wipe out something
329. Effect: (noun) 1. a result, 2. an impression given or produced
330. Effeminate: (adjective) of a man: having features of behaviour or appearance more typical of a woman; not manly
331. Egalitarian: (adjective) relating to, promoting or believing in the principle that all human beings are equal and should enjoy the same rights
332. Egoist: (noun) a person who is excessively self-centred or focused solely on their own interests and desires, often to the detriment of others
333. Electorate (noun) all the electors of a city, country, etc.
334. Elegant: (adjective) having or showing good taste in dress or style, combined with dignity and gracefulness

335. Elf: (noun) a tiny supernatural being with a human form
336. Eligible: (adjective) suitable or deserving to be chosen (for a job, as a husband, etc.)
337. Elope: (verb) to run away secretly in order to get married
338. Eloquent: (adjective) fluent, persuasive and expressive in speech or writing
339. Elysium: (noun) in Greek mythology: the place where the blessed were supposed to rest after death
340. Emancipation: (noun) the act of setting someone free from oppression, restraint or control, particularly in the context of legal or social liberation from slavery, servitude or oppression
341. Embargo: (noun) an official order forbidding something especially trade with another country
342. Embed: (verb) to set or fix something firmly and deeply
343. Ember: (noun) a piece of glowing or smouldering coal or wood
344. Embezzle: (verb) to take or use dishonestly (money or property with which one has been entrusted)
345. Embody: (verb) to be an expression or representation of something in words, actions or form
346. Emeritus: (adjective) retired or honourably discharged from office, but retaining a former title as an owner

> Effeminate is a term with complex historical and cultural connotations. Initially used to describe behaviours or characteristics deemed typical of or suitable for women, it has evolved over time to encompass a wide range of expressions and identities. In many cultures, effeminacy has been stigmatized, associated with weakness or inferiority, while in others, it's celebrated as an expression of gender diversity and fluidity. The term has been a subject of debate and scrutiny, reflecting changing attitudes toward gender roles and identities. Today, discussions around effeminacy intersect with broader conversations about gender norms, masculinity and inclusivity, highlighting the ongoing evolution of societal perceptions and acceptance of diverse gender expressions.

347. Emigrant: (noun) a person who leaves their own country to settle permanently in another; someone who migrates out of their homeland
348. Emissary: (noun) a person sent on a mission especially on behalf of a government
349. Empathy: (noun) the ability to share, understand and feel another person's feelings
350. Employer: (noun) a person or company that employs workers
351. Encyclopaedia: (noun) a reference work containing information on every branch of knowledge or on one particular branch, usually arranged in alphabetical order
352. Endemic: (adjective) of a disease, etc.: regularly occurring in a particular area or among a particular group of people
353. Engulf: (verb) to swallow something up completely
354. Enshrine: (verb) to enter and protect (a right, an idea, etc.) in the laws or constitution of a state, the constitution of an organization, etc.
355. Entomology: (noun) the scientific study of insects
356. Enviable: (adjective) likely to cause envy
357. Epic: (noun) a long narrative poem telling of heroic acts, the birth and death of nations, etc.
358. Epicure: (noun) someone who has refined taste, especially one who enjoys good food and drink
359. Epicurean: (noun) someone who likes pleasure and good living
360. Epidemic: (noun) a sudden outbreak of infectious disease which spreads rapidly and widely in a particular area for a limited period of time
361. Epilepsy: (noun) any of a group of disorders of the nervous system characterized by recurring attacks that involve impairment or sudden loss, of consciousness
362. Epilogue: (noun) the closing section of a book, programme, etc.
363. Epistle: (noun) a letter, especially a long one, dealing with important matters

364. Epitome: (noun) a miniature representation of a larger or wider idea, issue, etc.
365. Equator: (noun) the imaginary great circle that passes around the Earth at latitude 0 at an equal distance from the north and south poles
366. Equinox: (noun) either of the two occasions on which the Sun crosses the equator, making night and day equal in length, occurring about 21 March and 23 September
367. Eradicable: (verb) capable of being eradicated or eliminated, particularly of diseases
368. Erase: (verb) to remove all trace of something
369. Err: (verb) to make a mistake, be wrong or do wrong
370. Erratum: (noun) an error in writing or printing
371. Erudition: (noun) deep, extensive knowledge acquired through study or learning; scholarly expertise in a particular field or multiple subjects
372. Escort: (noun) one or more people, vehicles, etc. accompanying another or others for protection or guidance or as a mark of honour
373. Esteem: (verb) to value, respect or think highly of someone or something
374. Eternal: (adjective) without beginning or end
375. Ethics: (noun) the study or the science of morals
376. Etiolate: (verb) to become pale or weak due to lack of sunlight or nutrition, often used to describe plants that have grown in darkness. It can also mean to make someone or something weak or feeble
377. Etiquette: (noun) conventions of correct or polite social behaviour
378. Etymology: (noun) the study of the origin and development of words and their meanings
379. Eugenics: (noun) the now largely discredited science of improving the human race by selective breeding
380. Eulogy: (noun) a speech or piece of writing in praise of someone or something

381. Euphemism: (noun) a mild or inoffensive term used in place of one considered offensive or unpleasantly direct
382. Euphoria: (noun) a feeling of wild happiness and well-being
383. Euthanasia: (noun) the act or practice of ending the life of a person who is suffering from an incurable illness
384. Evict: (verb) to put someone out of a house or off land by force of law
385. Evolution: (noun) the process of evolving; a gradual development
386. Exaggerate: (verb) to regard or describe something as being greater or better than it really is
387. Excerpt: (noun) a short passage or part taken from a book, film, musical work, etc.
388. Excise: (noun) the tax or duty payable on goods produced and sold within a country, and on certain trading licences
389. Exclusive: (adjective) involving the rejection or denial of something else or everything else
390. Excursion: (noun) a short trip, usually one made for pleasure
391. Exegesis: (noun) a critical explanation of a text, especially of the Bible
392. Exertion: (noun) bringing something into use or action forcefully
393. Exhilarating: (adjective) filling someone with a lively cheerfulness
394. Exodus: (noun) a mass departure of people
395. Exonerate: (verb) to free someone from blame or acquit them of a criminal charge
396. Expanse: (noun) a wide area or space
397. Expatriate: (adjective) living abroad, especially for a long but limited period; exiled
398. Expiate: (verb) to make amends for (a wrong)
399. Expire: (verb) to come to an end or cease to be valid
400. Explicable: (adjective) able to be explained
401. Expurgate: (verb) to revise a book by removing objectionable or offensive words or passages
402. Extempore: (adjective) without planning or preparation

403. Exterminate: (verb) to get rid of or completely destroy (something living)
404. Extinguish: (verb) to put out a fire
405. Extradite: (verb) to return (a person accused of a crime) for trial in the country where the crime was committed
406. Extravagant: (adjective) using, spending or costing too much
407. Exuberant: (adjective) in very high spirits
408. Fable: (noun) a story with a moral, usually with animals as characters
409. Facile: (adjective) of success, etc.: too easily achieved
410. Facsimile: (noun) an exact copy made, e.g., of a manuscript, picture, etc.
411. Fallacy: (noun) a mistaken notion
412. Fallible: (adjective) capable of making mistakes
413. Fallow: (adjective) of land: left unplanted after ploughing, to recover its natural fertility
414. Fanatic: (noun) someone with an extreme or excessive enthusiasm for something, especially a religion or religious issues
415. Fantasy: (noun) a pleasant daydream
416. Farce: (noun) a comedy involving a series of ridiculously unlikely turns of events
417. Fastidious: (adjective) particular in matters of taste and detail, especially excessively so
418. Fatal: (adjective) causing death
419. Fatalism: (noun) a belief or the philosophical doctrine that all events are predestined and humans cannot alter them
420. Fatalist: (noun) a person who believes that all events are predetermined and inevitable, leading to a passive acceptance of fate or destiny
421. Feasible: (adjective) capable of being done or achieved
422. Felicitous: (adjective) of wording: well-chosen; elegantly apt
423. Feminist: (noun) a person who supports the advocacy of women's rights and equality between the sexes, seeking to address issues such as gender discrimination, stereotyping, and oppression

424. Ferry: (noun) a boat that carries passengers and offers cars across a strip of water, especially as a regular service
425. Feud: (noun) a long-drawn-out bitter quarrel between families, individuals or clans
426. Fiancée: (noun) a man or woman to whom one is engaged to be married
427. Fiasco: (noun) a ludicrous or humiliating failure
428. Fictitious: (adjective) imagined
429. Figment: (noun) something imagined or invented
430. Filicide: (noun) the act of killing one's own child
431. Fixation: (noun) an (open abnormal) attachment, preoccupation or obsession
432. Flamboyant: (adjective) of a person or behaviour: colourful, exuberant and showy
433. Flannel: (noun) soft woollen cloth with a slight nap used to make clothes
434. Fleet: (noun) 1. a number of ships under one command and organized as a tactical unit, 2. a number of buses, aircraft, etc. operating under the same ownership or management
435. Flexible: (adjective) bending easily
436. Flick: (verb) to move or touch something with a quick light movement
437. Flogging: (noun) whipping repeatedly particularly as a form of punishment
438. Florist: (noun) someone who grows, sells or arranges flowers
439. Flounder: (verb) to thrash about helplessly, as if caught in a bog
440. Fluke: (noun) a success achieved by accident or chance
441. Flux: (noun) 1. the flow of matter; a process or act of flowing, 2. constant change
442. Follow: (verb) to go or come after (someone or something)
443. Foreman: (noun) a worker who supervises other workers
444. Foresight: (noun) the ability to foresee
445. Forfeited: (verb) something that has been lost or surrendered as a penalty for a wrongdoing or failure to fulfil an obligation or condition

446. Forgery: (noun) the act or an instance of making a copy of a picture, a bank note, etc. for a fraudulent purpose
447. Fortuitous: (adjective) happening by chance
448. Fossil: (noun) an impression or cast of an animal or plant preserved within a rock
449. Foundling: (noun) an abandoned child of unknown parents
450. Foyer: (noun) an entrance hall of a theatre, hotel
451. Fragile: (adjective) easily broken
452. Fragrant: (adjective) having a pleasant or sweet smell; emitting a strong, pleasant odour
453. Freight: (noun) transport of goods by rail, road, sea or air
454. Frenzy: (noun) wild agitation or excitement
455. Fugitive: (noun) a person who is fleeing someone or something, usually some kind of authority, such as the law, an army, etc.
456. Fumigate: (verb) to disinfect (a room, a building, etc.) with fumes in order to destroy pests
457. Funambulist: (noun) a tightrope walker or acrobat who performs balancing acts on a tightrope or high wire
458. Fungus: (noun) an organism that superficially resembles a plant, but does not have leaves and roots, and lacks chlorophyll, so that it must obtain its nutrients from other organisms
459. Fur: (noun) the thick fine soft coat of a hairy animal
460. Fuselage: (noun) the main body of an aircraft to which the wings and tail unit are attached
461. Gallant: (adjective) 1. brave, 2. of a man: courteous and attentive to women
462. Gallery: (noun) 1. a room or building used to display works of art, 2. a balcony along an inside upper wall, e.g., of a church or hall, providing extra seating or reserved for musicians, etc.
463. Galling: (adjective) irritating
464. Gamble: (verb) to bet (usually money) on the result of a card game, horse race, etc.
465. Garage: (noun) a building in which motor vehicles are kept

466. Garbled: (adjective) of a report or account: muddled
467. Gargle: (verb) to cleanse, treat or freshen the mouth and throat by breathing out through a medicinal liquid that is held there for a while before spitting it out
468. Garrison: (noun) a body of soldiers stationed in a town or fortress
469. Garrulous: (adjective) of a person: tending to talk a lot, especially about trivial things
470. Gatekeeper: (noun) a person or entity that controls access to something, such as information, resources or opportunities. It can also refer to a person who monitors or regulates interactions, decisions or processes
471. Genetics: (noun) the scientific study of heredity and of the mechanisms by which characteristics are transmitted from one generation to the next
472. Geology: (noun) the scientific study of the origins and structure, composition, etc. of the Earth, especially its rocks
473. Geriatrics: (noun) the branch of medicine concerned with health and care of the elderly
474. Gesture: (noun) a movement of a part of the body as an expression of meaning
475. Ghastly: (adjective) extremely frightening or horrific
476. Ghetto: (noun) a poor area densely populated by people from a deprived social group, especially racial minority
477. Glacier: (noun) a large slow-moving body of ice
478. Glamorous: (adjective) full of glamour
479. Glutton: (noun) someone who eats too much
480. Gnaw: (verb) to bite something with a scraping action, causing a gradual wearing away
481. Gourmet: (noun) someone who has expert knowledge of, and the passion for, good food and wine
482. Graffiti: (noun) words or drawings, usually humorous, political or rude, scratched, spread or painted on walls, etc. in public places
483. Granary: (noun) a building where grain is stored
484. Gratis: (adjective) free; without charge

485. Gratuitous: (adjective) done without good reason; unjustified
486. Gregarious: (adjective) very sociable
487. Gullible: (adjective) easily tricked
488. Gulp: (verb) to swallow (food, drink, etc.) eagerly or in large mouthfuls
489. Gust: (noun) a sudden blast or rush, e.g., of wind or smoke
490. Hallucination: (noun) seeing something that is not actually present or which may not even exist
491. Hamlet: (noun) a small village
492. Hamper: (verb) to hinder the progress or movement of (someone or something)
493. Handicraft: (noun) an activity which requires skillful use of the hands, e.g., pottery
494. Hangar: (noun) a large shade or building in which aircraft are kept

The word 'ghetto' has a complex history, originally referring to restricted areas in European cities where Jewish communities were compelled to live during the Middle Ages. Over time, its meaning expanded to denote impoverished urban neighbourhoods inhabited primarily by minority or marginalized groups. The term gained prominence during the Holocaust, where it became synonymous with the Nazi regime's segregation and persecution of Jews. In modern usage, 'ghetto' often carries negative connotations, evoking images of poverty, crime and social isolation. However, it has also been reclaimed by some communities as a symbol of resilience and cultural identity. Today, discussions surrounding the ghetto intersect with broader conversations about systemic inequality, urban development, and the ongoing struggle for social justice and inclusion.

495. Harass: (verb) to pester, torment or trouble (someone) by continually questioning or attacking them
496. Harbour: (noun) a place of shelter for ships
497. Harrowing: (adjective) extremely distressing, agonizing or traumatic; causing intense feelings of fear, sorrow or anguish
498. Hassle: (noun) trouble, annoyance or inconvenience or a cause of this

499. Haven: (noun) a place of safety or rest
500. Hawker: (noun) a person who travels around selling goods, typically by shouting out to attract customers or by using a mobile stall or cart
501. Hearse: (noun) a vehicle used for carrying a coffin at a funeral
502. Heartily: (adverb) in very friendly and warm in manner
503. Heckle: (verb) to interrupt (a public speaker) with critical or abusive shouts and jeers
504. Heightened: (adjective) increased or intensified in degree, intensity or magnitude
505. Heir: (noun) someone who by law receives or is entitled to receive property, wealth, a title, etc. when the previous owner or holder dies
506. Herbarium: (noun) a classified collection of preserved plants (in a room or building, etc.)
507. Herculean: (adjective) describing a task or action that requires great strength, effort or endurance, often in reference to the legendary strength of the mythological hero Hercules
508. Heresy: (noun) an opinion that contradicts a conventional or traditional belief
509. Heterogenous: (adjective) composed of parts, people, things, etc. that are not related to each other or are of different kinds
510. Hexagon: (noun) a plane figure with six sides and angles
511. Hibernate: (verb) of certain animals: to pass the winter in a dormant state; to be completely inactive
512. Highbrow: (adjective) something that is highly intellectual, educated or cultured or to cultural activities or products that are considered sophisticated or refined
513. Hijack: (verb) to take control of a vehicle, especially an aircraft, and force it to go to an unscheduled destination, often taking any passengers present as hostages
514. Hinterland: (noun) the region lying inland from the coast or the banks of a river
515. Hiss: (noun) a sharp sibilant sound like a sustained 's'
516. Historic: (adjective) famous, important or significant in history

517. Histrionic: (adjective) of behaviour, etc.: theatrical, melodramatic, expressing too much emotion
518. Holocaust: (noun) a large-scale slaughter or destruction of life, often by fire
519. Homeopathy: (noun) a system of alternative medicine where a disease is treated by prescribing small doses of drugs which produce symptoms similar to those of the disease itself
520. Homicide: (noun) the murder or manslaughter of one person by another
521. Homogenous: (adjective) made up of parts or elements that are all of the same kind or nature
522. Homonym: (noun) a word with the same sound and spelling as another but with a different meaning
523. Honorarium: (noun) a fee paid to a professional person in return for services carried out on a voluntary basis
524. Honorary: (adjective) conferring or bestowing honour
525. Horde: (noun) a huge crowd or multitude, especially a noisy one
526. Horizon: (noun) the line at which the earth and the sky seem to meet
527. Horrendous: (adjective) causing great shock fear or terror; dreadful or horrifying
528. Horticulture: (noun) an intensive cultivation of fruit, vegetables, flowers and ornamental shrubs
529. Hospitable: (adjective) generous and welcoming towards guests
530. Hostage: (noun) someone who is held prisoner as a guide or security that the captor's demands and conditions are carried out and fulfilled
531. Hostess: (noun) a female host
532. Hub: (noun) the centre of a wheel
533. Huffy: (adjective) easily offended; touchy
534. Hutch: (noun) a box usually made of wood and with a wire-netting front, in which small animals, e.g., rabbits, are kept
535. Hydrography (noun) the science of charting and mapping seas, rivers and lakes, and of studying tides, currents winds, etc.

536. Hymn: (noun) a song of praise, especially to God, but also to a nation, etc.
537. Hyperbole: (noun) an overstatement or exaggeration used for effect and not meant to be taken literally
538. Hypochondria: (noun) a condition characterized by excessive or morbid concern over one's health and sometimes the belief that one is seriously ill
539. Hypochondriac: (adjective) a person who is excessively worried about their health and often imagines or exaggerates symptoms of illness without actual medical cause
540. Hypocrisy: (noun) the practice of pretending to have feelings, beliefs or principles which one does not actually have
541. Hypocrite: (noun) a person who practises hypocrisy
542. Iconoclast: (noun) someone who rejects the use of religious images, often destroying them
543. Idealism: (noun) a tendency to see things in an ideal or idealized form rather than they really are
544. Idolatry: (noun) the worship of idols
545. Idyllic: (noun) a peaceful, picturesque scene or experience, often idealized and romanticized, typically in a rural or pastoral setting; a short poem or prose work that describes a charming, peaceful, or idealized scene, especially in nature
546. Illegal: (adjective) not legal; not authorized by law
547. Illegible: (adjective) difficult or impossible to read
548. Illiterate: (adjective) unable to read or write
549. Illuminate: (verb) to light something up or make it bright
550. Imaginary: (adjective) existing only in the mind or imagination; not real
551. Immigrant: (noun) a person who comes permanently to live in a foreign country
552. Immobile: (adjective) not able to move or be moved
553. Immortal: (adjective) living forever; lasting forever
554. Immune: (adjective) having a natural resistance to or protected by inoculation from (a particular disease)
555. Impale: (verb) to pierce with or as if with, a long, pointed object
556. Impalpable: (adjective) not able to be felt by touch

557. Impartial: (adjective) fair and unbiased
558. Impenetrable: (adjective) incapable of being entered or passed through
559. Imperceptible: (adjective) to small, slight or gradual to be seen, heard or noticed, etc.
560. Impertinent: (adjective) disrespectful
561. Impervious: (adjective) of a substance, material, etc.: not allowing (e.g., water) to pass through or penetrate it
562. Impiety: (noun) disrespect or irreverence towards religious beliefs, practices or sacred things
563. Implacable: (adjective) not able to be calmed, satisfied or placated
564. Implicit: (adjective) implied but not stated directly
565. Imposter: (noun) someone who pretends to be someone else in order to deceive others
566. Impromptu: (adjective) made or done without preparation or rehearsal
567. Improve: (verb) to make or become better or of higher quality or value; to make or cause something to make progress
568. Improvident: (adjective) not considering or providing for likely future needs
569. Impunity: (noun) freedom or exemption from punishment, injury, loss, etc.
570. Inaccessible: (adjective) difficult or impossible to approach, reach or obtain
571. Inadmissible: (adjective) not allowable or able to be accepted
572. Inanimate: (adjective) without life; not living
573. Inaudible: (adjective) not loud enough to be heard
574. Incarnate: (verb) to give bodily, especially human, form to (a spirit or god)
575. Incendiary: (adjective) relating to the deliberate and illegal burning of property or goods
576. Incentive: (noun) something, such as extra money, that motivates or encourages an action, work, etc.
577. Incognito: (adjective) keeping one's identity secret, e.g., by using a disguise and a false name

578. Incorrigible: (adjective) of a person, their bad behaviour or a bad habit: not able to be improved, corrected or reformed
579. Incredible: (adjective) difficult or impossible to believe
580. Incurable: (adjective) of a disease: not curable
581. Indebted: (adjective) having reason to be grateful or obliged to (somebody)
582. Indefatigable: (adjective) without tiring
583. Indefensible: (adjective) unable to be excused or justified
584. Indemnity: (noun) compensation for damage or loss
585. Indigenous: (adjective) of plants or animals: belonging naturally to or occurring naturally in a country or area
586. Indignant: (adjective) feeling or showing anger or a sense of having been treated unjustly
587. Indignation: (noun) strong displeasure or anger aroused by a perceived injustice, unfairness or wrongdoing
588. Indispensable: (adjective) necessary
589. Inedible: (adjective) not fit or suitable to be eaten
590. Ineffable: (adjective) unable to be described or expressed in words
591. Ineligible: (adjective) not qualified to stand for election; not suitable to be chosen
592. Inept: (adjective) done without or not having, skill
593. Inert: (adjective) tending to remain in a state of rest or uniform motion in a straight line unless acted upon by an external force
594. Inexorable: (adjective) refusing to change opinion, course of action, etc.
595. Inexplicable: (adjective) impossible to explain or understand
596. Infallible: (adjective) of a person: incapable of error
597. Infinite: (adjective) having no limits in size, extent, time or space
598. Infirmary: (noun) a hospital
599. Inflammable: (adjective) easily set on fire
600. Inflate: (verb) to swell or cause something to swell or expand with air or gas
601. Inflorescence: (noun) the flower-head and stem of a flowering plant

602. Inheritance: (noun) something (e.g., money, property, a title, a physical or mental characteristic) that is or may be inherited
603. Inimitable: (adjective) too good, skillful, etc. to be satisfactorily imitated by others
604. Innate: (adjective) existing from birth
605. Innocuous: (adjective) harmless
606. Innuendo: (noun) an indirectly unpleasant, critical or spiteful remark, e.g., about someone's character
607. Insatiable: (adjective) not able to be satisfied
608. Inscribe: (verb) to write, print or engrave words on paper, metal stone, etc.
609. Inscription: (noun) words written, printed or engraved, e.g., as a dedication in a book or as an epitaph on a gravestone
610. Insolvent: (adjective) not having enough money to pay debts, etc.
611. Insulated: (adjective) protected or shielded from external influences or impacts
612. Insurgent: (adjective) opposed to and fighting against the government of the country
613. Intangible: (adjective) not perceptible by touch
614. Interloper: (noun) someone who interferes with other people's affairs or goes to places where they have no right to be
615. Interlude: (noun) a short period between two events or a short period of a different activity
616. Interment: (noun) burial, especially with appropriate ceremony
617. Interminable: (adjective) seemingly without an end, especially because of being extremely dull and tedious
618. Internment: (noun) the confinement or detention of individuals, especially during wartime, often based on their nationality, ethnicity or perceived threat to national security
619. Interpolate: (verb) to add (words) to a book or manuscript, especially to make the text misleading or corrupt
620. Interpose: (verb) to put something or come, between two other things

621. Intestate: (adjective) of a person: not having made a valid will before their death
622. Intimidate: (verb) to coerce, especially with threats; to frighten, scare or overawe
623. Intolerable: (adjective) too bad, difficult, painful, etc. to be put up with
624. Introspection: (noun) the examination of one's own thoughts, feelings, etc.
625. Introvert: (noun) someone who is more interested in the self and inner feelings than in the outside world and social relationships
626. Intruder: (noun) a person who enters a place, such as a building or property, without permission, often with the intent to commit a crime or cause disturbance
627. Intuition: (noun) the power of understanding or realizing something without conscious rational thought or analysis
628. Inundate: (verb) to cover with water; to swamp
629. Invalid: (adjective) of a document, agreement, etc.: having no legal force, 2. of an argument, reasoning, etc.: based on false reasoning or a mistake and therefore not valid, correct or reliable
630. Inventory: (noun) 1. a list of the articles, goods, etc. in a particular place, 2. the items on such a list
631. Invigilator: (noun) a person who supervises and maintains order during examinations, ensuring that rules are followed and preventing cheating or misconduct
632. Invigorate: (verb) to give fresh life, energy and health to something or someone; to strengthen or animate
633. Invincible: (adjective) indestructible; unable to be defeated
634. Invocation: (noun) the act of calling upon a higher power, deity or spiritual force for assistance, guidance or blessing, often as part of a religious or ceremonial ritual
635. Invulnerable: (adjective) incapable of being hurt, damaged or attacked
636. Irrefutable: (adjective) not able to be denied or proved false
637. Irrelevant: (adjective) not connected with the subject in hand

638. Irreparable: (adjective) not able to be restored or put right
639. Irreverent: (adjective) lacking respect or reverence (e.g., for things considered sacred or for important people)
640. Irrevocable: (adjective) unable to be changed, stopped or undone
641. Irrigate: (verb) to provide (land) with the supply of water
642. Isolated: (adjective) placed or standing alone or apart; separate
643. Isthmus: (noun) a narrow strip of land, bounded by water on both sides, that joins two larger areas of land
644. Itinerant: (adjective) travelling from place to place, e.g., on business
645. Jacket: (noun) a short coat, especially a long-sleeved, hip-length one
646. Janitor: (noun) a caretaker, especially of a school
647. Jargon: (noun) the specialized vocabulary of a particular trade, profession, group or activity
648. Jaunt: (noun) a short journey for pleasure
649. Jaywalk: (verb) to cross streets wherever one likes, regardless of traffic signals
650. Jinx: (noun) an evil spell or influence, held responsible for misfortune
651. Jockey: (noun) a rider, especially a professional one, in horse races
652. Journal: (noun) 1. a magazine or periodical, e.g., one dealing with specialized subject, 2. a diary in which one recounts one's daily activities
653. Journalism: (noun) the profession of writing for newspapers and magazines or for radio and television
654. Journey: (noun) a process of travelling from one place to another
655. Judge: (noun) 1. a public official who hears and decides cases in a law court, 2. a person appointed to decide the winner of a contest
656. Judiciary: (noun) the branch of government concerned with the legal system and the administration of justice

657. Judicious: (adjective) shrewd, sensible or tactful
658. Junta: (noun) a group or faction, usually of army officers, in control of a country after a coup d'etat
659. Jury: (noun) a body of people sworn to give an honest verdict on the evidence presented to a court of law on a particular case
660. Juvenile: (adjective) young
661. Juxtapose: (verb) to place (things) side by side
662. Kennel: (noun) a small shelter for a dog
663. Kernel: (noun) the inner part of a seed, e.g., the edible part of a nut

> The term 'junta', originating from Spanish and Portuguese, carries a weighty historical significance, particularly in Latin American politics. Typically associated with military or political groups, 'juntas' often emerge during times of political upheaval or transition, exercising authoritarian control over the government. Throughout history, they have been involved in revolutions, coups and transitions of power, leaving a lasting impact on the countries they govern. Notable examples include the Junta of National Reconstruction in Spain during the Spanish Civil War and the National Reorganization Process in Argentina.

664. Kleptomania: (noun) an irresistible urge to steal, especially objects that are not desired for themselves and are of little monetary value
665. Knave: (noun) a scoundrel
666. Knell: (noun) the tolling of a bell announcing a death or funeral
667. Laceration: (noun) a deep cut or tear in the skin or flesh, typically caused by a sharp object or trauma
668. Laconic: (adjective) using few words; neatly concise and to the point
669. Lagoon: (noun) a relatively shallow body of water separated from the open sea by a barrier, such as a reef or a narrow bank of sand
670. Lair: (noun) a wild animal's den
671. Laminate: (verb) 1. to beat (a material, especially metal) into thin sheets, 2. to cover or overlay (a surface) with a thin sheet of protective material, e.g., transparent plastic film

672. Lancet: (noun) a small pointed surgical knife which has both edges sharpened
673. Laudable: (adjective) worthy of praise
674. Laundry: (noun) 1. a place where clothes, linen, etc. are washed, 2. clothes, linen, etc. for washing or newly washed
675. Lazy: (adjective) disinclined to work or do anything requiring effort
676. Lease: (noun) a contract by which the owner of a house, land, etc. agrees to let someone else use it for a stated period of time in return for payment
677. Leer: (noun) a lecherous look or grin
678. Legal: (adjective) allowed by the law
679. Legible: (adjective) especially of handwriting: clear enough to be read
680. Lengthened: (verb) made longer or extended in length
681. Leonine: (adjective) relating to or like a lion
682. Lethal: (adjective) causing or enough to cause death
683. Liable: (adjective) legally bound or responsible
684. Libertarian: (noun) someone who believes that people should be completely free to express themselves as they like
685. Ligaments: (noun) bands of tough connective tissue that hold two bones together at a joint
686. Linguist: (noun) someone skilled in languages or linguistics
687. Literati: (noun) literary or learned people
688. Lullaby: (noun) a soft soothing song to help send a child to sleep
689. Lunar: (adjective) relating to, like or caused by the moon
690. Maiden: (noun) a young, unmarried woman
691. Malapropism: (noun) the unintentional misuse of a word, usually with comic effect, through confusion with another word that sounds similar but has a different meaning
692. Malediction: (noun) a curse or defamation
693. Malleable: (adjective) of certain metals and alloys, etc.: able to be beaten into a different shape without breaking
694. Mammals: (noun) any warm-blooded, vertebrate animal characterized by the possession in the female of mammary glands which secrete milk to feed its young

695. Manifesto: (noun) a written public declaration of policies, intentions, opinions or motives, especially one produced by a political party or candidate
696. Mannequin: (noun) 1. a fashion model, especially a woman, employed to model clothes, 2. a life-size dummy of the human body, used in the making or displaying of clothes
697. Manoeuvre: (noun) a movement requiring or performed with, skill or intelligence
698. Mansion: (noun) a large house, usually a grand or luxurious one
699. Manuscript: (noun) an author's handwritten or typed version of a book, play, etc. before it has been printed
700. Marine: (adjective) belonging to or concerned with the sea
701. Marooned: (verb) stranded or abandoned in a remote or isolated place, typically without means of escape or assistance
702. Martial: (adjective) belonging or relating to or suitable for war or the military
703. Martinet: (noun) someone who maintains strict discipline
704. Martyr: (noun) someone who chooses to be put to death as an act of witness to their faith
705. Mascot: (noun) a person, animal or thing thought to bring good luck and adopted for this purpose by a person, team, etc.
706. Masochist: (noun) someone who finds enjoyment in experiencing pain or humiliation
707. Massacre: (noun) a cruel and indiscriminate killing of large numbers of people or animals
708. Materialistic: (adjective) having excessive interest in or devotion to material possessions and financial success
709. Matinee: (noun) an afternoon performance of a play or showing off a film
710. Matins: (noun) the daily morning service
711. Matriarch: (noun) the female head of a family, community or tribe
712. Matrimony: (noun) the state of being married
713. Mausoleum: (noun) a grand or monumental tomb
714. Maxim: (noun) a saying that expresses a general truth

715. Mediate: (verb) to act as the agent seeking to reconcile the two sides in a disagreement
716. Medieval: (adjective) belonging or relating to or characteristic of, the Middle Ages
717. Mediocre: (adjective) only ordinary or average
718. Medley: (noun) a piece of music made up of pieces from other songs, tunes, etc.
719. Melancholic: (adjective) a deep, pensive sadness or a feeling of gloominess, often accompanied by introspection or reflection
720. Melodious: (adjective) pleasant to listen to
721. Memento: (noun) a thing that serves as a reminder of the past
722. Menace: (noun) a source of threatening danger
723. Metamorphosis: (noun) a change of form, appearance, character, etc.
724. Meticulous: (adjective) paying or showing, very careful attention to detail
725. Microphobia: (noun) a fear or aversion towards small objects or things
726. Microscope: (noun) an instrument consisting of a system of lenses which produce a magnified image of objects that are too small to be seen with naked eye
727. Migrant: (noun) a person or animal that migrates
728. Migration: (noun) movement of individuals or groups from one place to another, often for reasons such as seasonal changes, environmental conditions or seeking better opportunities
729. Militia: (noun) a civilian fighting force used to supplement a regular army in emergencies
730. Millenium: (noun) a period of thousand years
731. Mimic: (verb) to imitate someone or something, especially for comic effect
732. Misandrist: (noun) someone who harbours a strong dislike or prejudice against men
733. Misanthrope: (noun) someone who has an irrational hatred or distrust of people in general

734. Mishap: (noun) an unfortunate incident, especially a minor one
735. Misologist: (noun) a person who has a strong dislike or distrust of reasoning, logic or intellectual discussion
736. Mobilize: (verb) to organize or prepare something or someone for use, action, etc.
737. Momentary: (adjective) lasting only for a moment
738. Momentous: (adjective) describing something of great importance or significance
739. Monarchy: (noun) a form of government in which the head of state is a monarch
740. Monastery: (noun) the home of a community of monks
741. Monetary: (adjective) belonging or relating to or consisting of, money
742. Monition: (noun) a warning or caution
743. Monogamist: (noun) a person who practices or advocates monogamy, being married to or in a relationship with one person at a time
744. Monologue: (noun) a long speech by one actor in a film or play
745. Monomania: (noun) domination of the mind by a single subject to an excessive degree
746. Monument: (noun) something, e.g., a statue, built to preserve the memory of a person or event
747. Moor: (noun) a large area of open, uncultivated upland with an acid peaty soil
748. Mores: (noun) social customs that reflect the basic moral and social values of a particular society
749. Mortality: (noun) the state of being mortal
750. Mortuary: (noun) a building or room in which dead bodies are laid out for identification or kept until they are buried or cremated
751. Mosaic: (noun) a design or piece of work formed by fitting together lots of small pieces of coloured stone, glass, etc.
752. Muffle: (verb) to make something quieter
753. Mundane: (adjective) ordinary; dull

754. Museum: (noun) a place where objects of artistic, scientific or historical interest are displayed to the public, preserved and studied
755. Muslin: (noun) a fine cotton cloth with a gauze-like appearance
756. Mutiny: (noun) rebellion or an act of rebellion, against established authority
757. Myopic: (adjective) short-sighted
758. Mystery: (noun) an event or phenomenon that cannot be or has not been explained
759. Narcissism: (noun) excessive admiration for oneself or one's appearance
760. Nausea: (noun) a feeling that one is about to vomit
761. Navigate: (verb) to direct the course of a ship, aircraft or other vehicle
762. Negligible: (adjective) small or unimportant enough to be ignored
763. Neigh: (noun) the cry of a horse
764. Nemesis: (noun) retribution or just punishment
765. Neologism: (noun) a new word or expression
766. Niche: (noun) 1. a position in life in which one feels fulfilled or at least, 2. a group identified as a market for a particular range of products or services
767. Nirvana: (noun) the ultimate state of spiritual tranquillity attained through release from everyday concerns and extinction of individual passions
768. Nocturnal: (adjective) of animals or birds active at night
769. Nomads: (noun) people without a permanent home, who travel from place to place seeking food and pasture
770. Nomenclature: (noun) a classified system of names, especially in science; terminology
771. Nonentity: (noun) someone of no significance, character, ability, etc.
772. Nostalgia: (noun) a yearning for the past
773. Notorious: (adjective) famous for something disreputable
774. Novice: (noun) someone new in anything

775. Numismatics: (noun) the study or collecting of coins and medals
776. Nursery: (noun) 1. a place where children are looked after while their parents are at work, 2. a place where plants are grown for sale
777. Oasis: (noun) a fertile area in a desert where water is found and plants grow
778. Obese: (adjective) very or abnormally fat
779. Obligatory: (adjective) legally or morally binding
780. Obscure: (adjective) 1. dark, dim, 2. not clear, hidden, 3. not well known
781. Obsolete: (adjective) no longer in use or in practice
782. Occidental: (adjective) relating to the Western world or Western countries
783. Octagon: (noun) a plane figure with eight straight sides and eight angles
784. Oligarchy: (noun) government by a small group of people
785. Ominous: (adjective) threatening; containing a warning of something evil or bad
786. Omnibus: (noun) a book that contains reprints of a number of works by a single author or several works on the same subject or of a similar type
787. Omnipotent: (adjective) of God or a deity: all-powerful
788. Omnipresent: (adjective) especially of God: present everywhere at the same time
779. Omniscient: (adjective) especially a God: with infinite knowledge or understanding
790. Opaque: (adjective) not allowing light to pass through
791. Ophiology: (noun) study of snakes
792. Opinionated: (adjective) with very strong opinions that one is very unwilling to change
793. Opprobrium: (noun) public shame, disgrace or loss of favour
794. Optician: (noun) someone who fits and sells glasses and contact lenses, but is not qualified to prescribe them
795. Optimist: (noun) a person who tends to expect the best possible outcome

796. Opus: (noun) an artistic work, especially a musical composition, often used with a number to show the order in which a composer's works were written or catalogued
797. Oration: (noun) a formal or ceremonial public speech delivered in dignified language
798. Orator: (noun) someone who is skilled in persuading, moving or exciting people through public speech
799. Orchard: (noun) a garden or piece of land where fruit trees are grown
800. Orchestra: (noun) a large group of instrumentalists who play together
801. Orifice: (noun) a usually small opening or hole, especially one in the body
802. Orthodox: (adjective) believing in, living according to or confirming with established or generally accepted opinions
803. Ostler: (noun) someone who attends to horses at an inn
804. Ostracise: (verb) to exclude (someone) from a group or society, etc.
805. Outlaw: (noun) someone excluded from, and deprived of the protection of, the law
806. Ovine: (adjective) relating to or a characteristic of a sheep or sheep
807. Oviparous: (adjective) animals that lay eggs to reproduce
808. Pachyderm: (noun) any large, thick-skinned non-ruminant mammal, especially the elephant, rhinoceros or hippopotamus
809. Pacifist: (noun) someone who believes that violence is unjustified and refuses to take part in making war
810. Pageant: (noun) 1. a series of tableaux or dramatic scenes, usually depicting local historical events or other topical matters, 2. any colourful and varied spectacle, especially involving a procession
811. Palatable: (adjective) having a pleasant taste
812. Palindrome: (noun) a word or phrase that reads the same backwards and forwards
813. Palliation: (noun) relief or alleviation of pain or symptoms, especially in medical contexts

814. Palmtop: (noun) a portable computer small enough to be held in the hand
815. Palpable: (adjective) easily detected
816. Panacea: (noun) a cure for any ill, problem, etc.
817. Pandemonium: (noun) any very disorderly or noisy place or assembly
818. Pander: (verb) to indulge or gratify somebody or their wishes or tastes
819. Panorama: (noun) an open and extensive or all-round view, e.g., of a landscape
820. Pantheism: (noun) the belief that equates all the matter and forces in the universe with God
821. Pantheon: (noun) all the gods of a particular people
822. Pantry: (noun) a small room or cupboard for storing food, cooking utensils, etc.
823. Parable: (noun) a story intended to convey a moral or religious lesson
824. Paradox: (noun) a statement that seems to contradict itself
825. Parasite: (noun) a plant or animal that for all or part of its life obtains food and physical protection from a living organism of another species which never benefits from its presence
826. Parasol: (noun) a light umbrella used as a protection against the sun
827. Parole: (noun) the release of a prisoner before the end of their sentence, on promise of good behaviour
828. Parricide: (noun) the act of killing one's own parent or near relative
829. Parvenu: (noun) a man or woman who has recently acquired wealth but lacks the social refinement sometimes thought necessary to go with it
830. Patent: (noun) an official licence from the government granting person or business the sole right, for a certain period, to make and sell a particular article
831. Patriarchy: (noun) a social system in which a male is head of the family and descent is traced through the male line
832. Patricide: (noun) the act of killing one's own father

833. Patrimony: (noun) property inherited from one's father or ancestor
834. Patriot: (noun) someone who loves and serves their fatherland or country devotedly
835. Pauper: (noun) a poverty-stricken person
836. Peculation: (noun) embezzlement or theft of public funds
837. Pedant: (noun) someone who is overconcerned with correctness or detail, especially in academic matters
839. Pedestrian: (noun) someone travelling on foot, especially on a street
839. Penalty: (noun) a punishment such as imprisonment, a fine, etc., imposed for wrongdoing, breaking a contract or rule, etc.
840. Penchant: (noun) a taste, liking or tendency
841. Pendant: (noun) an ornament suspended from a neck chain, bracelet, etc.
842. Peninsula: (noun) a piece of land, projected into water from a large landmass and almost completely surrounded by water
843. Pensive: (adjective) preoccupied with one's thoughts
844. Perceptible: (adjective) able to be perceived; noticeable
845. Perpetual: (adjective) everlasting; eternal; continuous
846. Persecute: (verb) to ill-treat, oppress, torment or put to death (a person or people), especially for their religious or political beliefs
847. Perseverance: (noun) the act or state of persevering; continued effort to achieve something one has begun, despite setbacks
848. Personnel: (noun) the people employed in a business company, an armed service or other organization
849. Perspicacious: (adjective) shrewd; astute; perceptive or discerning
850. Perversion: (noun) the process of perverting or condition of being perverted
851. Pessimist: (noun) a person who tends to expect the worst possible outcome
852. Pesticide: (noun) any of various chemical compounds that are used to kill pests

853. Pestle: (noun) a club-shaped utensil for pounding, crushing, and mixing substances in a mortar
854. Peter: (verb) to dwindle away to nothing
855. Philanthropist: (noun) a person who seeks to promote the welfare of others, often through charitable donations
856. Philistine: (adjective) having no interest in or appreciation of art, literature, music, etc.
857. Phobia: (noun) an obsessive and persistent fear of a specific object or situation
858. Phonetics: (noun) the branch of linguistics that deals with speech sounds, especially how they are produced and perceived
859. Physician: (noun) in UK: a registered medical practitioner who specializes in medical as opposed to surgical treatment of diseases and disorders; in other parts of the world: anyone who is legally qualified to practise medicine
860. Physiology: (noun) the branch of biology that is concerned with the internal processes and functions of living organisms, as opposed to their structure
861. Picturesque: (adjective) 1. of places or buildings: charming to look at, especially if rather quaint, 2. of language: colourful, expressive or graphic
862. Pigment: (noun) any insoluble colouring matter that is used in suspension in water, oil or other liquids to give colour to paint, paper, etc.
863. Pilferage: (noun) petty theft or stealing small items
864. Pioneer: (noun)1. an explorer of or settler in, hitherto unknown or wild country, 2. someone who breaks new ground in anything
865. Pirate: (noun) 1. someone who attacks and robs ships at sea, 2. someone who publishes material without permission from the copyright holder or otherwise uses someone else's work illegally
866. Placate: (verb) to pacify or appease (someone who is angry, etc.)

867. Placid: (adjective) calm
868. Plagiarism: (noun) copying someone else's work or ideas without giving credit
869. Plaintiff: (noun) someone who brings a case against another person in a court of law
870. Plaque: (noun) 1. a commemorative inscribed tablet fixed to or set into a wall, 2. a thin layer of food debris, bacteria and calcium salts that forms on the surface of teeth and may cause tooth decay
871. Plausible: (adjective) of an explanation or excuse: credible, reasonable or likely
872. Plebian: (noun) a member of the common people, especially of ancient Rome
873. Pledge: (noun) a solemn promise
874. Plumber: (noun) someone who fits and repairs water pipes, and water- or gas-using appliances
875. Podium: (noun) a small platform for a public speaker, orchestra conductor, etc.
876. Polyandry: (noun) the custom or practice of having more than one husband at the same time
877. Polygon: (noun) a plane figure with a number of straight sides, usually more than three
878. Portable: (adjective) easily carried or moved, and usually designed to be so
879. Posthumous: (adjective) coming or occurring after death
880. Potable: (adjective) fit or suitable for drinking
881. Potion: (adjective) a draught of medicine, poison or some magic elixir
882. Pragmatist: (noun) a person who is practical and focused on reaching effective solutions
883. Predator: (noun) any animal that obtains food by catching, usually killing and eating other animals
884. Predecessor: (noun) the person who formerly held a job or position now held by someone else
885. Predicting: (verb) forecasting or estimating a future event
886. Preface: (noun) an explanatory statement at the beginning of a book

887. Prejudiced: (noun) having an unfair or biased opinion
888. Prelude: (noun) an introductory passage or first movement, e.g., of a fugue or suite
889. Premiere: (noun) the first public performance of a play or showing of a film
890. Premonition: (noun) a feeling that something is about to happen, before it actually does
891. Prepare: (verb) to make or get ready
892. Prerequisite: (noun) a preliminary recruitment that must be satisfied
893. Prerogative: (noun) an exclusive right or privilege arising from one's rank or position
894. Prescient: (adjective) having foresight or knowing about events before they happen
895. Pride: (noun) a feeling or pleasure and satisfaction at one's own or another's accomplishments, possessions, etc.
896. Privilege: (noun) a right granted to an individual or a select few, bestowing an advantage not enjoyed by others
897. Probationer: (noun) someone on probation
898. Prodigy: (noun) 1. something that causes astonishment, 2. someone, especially a child, of extraordinary talent
899. Profile: (noun) 1. a side view of something especially of a face or head, 2. a brief outline, sketch or assessment
900. Profligate: (adjective) immoral and irresponsible; licentious and dissolute
901. Proletariat: (noun) the working class, especially unskilled labourers and industrial workers
902. Prologue: (noun) a speech addressed to the audience at the beginning of a play; a preface to a literary work
903. Prolonged: (adjective) extended or lengthened in duration
904. Prop: (noun) a portable object or a piece of furniture used on stage
905. Propellant: (noun) a compressed inert gas in an aerosol that is used to release the liquid contents as a fine spray when the pressure is released
906. Prophet: (noun) someone who is able to express the will of God or a god

907. Proponent: (noun) a supporter or advocate of something
908. Propriety: (noun) conformity to socially acceptable behaviour, especially between the sexes; modesty or decorum
909. Propulsion: (noun) the act of causing something to move forward
910. Protagonist: (noun) the main character in a play, story, film, etc.
911. Protocol: (noun) correct formal or diplomatic etiquette or procedure
912. Provender: (noun) dry food for livestock
913. Provisional: (adjective) for the time being or immediate purposes only; liable to be altered
914. Prowler: (noun) someone who moves about stealthily, typically with criminal intent
915. Prudent: (adjective) wise or careful in conduct
916. Pulmonary: (adjective) Belonging or relating to or affecting, the lungs
917. Punctilious: (adjective) carefully attentive to details of correct, polite or considerate behaviour; making a point of observing a rule or custom
918. Punter: (noun) 1. someone who places bets, 2. the average consumer, customer or member of the public
919. Pursue: (verb) 1. to follow someone or something in order to overtake, capture or attack them or it, etc., 2. to put effort into achieving (a goal, aim, etc.)
920. Putrefy: (verb) of flesh or other organic matter: to go bad, rot or decay
921. Putrid: (adjective) 1. of organic matter: decayed, 2. foul, disgusting
922. Quack: (noun) someone who practises medicine or who claims to have medical knowledge but who has no formal training in the subject
923. Quadruped: (noun) an animal, especially a mammal, that has its four limbs specially adapted for walking
924. Quaver: (verb) of a voice, a musical sound, etc.: to shake or tremble
925. Quest: (noun) a search or hunt

926. Quill: (noun) 1. a large stiff feather from a bird's wing or tail, 2. a pen that is made by sharpening and splitting the end of a feather, especially a goose feather
927. Quiver: (verb) to shake or tremble slightly; to shiver
928. Quixotic : (adjective) 1. absurdly generous or chivalrous, 2. naively romantic, idealistic, impractical, etc.
929. Raconteur: (noun) someone who tells anecdotes
930. Radiation: (noun) energy, usually electromagnetic radiation, e.g., radio waves, visible light or X-rays, that is emitted from a source and travels in the form of waves or particles
931. Radical: (adjective) 1. concerning or relating to the basic nature of something, 2. in favour of or tending to produce reforms
932. Rancid: (adjective) of stale butter, oil, etc.: tasting or smelling sour
933. Rancorous: (adjective) characterized by bitterness or resentment
934. Ransom: (noun) money demanded in return for the release of a kidnapped person or for the return of property, etc.
935. Rapport: (noun) a feeling of sympathy and understanding
936. Rebate: (noun) a refund of part of a sum of money paid
937. Recant: (verb) to revoke a formal declaration, belief, etc.
938. Receptacle: (noun) anything that holds something
939. Receptive: (adjective) willing to accept new ideas, suggestions, etc.
940. Recipient: (noun) a person or thing that receives something
941. Reciprocate: (verb) to give and receive mutually; to return (affection, love, etc.)
942. Recluse: (noun) someone who lives alone and has little contact with society
943. Reconcile: (verb) to put on friendly terms again, especially after a quarrel
944. Redundancy: (noun) unnecessary repetition or surplus
945. Redundant: (adjective) not needed
946. Referendum: (noun) the practise of giving people a chance to state their opinions on a particular matter by voting for or against it

947. Reflation: (noun) an increase in economic activity and in the amount of money and credit available, designed to increase industrial production after a period of deflation
948. Reflex: (noun) a response to a sensory, physical or chemical stimulus
949. Reformism: (noun) any doctrine or movement that advocates gradual social and political change
950. Refugee: (noun) someone who seeks refuge, especially from religious or political persecution, in another country
951. Regalia: (noun) the insignia of royalty such as the crown, sceptre and orb
952. Rehabilitate: (verb) to help (someone who has been ill or sick, or a formal prisoner) adapt to normal life again
953. Reinforce: (verb) to strengthen or give additional support to something
954. Remand: (verb) to send (an accused person) back into custody to await trial
955. Reminded: (verb) cause someone to remember something or bring something back to their attention
956. Reminiscence: (noun) the act of thinking, talking or writing about the past
957. Remission: (noun) 1. a lessening in force or effect, especially in the symptoms of a disease such as cancer, 2. pardon; forgiveness from sin
958. Rendition: (noun) a performance or interpretation of a piece of music, a dramatic role, etc.
959. Renegade: (noun) someone who deserts the religious or political group which they belong to, and joins a rival group
960. Renovate: (verb) to renew or make new again
961. Repentance: (noun) act of feeling regret or remorse for one's wrongdoing and seeking to change one's behaviour
962. Replica: (noun) an exact copy, especially of a work of art
963. Repository: (noun) a storage place or container
964. Reprieve: (verb) to delay or cancel (punishment)
965. Repulsive: (adjective) provoking a feeling of disgust

966. Requisition: (noun) a formal demand for supplies or the use of something, e.g., by the army
967. Respiration: (noun) an act or instance or the process of breathing
968. Respite: (noun) a period of rest or relief from, a temporary stopping of, something unpleasant, difficult, etc.
969. Retrace: (verb) to go back over (a route, etc.)
970. Retreat: (verb) of a military force, army, etc.: to move back or away from the enemy or retire after defeat
971. Retribution: (noun) the act of punishing or taking vengeance for sin or wrongdoing
972. Retrospective: (adjective) inclined to look back on and evaluate past events
973. Reveille: (noun) a military wake-up call, usually by a drum or bugle
974. Revel: (verb) to take great delight in (something)
975. Revile: (verb) to abuse or criticize bitterly or scornfully
976. Rhetoric: (noun) the art of using language elegantly, effectively or persuasively
977. Rheumatism: (noun) a disease causing painful swelling of the joints, muscles and fibrous tissues
978. Richter: (noun) Richter scale, a scale used to measure the magnitude of earthquakes
979. Rigid: (adjective) completely stiff and inflexible
980. Rotunda: (noun) a round, usually domed, building or hall
981. Ruins: (noun) the remains of something which has been broken or destroyed or has decayed or collapsed, especially a building
982. Sacrilege: (noun) a profanation or extreme disrespect for something holy or greatly respected
983. Sadistic: (adjective) deriving pleasure from inflicting pain or suffering on others
984. Salience: (noun) quality of being noticeable or prominent
985. Salvo: (noun) a burst of gunfire from several guns firing simultaneously

986. Samaritan: (noun) a kind, considerate or helpful person
987. Sanatorium: (noun) a hospital for the chronically ill or convalescents
988. Sanctity: (noun) the quality of being holy or sacred
989. Sarcasm: (noun) an often ironical expression of scorn or contempt
990. Savoring: (noun) enjoying or relishing something deeply
991. Scabbard: (noun) a sheath, especially for a sword or dagger
992. Scaffold: (noun) a temporary framework of metal poles and planks used as a platform from which building repairs or construction can be carried out
993. Scandal: (noun) widespread public outrage and loss of reputation
994. Scant: (adjective) in short supply; deficient
995. Scapegoat: (noun) someone made to take the blame or punishment for the errors and mistakes of others
996. Scarcity: (noun) a shortage or insufficiency of something relative to its demand
997. Scatterbrain: (noun) a person incapable of organized thought
998. Scavenge: (verb) to search among waste (for usable items)
999. Sceptic: (noun) someone with a tendency to disbelieve or doubt the veracity or validity of other people's motives, ideas, opinions, etc.
1000. Sceptre: (noun) a ceremonial staff or baton carried by a monarch as a symbol of sovereignty
1001. Scholarship: 1. the achievements or learning of a scholar, 2. a sum of money awarded, usually to an outstanding student, for the purposes of further study
1002. Scintillating: (adjective) brilliant or sparkling; full of interest or wit
1003. Score: (noun) a total number of points gained or achieved e.g., in a game; (verb) to gain or achieve (a point) in a game
1004. Screech: (noun) a harsh, shrill and sudden cry, voice or noise
1005. Scullery: a room attached to the kitchen where basic chores are carried out

1006. Sculptor: a person who practises the art of sculpture
1007. Secular: (adjective) relating to the present world rather than to heavenly or spiritual things; not religious or ecclesiastical
1008. Sedative: (noun) any agent, especially a drug, that has a calming effect
1009. Seminar: (noun) a group of advanced students working in a specific subject of study under the supervision of a teacher
1010. Senility: (noun) mental and physical decline associated with old age, typically characterized by memory loss and confusion
1011. Sentinel: (noun) someone posted on guard; a sentry
1012. Serendipity: (noun) the state of frequently making lucky or beneficial finds
1013. Serial: 1. (adjective) in series; in a row, 2. (noun) a story, television programme, etc. published or broadcast in regular instalments
1014. Sermon: (noun) a public speech or discourse, especially one forming part of a church service
1015. Sever (verb) to cut off physically
1016. Shaft: (noun) the long, straight part or handle of anything
1017. Shoal: (noun) a multitude of fish swimming together
1018. Shrapnel: (noun) a shell, filled with pellets or metal fragments, which explodes shortly before impact
1019. Siesta: (noun) in hot countries: a sleep or rest after the midday meal
1020. Silhouette: (noun) a dark shape or shadow seen against a light background
1021. Simile: (noun) a figure of speech in which a thing is described by being likened to something
1022. Sinecure: (noun) a paid job involving little or no work
1023. Slacken : (verb) to become slower; to slow one's working pace through tiredness or laziness
1024. Slobber: (verb) to let saliva run from the mouth
1025. Smother: (verb) to kill with or die from lack of air, especially with an obstruction over the mouth and nose
1026. Snippet: (noun) a scrap of information, news, etc.
1027. Sojourn: (noun) a short stay

1028. Solecism: (noun) a grammatical mistake in the use of language
1029. Soliloquy: (noun) a speech, especially in a play in which someone reveals their thoughts by talking aloud
1030. Solitude: (noun) the state of being alone
1031. Solvent: (adjective) able to pay all one's debts
1032. Sonnet: (noun) a short poem with 14 lines of 10 or 11 syllables each and a regular rhyming pattern
1033. Sonorous: (adjective) sounding impressively loud and deep
1034. Soporific: (adjective) causing sleep
1035. Sorcery: (noun) the art of use of magic
1036. Spasm: (noun) a sudden uncontrollable contraction of a muscle or muscles
1037. Speculation: (noun) making guesses or conjectures about something without solid evidence
1038. Spinster: (noun) a woman who has never been married
1039. Sporadic: (adjective) occurring from time to time, at irregular intervals
1040. Spurious: (adjective) false, counterfeit or untrue
1041. Stampede: (noun) an excited or historical rush by a crowd of people
1042. Statute: (noun) a law made by the legislative assembly of a country and recorded in a formal document
1043. Stellar: (adjective) referring or relating to or resembling a star or stars
1044. Sterile: (adjective) 1. biologically incapable of producing offspring, fruit or seeds, 2. free of germs
1045. Stevedore: (noun) a person whose job is to load and unload ships; a docker
1046. Stoic: (noun) someone who can repress emotions and show patient resignation under difficult circumstances
1047. Strangulate: (verb) to press or squeeze so as to stop the flow of blood or air
1048. Stratagem: (noun) a trick or plan, especially one for deceiving an enemy
1049. Strict: (adjective) demanding obedience or close observance of rules

1050. Strife: (noun) bitter conflict or fighting
1051. Stringent: (adjective) of rules, terms, etc.: strictly enforced
1052. Sublime: (adjective) of something in nature or art: overwhelmingly great or awe-inspiring
1053. Subservient: (adjective) ready or eager to submit to the wishes of others, often excessively so
1054. Subsidy: (noun) a sum of money given, e.g., by a government to an industry, to help with running costs or to keep product prices low
1055. Subsistence: (noun) basic necessities required for survival, such as food, shelter, and clothing
1056. Succulent: (adjective) juicy; tender and tasty
1057. Suede: (noun) a soft leather, where the flesh side is brushed so that it has a velvety finish
1058. Suicide: (noun) the act or an instance of killing oneself deliberately
1059. Summary: (noun) a short account that outlines or picks out the main points
1060. Sumptuous: (adjective) widely expensive; extravagantly luxurious
1061. Superlative: (adjective) of adjectives or adverbs: expressing the highest degree of a particular quality
1062. Superstition: (noun) belief in an influence that certain (especially commonplace) objects, actions or occurrences have on events, people's lives, etc.
1063. Supplicate: (verb) to humbly and earnestly request something
1064. Surge: (noun) 1. a sudden powerful mass movement of a crowd, especially forward, 2. a sudden sharp increase, e.g., in prices, electrical current, etc.
1065. Surreal: (adjective) dream-like; very odd or a bizarre
1066. Swarm: (noun) a large group of flying bees, laid by a queen, that have left their hive in order to set up a new home
1067. Sycophant: (noun) someone who flatters in a servile way
1068. Syllable: (noun) a segment of a spoken word consisting of one sound or of two or more sounds said as a single unit of speech
1069. Symphony: (noun) a long musical work divided into several movements, played by a full orchestra

1070. Synagogue: (noun) a Jewish place of worship and religious instruction
1071. Tantrum: (noun) an outburst of childish or petulant bad temper
1072. Tartar: (noun) 1. a hard deposit that forms on the teeth, 2. a fierce, ill-tempered, etc. person
1073. Tattoo: (verb) to mark (a coloured design) on (the body) by pricking the skin and putting in indelible dyes
1074. Tautology: (noun) the use of words which repeat the meaning of words already used
1075. Taxonomy: (noun) the science of classification of animals, plants, fossils, languages, etc.
1076. Teetotaller: (noun) a person who abstains completely from alcoholic beverages
1077. Telepathy: (noun) the apparent communication of thoughts directly from one person's mind to another's without using any of the five known senses
1078. Tempest: (noun) a violent storm with very strong winds
1079. Temporary: (adjective) lasting, acting or used for a limited period of time only
1080. Terminate: (verb) to end
1081. Terminus: (noun) the end of a railway line or bus route
1082. Theist: (noun) a person who believes in the existence of a god or gods
1083. Theocracy: (noun) government by a deity or by priests representing a deity
1084. Theologian: (noun) a person who studies or is an expert in theology, the study of religious beliefs and doctrines
1085. Theology: (noun) the study of God and religious affairs
1086. Thorough: (adjective) of a person: extremely careful and attending to every detail
1087. Timid: (adjective) easily frightened or alarmed; nervous
1088. Tirade: (noun) a long angry speech, harangue or denunciation
1089. Toddler: (noun) a child who is just beginning or has just learned, to walk

1090. Torrent: (noun) a great rushing stream or downpour of water or lava, etc.
1091. Totalitarianism: (noun) a system of government by a single party which allows no opposition and which demands complete obedience to the State
1092. Toxic: (adjective) poisonous
1093. Traitor: (noun) someone who betrays their country, sovereign, government, etc.
1094. Tranquil: (adjective) serenely quiet or peaceful
1095. Transformer: (noun) an electromagnetic device designed to transfer electrical energy from one alternating current circuit to another, with an increase or decrease in voltage
1096. Transgender: (adjective) a person whose gender identity differs from the sex they were assigned at birth
1097. Transgressor: (noun) someone who violates a law, command or moral code
1098. Transient: (adjective) lasting, staying, etc. for only a short time
1099. Transitory: (adjective) short-lived; lasting only for a short time
1100. Translucent: (adjective) allowing light to pass diffusely
1101. Transmute: (verb) to change the form substance or nature of
1102. Transonic: (adjective) speeds near or just below the speed of sound
1103. Transparent: (adjective) able to be seen through
1104. Travesty: (noun) a ridiculous or crude distortion
1105. Treason: (noun) disloyalty to or betrayal of one's country, sovereign or government
1106. Tremor: (noun) a shaking or quivering
1107. Trespassers: (noun) people who enter or use someone else's property without permission
1108. Triennial: (adjective) 1. happening once every three years, 2. lasting for three years
1109. Trilogy: (noun) a group of three related plays, novels, poems, operas, etc.

1110. Tripod: (noun) a three-legged stand or support, e.g., for a camera, etc.
1111. Triumvirate: (noun) a group of three people who share an official position, power, authority, etc. equally
1112. Truant: (noun) someone who stays away from school or work without good reason or without permission
1113. Truculent: (adjective) aggressively defiant, quarrelsome or discourteous
1114. Truism: (noun) a statement so obviously true that it requires no discussion
1115. Turncoat: (noun) someone who turns against or leaves his or her political party, principles, etc. and joins the opposing side

> There are various types of acts of killing. Some of them are:
>
> **Regicide**: the act of killing a king
>
> **Fratricide**: the act of killing one's brother
>
> **Matricide**: the act of killing one's mother
>
> **Sororicide**: the act of killing one's sister
>
> **Infanticide**: the act of killing an infant
>
> **Genocide**: deliberate killing of a large number of people from a particular nation or ethnic group, with the aim of destroying that group

1116. Tutelage: (noun) 1. the state or office of being a guardian, 2. the state of being under the care of a guardian, 3. tuition or instruction, especially as given by a tutor
1117. Tyrant: (noun) a cruel, unjust and oppressive ruler with absolute power
1118. Unanimous: (adjective) all in complete agreement; of one mind
1119. Unfeigned: (adjective) genuine or sincere, without pretence or deceit
1120. Unique: (adjective) sole or solitary; of which there is only one
1121. Unisex: (adjective) suited to, for use by or to be worn by, both men and women
1122. Universal: (adjective) relating to the universe
1123. Unknowable: (adjective) unable to be known or understood
1124. Unprecedented: (adjective) without precedent; not known to have ever happened before; unparalleled

1125. Unscrupulous: (adjective) without scruples or moral principles
1126. Unspoilt: (adjective) in its original or natural state, untouched or unmarred by human influence
1127. Unsurpassed: (adjective) unmatched or superior to all others
1128. Upthrust: (adjective) something that has been thrust or pushed upward
1129. Urn: (noun) 1. a vase or vessel with a rounded body, usually a small narrow neck and a base or foot, 2. such a vase used to contain the ashes of a dead person
1130. Usher: (noun) someone whose job is to show people to their seats, e.g., in a theatre, cinema, etc.
1131. Usurer: (noun) someone who lends money, especially one charging exorbitant rates of interest
1132. Usurper: (noun) someone who seizes power or position illegally or by force
1133. Utopia: (noun) any imaginary place, state or society of idealized perfection
1134. Uxorious: (adjective) excessively or submissively fond of one's wife
1135. Vagrant: (noun) someone who has no permanent home or place of work
1136. Vandal: (noun) someone who wantonly damages or destroys personal and public property
1137. Vaticide: (noun) the killing or murder of a prophet or seer
1138. Vegetarian: (noun) someone who does not eat meat or fish
1139. Vehement: (adjective) expressed with strong feeling or firm conviction
1140. Velocity: (noun) rate of motion, ie distance per unit of time, in a particular direction
1141. Venerate: (verb) to regard someone or something with deep respect or awe
1142. Vengeful: (adjective) eager for revenge
1143. Venial: (adjective) of sin: pardonable or excusable
1144. Venture: (noun) 1. an exercise or operation involving danger or uncertainty, 2. a business project, especially one involving risk or speculation

1145. Veracity: (noun) truthfulness
1146. Verbatim: (adjective)(adverb) using exactly the same words
1147. Verbiage: (noun) the use of language that is wordy or needlessly complicated
1148. Verbose: (adjective) using or containing too many words; boringly or irritatingly long-winded
1149. Verdict: (noun) a decision arrived at by a jury in a court of law, 2. any decision, opinion or judgment
1150. Versatile: (adjective) adapting easily to different tasks
1151. Vespers: (noun) the sixth of the canonical hours, taking place towards evening
1152. Veteran: (noun) 1. someone with many years of experience in a particular activity, 2. an old and experienced member of the armed forces
1153. Vicinity: (noun) a neighbourhood; the area immediately surrounding a place
1154. Villain: (noun) 1. the principal wicked character in a story, 2. any violent, wicked or unscrupulous person
1155. Vindicate: (verb) to clear someone of blame or criticism
1156. Virtuoso: (noun) someone with remarkable artistic skill, especially a brilliant music performer
1157. Virulent: (adjective) of a disease: having a rapidly harmful effect
1158. Virus: (noun) an infectious particle, only visible under an electron microscope, that invades the cells of animals, plants and bacteria, and can only survive and reproduce within such cells
1159. Visionary: (adjective) showing great foresight or imagination
1160. Viticulture: (noun) the cultivation of grapes for making wine
1161. Vivacious: (adjective) attractively lively and animated
1162. Volatile: (adjective) 1. changing quickly from a solid or liquid into a vapour, 2. easily becoming angry or violent, 3. of a situation, etc.: liable to change quickly, especially verging on violence
1163. Volition: (noun) the act of willing or choosing

1164. Volley: (noun) a firing of several guns or other weapons simultaneously
1165. Voluntary: (adjective) done or acting by free choice, not by compulsion
1166. Volunteer: (verb) to offer one's help or services freely, without being persuaded or forced
1167. Voracious: (adjective) 1. eating or craving food in large quantities, 2. extremely eager in some respect
1168. Voyage: (noun) a long journey to a distant place, especially by air or sea
1169. Vulnerable: (adjective) easily hurt or harmed physically or emotionally
1170. Wag: (verb) to wave (something) to and fro vigorously
1171. Wager: (noun) a bet on the result of something
1172. Walkway: (noun) a paved path or message for pedestrians
1173. Wardrobe: (noun) a tall cupboard for clothes
1174. Waterfall: (noun) a sudden interruption in the course of a river or stream where water falls more or less vertically, e.g., over the edge of a cliff
1175. Waybill: (noun) a list that gives details of goods or passengers being carried by a public vehicle
1176. Whisk: (verb) to transport (someone or something) rapidly
1177. Whittle: (verb) 1. to cut, carve or pare (a stick or piece of wood, etc.) with a knife, 2. to wear (something) away or reduce it gradually
1178. Wholesale: (noun) the sale of goods in large quantities to a retailer
1179. Widow: (noun) a woman whose husband is dead and who has not remarried
1180. Windfall: (noun) a fruit blown down from its tree
1181. Winnow: (verb) to separate (chaff) from (grain) by blowing a current of air through it
1182. Wreath: (noun) a ring-shaped garland of flowers and foliage placed on a grave or memorial as a tribute
1183. Wreathe: (verb) to hang or encircle something with flowers, etc.

1184. Wreckage: (noun) the remains of things that have been wrecked
1185. Yacht: (noun) a boat or small ship, usually with sails and often with an engine, built for racing or cruising
1186. Yearning: (noun) feeling a great desire for something
1187. Zealot: (noun) a single-minded and determined supporter of a cause
1188. Zenith: (noun) the point on the celestial sphere directly above the observer
1189. Zodiac: (noun) 1. the band of sky that extends 8° on either side of the sun's ecliptic, divided into 12 equal parts, each of which once contained one of the zodiacal constellations, though some no longer do, 2. a chart or diagram (usually a circular one), representing this band of sky and the signs of the zodiac contained within it

A few terms to understand English language better:

Ambigram: An ambigram is a word that the same right side up and upside down. For example, the word 'swims'

Contronyms: A contronym is a word that has two opposite meanings. For example 'cleave' can mean both to 'split apart' and 'stick together'

Palindrome: A palindrome is a word, phrase or number that reads the same backward as forward. For example, 'racecar' and 'madam'

Homophones: Homophones are words that sound the same but have different meanings and spellings such as 'bare' and 'bear'

Tautonyms: Tautonyms are words in which a syllable or word is repeated. Example: 'bye-bye' and 'choo-choo'

Eponym: An eponym is word derived from the name of a person or place. Example: 'sandwich' (named after the Earl of Sandwich) and 'pasteurize' (named after Louis Pasteur)

Anagram: An anagram is a word of phrase formed by rearranging the letters of another. For example, 'listen' can be rearranged to form 'silent'

COLLOCATIONS:

Collocations are pairs or groups of words that often occur together in natural language due to the way they are commonly used by speakers of a particular language. These word combinations have a tendency to co-occur frequently, either due to semantic associations, grammatical rules or cultural conventions. Collocations can be common phrases, idiomatic expressions or even specific word combinations that have become established through common usage. They are an essential aspect of fluency in any language and play a significant role in natural-sounding speech and writing.

1. Above average: Better than the typical or expected level.
2. Absolutely necessary: Completely essential or required.
3. Accept defeat: Acknowledge and come to terms with losing.
4. Accept a challenge: Agree to take on a difficult task or contest.
5. Achieve a goal: Successfully reach a desired outcome or objective.
6. Act suspiciously: Behave in a manner that raises doubts or mistrust.
7. Active ingredient: The component in a substance that produces the desired effects.
8. Active volcano: A volcano that is currently erupting or has erupted recently.
9. Against the law: Illegal or not permitted by legal standards.
10. All alone: Completely by oneself, without anyone else present.
11. All along: From the very beginning throughout a period of time.
12. All over: Spread across the entirety of something or everywhere.
13. Almost certainly: Very likely or nearly guaranteed.
14. Alternative medicine: Medical treatments that are not part of standard Western practices, such as herbal remedies or acupuncture.
15. Answer a letter: Write a reply to a received correspondence.
16. Any more: No longer or no more of something.

17. Apply for a job: Submit a request or application to be considered for employment.
18. Arrive on time: Reach a destination at the expected or designated time.
19. Artificial limb: A prosthetic device that replaces a missing limb.
20. Ask for a favour: Request someone to do something for you.
21. Attract attention: Draw the interest or notice of others.
22. Awful lot: A large amount or quantity of something.
23. Back road: A minor or less-travelled road.
24. Back street: A secondary or less prominent street, often in a residential area.
25. Back taxes: Taxes that are owed from previous years.
26. Bad mood: A state of being unhappy or irritable.
27. Badly hurt: Seriously injured or harmed.
28. Bare essentials: The most basic and necessary items or requirements.
29. Basic right: A fundamental right that is considered to be universally entitled to all individuals.
30. Bear resemblance: To look similar to someone or something.
31. Bitterly disappointed: Extremely or severely let down or unhappy because something did not happen as expected.
32. Blind faith: Complete trust or confidence in something or someone without questioning or evidence.
33. Blissfully ignorant: Completely unaware of something, often because being aware would cause stress or unhappiness.
34. Blow your nose: The act of expelling mucus from the nose by forcefully breathing out through the nostrils, typically into a tissue.
35. Boost morale: To increase the confidence, enthusiasm, and discipline of a person or group.
36. Break a promise: To fail to do what one has committed to do.
37. Break a record: To surpass a previously set achievement, often in sports or other competitions.
38. Bright future: A promising and successful period of time ahead.

39. Bring about change: To cause a significant alteration or transformation in a situation.
40. Bring to justice: To ensure that someone is tried in court and punished for a crime they have committed.
41. Broken home: A family in which the parents are divorced or separated, often implying an unstable or troubled environment.
42. Call a name: To use a specific name to address or refer to someone.
43. Can't afford: Not having enough resources, typically money, to do something.
44. Can't help: Unable to avoid or resist doing something.
45. Carry weight: To have influence or importance.
46. Cast a spell: To use magic words or rituals to cause something to happen.
47. Cast doubt: To cause uncertainty or distrust about something.
48. Casual relationship: A relationship without deep emotional commitment or seriousness.
49. Catch a glimpse: To see something briefly or partially.
50. Catch a whiff: To detect a brief, faint smell.
51. Centre of attention: The focus of everyone's interest or activity.
52. Certain amount: A specific quantity of something, though not always precisely defined.
53. Change course: To alter the direction or path of action.
54. Claim responsibility: To accept or state that one is the cause of something, often something negative.
55. Close the gap: To reduce the difference or distance between two things, often in context of progress or achievement.
56. Come alive: To become lively or animated; to become active or exciting.
57. Come to a realization: To suddenly understand or become aware of something.
58. Come to expect: To develop the habit of anticipating something as a norm.
59. Commit suicide: To intentionally take one's own life.

60. Common knowledge: Information that is generally known by many people.
61. Common language: A language shared by people who might have different native languages, used for clear communication.
62. Completely different: Utterly dissimilar in every way.
63. Conduct research: To systematically investigate or study a subject to discover or establish facts or principles.
64. Consider a possibility: To think about the potential of something happening.
65. Crystal clear: Extremely clear; easily understood or transparent.
66. Cut costs: To reduce expenses.
67. Dead ahead: Directly in front.
68. Dead end: A situation or path that leads nowhere, with no prospects of progress or success.
69. Dead tired: Extremely exhausted.
70. Deadly weapon: A weapon capable of causing death.
71. Deafening silence: A very noticeable and complete lack of sound, often felt as uncomfortable or ominous.
72. Declare war: Formally announce the beginning of a war against another country.
73. Desk job: An occupation that involves working at a desk, typically in an office setting.
74. Diametrically opposed: Completely opposite in views or opinions.
75. Dirty laundry: Personal or private matters that one might not want others to know about.
76. Dirty player: An athlete who uses unfair or unethical tactics in a game.
77. Distant relative: A family member who is not closely related, such as a second cousin.
78. Do business with: Engage in commercial or financial transactions with someone.
79. Do damage: Cause harm or injury to something or someone.
80. Early start: Beginning an activity or journey earlier than usual.

81. Earn a living: Make enough money to support oneself financially.
82. Easy target: Someone or something that is vulnerable to attack or criticism.
83. Eating habits: The usual choices and patterns in someone's diet.
84. Empty promises: Commitments made without any intention of fulfilling them.
85. Express concern: Show worry or anxiety about a situation or issue.
86. Face down: Lying flat with the face towards the ground.
87. Fall asleep: Begin to sleep.
88. Fall dramatically: Decrease or drop sharply.
89. False impression: An incorrect or misleading understanding of something.
90. Fatal mistake: An error that results in severe consequences, often death.
91. Fatal accident: An incident that results in death.
92. Feel strongly about: Have intense emotions or opinions regarding something.
93. Flat tyre: A tyre that has lost air, making it unusable.
94. Follow advice: Act according to someone's recommendations or guidance.
95. Follow instructions: Do as directed or as outlined by given instructions.
96. Front row: The first row of seats, usually closest to the stage or screen.
97. Gain access: Obtain entry or the right to use something.
98. Generally accepted: Widely recognized or approved by most people.
99. Get married: Enter into a legal union with another person.
100. Happy hour: A period during which drinks are sold at reduced prices in bars or restaurants.
101. Hard to tell: Difficult to distinguish or determine.
102. Hard work: Effort and diligence put into a task.
103. Have a look: Take a glance or inspect something.

104. Healthy diet: A balanced and nutritious eating plan.
105. Heavy drinker: Someone who consumes large amounts of alcohol regularly.
106. Heavy smoker: Someone who smokes cigarettes frequently and in large quantities.
107. High level: A considerable degree of something, often indicating importance or difficulty.
108. High quality: Superior standard or excellence.
109. High standard: Elevated criteria or expectations.
110. Honest mistake: An unintentional error made without malice or deceit.
111. Human cost: The impact of an action or event in terms of human suffering or loss.
112. Human error: A mistake made by a person, often due to oversight, lack of knowledge or misjudgment.
113. Icy wind: A very cold wind, often associated with winter weather.
114. Immediate action: Prompt or urgent response to a situation.
115. Insect bite: A wound or mark on the skin caused by an insect.
116. Inside information: Confidential or privileged knowledge not available to the general public.
117. Intense pressure: Extreme stress or demands placed on someone.
118. Irreparable damage: Harm that cannot be fixed or undone.
119. Job interview: A meeting between an employer and a job applicant to assess the applicant's suitability for a position.
120. Job opportunity: A chance for employment.
121. Joint owners: Two or more individuals who own something together.
122. Jump to a conclusion: To make a decision or form an opinion too quickly without sufficient evidence.
123. Junk food: Food that is unhealthy and low in nutritional value.
124. Junk mail: Unwanted or unsolicited advertising sent by mail or email.
125. Just cause: A legitimate or valid reason for an action.

126. Keep a diary: To regularly write down personal experiences, thoughts or observations.
127. Keep fit: To maintain physical health and fitness.
128. Keep in touch: To continue to communicate with someone.
129. Keep records: To maintain detailed and accurate documentation or accounts.
130. Keep safe: To protect from harm or danger.
131. Keep score: To record or track points in a game or competition.
132. Keep the change: To allow someone to keep the remaining amount of money after a purchase.
133. Kill time: To engage in activities to pass the time, usually while waiting.
134. Know best: To have the most understanding or expertise about a situation.
135. Know the score: To understand the situation or the facts of a matter.
136. Language skills: The ability to communicate effectively in one or more languages.
137. Last long: To endure or remain in good condition over an extended period.
138. Late night: The period of time late in the evening, often after usual bedtime.
139. Laugh out loud: To laugh audibly and heartily.
140. Law and order: The condition of a society where legal rules are followed and authority is respected.
141. Lead the world: To be at the forefront or in a dominant position globally.
142. Leave a message: To provide information or a communication for someone who is not available at the moment.
143. Leave home: To depart from one's residence, often for an extended period or permanently.
144. Let go: To release or relinquish control; to stop holding on.
145. Little known: Not widely known or recognized.
146. Living conditions: The circumstances affecting the daily life of people, including housing, sanitation and safety.

147. Long ago: Refers to a distant point in time, typically in the past, often implying a significant amount of time has passed since the event being referenced.
148. Long overdue: Something that should have happened or been completed a while ago but has been delayed beyond what is appropriate or expected.
149. Lose control: To no longer have power or authority over a situation, emotion or oneself, often resulting in chaotic or undesirable consequences.
150. Lose faith: To stop believing in something or someone, often due to disappointment, doubt or disillusionment.
151. Lose money: To experience a financial loss, typically by spending more money than one earns or by making poor investment decisions.
152. Lose your temper: To become angry or lose control of one's emotions, often resulting in outbursts or aggressive behaviour.
153. Love dearly: To have deep affection or strong feelings of love towards someone or something.
154. Lucky escape: Narrowly avoiding a dangerous or undesirable situation, often by chance or good fortune.
155. Main course: The primary dish in a meal, typically consisting of the main protein or centrepiece.
156. Main road: A major or primary route, often designated for high volumes of traffic and connecting key destinations.
157. Make a decision: To reach a conclusion or choose a course of action after considering options or alternatives.
158. Make a difference: To have a positive impact or effect on a situation, often by bringing about change or improvement.
159. Make a fortune: To accumulate a large amount of wealth or money, typically through successful business ventures or investments.
160. Make a fuss: To react or behave in an exaggerated or attention-seeking manner, often in response to minor issues or inconveniences.
161. Make a living: To earn money or support oneself financially through employment or other means.

162. Make a profit: To earn more money from a venture or activity than what was initially invested or spent.
163. Make a reservation: To arrange or secure a booking or appointment, typically in advance.
164. Make amends: To apologize or take action to correct a wrong or injury caused to someone.
165. Make an appointment: To schedule a specific time or arrangement to meet with someone or attend an event.
166. Make an effort: To exert energy or attempt to accomplish something, often implying determination or willingness to overcome obstacles.
167. Make an offer: To propose or present something for consideration, often in a formal or business context.
168. Make believe: To pretend or imagine something to be true, often for amusement or as a form of play.
169. Make contact: To establish communication or connection with someone, typically after initial difficulty or effort.
170. Make progress: To advance or move forward, often towards a goal or desired outcome.
171. Make room: To create space or accommodate something or someone by clearing or rearranging objects or arrangements.
172. Married couple: A pair of individuals who are legally joined in marriage.
173. Mass market: The sale of goods or services to a large number of consumers, typically through broad distribution channels.
174. Murder mystery: A genre of fiction or entertainment involving a crime, typically homicide, and the subsequent investigation to uncover the perpetrator.
175. Nasty habit: An undesirable or unpleasant behaviour that is repeated regularly and may be difficult to stop.
176. Nasty shock: A sudden and unpleasant surprise or revelation that causes distress or discomfort.
177. Native speaker: Someone who speaks a particular language as their first or primary language, typically from birth or early childhood.

178. Natural causes: Refers to the biological processes or phenomena that lead to an event, often used in the context of death to indicate non-violent or non-criminal circumstances.
179. Neat and tidy: Orderly and well-organized; clean and free from clutter or mess.
180. Negative attitude: A pessimistic or unfavourable mindset or outlook towards people, situations or life in general.
181. New generation: Refers to the youngest group of people within a society or family, typically succeeding a previous generation.
182. Next time: Referring to a future occasion or opportunity; indicating a plan or intention to do something at a later point.
183. Occupational hazard: A risk or danger that is inherent in a particular job or occupation.
184. Odd number: A number that cannot be divided evenly by two, leaving a remainder of one when divided by two.
185. Odd socks: Pairs of socks that do not match in colour, pattern or design.
186. Offer an explanation: To provide clarification or justification for something, typically in response to a question or confusion.
187. Office hours: The period during the day when an office is open and employees are working.
188. Old age: The later stage of life, typically considered to be after the age of retirement.
189. Overall effect: The total impact or result of something.
190. Owe an apology: Need to express regret for a mistake or wrongdoing.
191. Pack of cards: A full set of 52 playing cards.
192. Painful memory: A recollection that causes emotional distress.
193. Painfully slow: Extremely slow, to the point of causing frustration.
194. Pair work: An activity where two people work together.
195. Pass a test: Successfully complete an examination.
196. Pay attention: Focus on or listen carefully to something.
197. Pay increase: A rise in salary or wages.

198. Peace and quiet: A state of calm and tranquility.
199. Perfectly normal: Completely typical or expected.
200. Pick your nose: Remove mucus from your nose with your finger.
201. Piece of information: A single fact or detail.
202. Quick fix: A rapid but temporary solution to a problem.
203. Quick reply: A prompt response.
204. Quiet life: A lifestyle with minimal noise, stress or excitement.
205. Quietly confident: Self-assured without being boastful.
206. Quite good: Fairly or moderately good.
207. Quite right: Absolutely correct.
208. Quite sure: Very certain.
209. Rainy day: A day when it is raining, often used metaphorically to refer to difficult times.
210. Raise a family: Bring up children.
211. Raise doubts: Cause uncertainty or suspicion.
212. Raise questions: Prompt inquiries or uncertainties.
213. Raise your voice: Speak louder, often due to anger or emphasis.
214. Reach an agreement: Come to a consensus or decision with others.
215. Readily available: Easily accessible or obtainable.
216. Real life: Actual life as opposed to fiction or imagination.
217. Reasonably happy: Fairly or moderately content.
218. Regain control: Recover the ability to direct or manage something.
219. Repair damage: Fix harm that has been done.
220. Resort to violence: Turn to physical force to achieve an end.
221. Return flight: The journey back to the original departure point
222. Return home: Go back to one's place of residence.
223. Rough draft: An initial version of a written work.
224. Rough idea: A general or approximate understanding.
225. Rough estimate: An approximate calculation.
226. Runny nose: A condition where nasal mucus flows out of the nose.

227. Safe and sound: Free from danger and unharmed.
228. Safe distance: A space that ensures safety from harm or danger.
229. Safety record: The documented history of safety performance.
230. Safety net: A system or arrangement that provides financial or other support to individuals or organizations in times of need or emergency.
231. Score a goal: To successfully achieve an objective or accomplish a task, often used metaphorically in contexts outside of sports.
232. Serious injury: Physical harm or trauma that is significant and may have long-lasting or permanent effects on health or well-being.
233. Serve a purpose: To fulfill a function or role; to be useful or meaningful in achieving a particular goal or objective.
234. Set a date: To choose or establish a specific day or time for an event or activity to take place.
235. Set menu: A fixed selection of dishes offered by a restaurant or catering service for a specific price.
236. Short memory: A tendency to forget things quickly or to have difficulty retaining information for extended periods.
237. Stay awake: To remain conscious and not fall asleep, often by making an effort or using techniques to remain alert.
238. Steady job: A stable and reliable employment position that provides regular income and benefits.
239. Straight answer: A direct and honest response to a question or inquiry, without evasion or ambiguity.
240. Take hostage: To capture or detain someone as a hostage, typically for ransom or as a means of exerting leverage or control.
241. Take medicine: To ingest or administer medication for the purpose of treating or alleviating a medical condition.
242. Take notes: To write down or record information, often during a lecture, meeting or presentation.
243. Take notice: To pay attention or become aware of something; to acknowledge or recognize its importance.

244. Tax cut: A reduction in the amount of taxes owed by individuals or businesses, typically implemented by a government as a fiscal policy measure.
245. Tell a lie: To intentionally make a false statement or deceive someone.
246. Tight grip: A firm or secure hold on something; a strong grasp or control.
247. Tight schedule: A timetable or agenda that allows little or no room for delays or deviations; a schedule with limited flexibility.
248. Top priority: The most important or highest-ranking task or objective; something that deserves immediate attention and action.
249. Try hard: To make a concerted effort or exert oneself to achieve a goal or overcome a challenge.
250. Turn around: To change direction or reverse course; to make a significant improvement or recovery after a period of decline or difficulty.
251. Ulterior motive: A hidden or underlying reason for doing something, often different from the one that is stated or apparent.
252. Ultimate goal: The highest or most important objective or aspiration; the desired outcome or endpoint of a process or journey.
253. Uncertain future: A future that is unpredictable or not fully determined; a lack of clarity or assurance regarding what lies ahead.
254. Unconditional love: Love that is given without limitations or conditions; affection and support that are not dependent on specific circumstances or behaviours.
255. Unrequited love: Feelings of romantic affection that are not reciprocated by the object of one's affection.
256. Unusually wealthy: Possessing a significant amount of wealth or assets that is uncommon or unexpected.
257. Upper deck: The upper level or floor of a multi-storey structure, typically referring to the upper seating area of a vehicle or venue.

258. Upper echelons: The highest levels or ranks within an organization or hierarchy; the top-tier leadership or management positions.
259. Urban development: The planning and construction of infrastructure, buildings and amenities in urban areas to accommodate population growth and improve quality of life.
260. Vague idea: A concept or notion that is unclear or not fully formed, lacking specificity or detail.
261. Vague memory: A recollection of past events or information that is unclear or indistinct, often lacking specific details.
262. Vary widely: To exhibit a broad range or diversity in characteristics, behaviours or outcomes.
263. Victory parade: A celebratory procession held in honour of a triumph or success, typically following a significant achievement in a competition or conflict.
264. Vital role: An essential or crucial function or responsibility that is necessary for the success or functioning of a system, organization or process.
265. Vocal music: Music that primarily features singing or vocalization, often accompanied by instrumental accompaniment.
266. Vote for: To express one's choice or preference in favour of a candidate, proposal or option in an election or decision-making process.
267. Wage increase: A rise in the amount of money paid to employees for their work, typically negotiated between employers and labour representatives.
268. Wage war: To engage in armed conflict or aggressive actions against an enemy or adversary.
269. Warm welcome: A friendly and enthusiastic reception or greeting extended to someone upon their arrival or return.
270. Warning sign: A visible indication or signal that alerts people to a potential danger, hazard or problem.
271. Waste of time: An activity or endeavor that consumes time and effort without producing any meaningful or valuable results.

272. Wave goodbye: To make a gesture with the hand or arm, typically moving it back and forth, as a way of bidding farewell.
273. Widely used: Utilized or employed by a large number of people or in many different contexts.
274. Wild animal: An undomesticated creature that lives in its natural habitat, typically exhibiting untamed behaviour.
275. Work hard: To exert a great deal of effort and diligence in performing tasks or achieving goals.
276. Worth a fortune: Valuable to an extremely high degree, often in terms of monetary value.
277. Wrong number: A telephone call made to an incorrect or unintended recipient.
278. Yawning gap: A significant disparity or difference between two things, often in terms of size, quality or understanding.
279. Yield results: To produce or generate outcomes or effects as a result of effort, action or process.
280. Zero tolerance: A strict policy or approach that allows no exceptions for a particular behaviour or activity, typically associated with swift and severe consequences for violations.
281. Zero visibility: A condition in which visibility is completely obscured or nonexistent, typically due to fog, smoke or darkness.

Match the following incomplete collocations:

1. Answer	______	a. Schedule
2. Diametrically	______	b. A whiff
3. Law and	______	c. Love
4. Odd	______	d. Tolerance
5. Perfectly	______	e. Normal
6. Rough	______	f. Opposed
7. Tight	______	g. The phone
8. Unrequited	______	h. Order
9. Zero	______	i. Number
10. Catch	______	j. Estimate

Complete the following dialogue with the collocations given

(take medicine, overall effect, lose your temper, heavy drinker, dirty laundry, bitterly disappointed)

Aziz : Meena, I'm feeling absolutely dreadful.

Meena : What's going on, Aziz?

Aziz : I've caught a nasty cold. The doctor told me to ______________, but it doesn't seem to be helping much.

Meena : That's tough. Have you noticed any ____________ since you started taking it?

Aziz : Not really. I'm still feeling terrible. I'm a __________________ of tea, but even that's not providing much relief.

Meena : It sounds like you're really struggling. Have you been able to rest?

Aziz : I've been trying, but I've got so much to do. I can't afford to be sick right now.

Meena : I understand. Being sick can be frustrating, especially when you have a lot on your plate.

Aziz : Exactly. And to make matters worse, I've got a big presentation tomorrow. I'll be ______________ if I don't do well.

Meena : Oh no, that's terrible timing.

Aziz : Yeah, I'm worried I'll ________________ if I'm not feeling well during the presentation.

Meena : Just try to stay calm and focused. You don't want to air your ________________ in front of everyone.

Aziz : You're right. I'll do my best. I just hope I can shake off this cold before tomorrow.

Meena : Hang in there, Aziz. We're all rooting for you.

Aziz : Thanks, Meena. I appreciate your support.

The phrases 'How are you?' and 'Thank you' have undergone many variations over time. Now-a-days instead of saying 'How are you?' we also use phrases like 'What's up?', 'How's life treating you?', 'How have you been?' or 'What's new with you?'.
Instead of saying 'Thank you' some of the common phrases to use these days are 'I owe you one', 'Thanks a million', 'I appreciate it' or 'Many thanks'.
The response to 'Thank you' is usually considered to be 'You're welcome'. However, we may also use responses such as:

1. No problem.
2. Sure thing.
3. Don't mention it.
4. No worries.
5. Glad I could help.

Philosophical terms:

1. A posteriori: Knowledge or justification that depends on empirical evidence or experience.
2. A priori: Knowledge or justification that is independent of experience, often based on logic or reason.
3. Deductivism: An approach in reasoning and argumentation that starts from general principles and derives specific conclusions from them.
4. Dualism: The belief that reality consists of two fundamentally different components, such as mind and body or good and evil.
5. Empiricism: The theory that all knowledge is derived from sensory experience.
6. Epistemology: The branch of philosophy that studies the nature, origin and limits of human knowledge.
7. Hermeneutics: The theory and methodology of interpretation, especially of scriptural and literary texts.
8. Idealism: The belief that reality is mentally constructed or otherwise immaterial.
9. Logic: The study of principles of reasoning, especially the structure of propositions and the nature of deductive inference.
10. Materialism: The belief that only physical matter exists and that all phenomena, including consciousness, can be explained in terms of material interactions.
11. Metaphysics: The branch of philosophy that examines the fundamental nature of reality, including concepts such as existence, causality and the nature of objects.
12. Postmodernism: A late-twentieth-century movement in philosophy and the arts that is characterized by a skeptical approach to grand narratives and ideologies, emphasizing the relative nature of truth and knowledge.
13. Pragmatism: A philosophical tradition that considers the practical consequences of beliefs as the basis for their truth and meaning.

14. Rationalism: The belief that reason and logic are the primary sources of knowledge and truth, as opposed to experience or sensory perception.
15. Archetypes: Universal symbols or patterns in human thought and culture, often found in myths and dreams, that are said to be innate and inherited.
16. Ataraxia: A state of serene calmness or emotional tranquility, often sought in philosophical schools such as Stoicism and Epicureanism.
17. Atheism: The absence of belief in the existence of deities or gods.
18. Fatalism: The belief that all events are predetermined and inevitable, rendering human effort futile.
19. Hedonism: The ethical theory that pleasure is the highest good and proper aim of human life.
20. Nihilism: The belief that life is meaningless, rejecting all religious and moral principles.
21. Socratic Method: A form of cooperative argumentative dialogue that uses questioning to stimulate critical thinking and to draw out ideas and underlying presumptions.
22. Theism: The belief in the existence of one or more deities.
23. Weltanschauung: A comprehensive worldview or philosophy of life.
24. Zen: A school of Mahayana Buddhism that emphasizes meditation, intuition and direct experience over theoretical knowledge.

Social Media terms:

1. **Hashtag (#)**: A word or phrase preceded by the hash symbol used to categorize content and make it searchable by keyword.
2. **Tweet**: A message posted on Twitter, limited to a certain number of characters (formerly 140, now 280.)
3. **Share**: Reposting content from another user to own profile or feed.
4. **Feed**: The main page where updates, posts, and content from followed users appear.
5. **Viral**: Content that becomes widely popular and spreads quickly across social media platforms.
6. **Influencer**: A person with a significant following on social media who can influence their audience's opinions and behaviours.
7. **Engagement**: Interactions with a post, including likes, comments, shares and reactions.
8. **Trending**: Topics or hashtags that are currently popular and widely discussed on social media platforms.
9. **Filter**: A tool that applies visual effects to photos or videos before posting them.
10. **Meme**: A humorous image, video or text that is copied and spread rapidly by internet users.
11. **Algorithm**: A set of rules used by social media platforms to determine what content appears in a user's feed.
12. **Troll**: A person who intentionally posts provocative or offensive messages to provoke others.
13. **Clickbait**: Content designed to attract attention and encourage users to click on a link, often using sensationalized or misleading headlines.
14. **Live stream**: Broadcasting live video content in real-time to an audience on social media platforms.
15. **Vlog**: A video blog, often documenting the daily life or activities of the vlogger.

Geography terms:

1. Acre: A unit of land area used in the imperial and US customary systems, equal to 4,840 square yards (4,047 square metres).
2. Alpine: Relating to high mountains, especially those in the Alps or describing anything resembling or associated with mountains.
3. Altitude: The height of an object or point in relation to sea level or ground level.
4. Anthropization: The process of transforming natural landscapes through human activity, including urbanization, agriculture and deforestation.
5. Anthropogenic: Resulting from or produced by human activities, typically used in the context of environmental and ecological changes.
6. Anticline: A type of fold in rock layers where the layers slope downward from a common crest, typically forming an arch-like shape.
7. Antemeridian: Relating to the time before noon; commonly abbreviated as 'a.m.'
8. Archipelago: A group or chain of islands clustered together in a sea or ocean.
9. Atlas: A collection of maps or charts, often bound together in a book.
10. Barrier reef: A long, narrow coral reef parallel to the shore but separated from it by a deep channel or lagoon.
11. Bedrock: The solid rock underlying loose deposits such as soil or alluvium.
12. Biota: The animal and plant life of a particular region, habitat or geological period.
13. Cairn: A man-made pile of stones, often used as a trail marker or memorial.
14. Cartography: The science or practice of drawing maps.
15. Continental shelf: The extended perimeter of each continent, which lies submerged under relatively shallow seas and oceans.

16. Dune: A mound or ridge of sand formed by the wind, typically found in deserts or near beaches.
17. Estuary: The tidal mouth of a large river, where the tide meets the stream.
18. Fissure: A long, narrow crack or opening in a surface, especially in rock or earth.
19. Glacial: Relating to or resulting from the presence or movement of ice, typically large masses of ice like glaciers.
20. Hemisphere: Half of the Earth, usually divided into northern and southern halves by the equator or into western and eastern halves by an imaginary line passing through the poles.
21. Isthmus: A narrow strip of land with sea on either side, forming a link between two larger areas of land.
22. Latitude: The measurement of distance north or south of the Equator, expressed in degrees.
23. Longitude: The measurement of distance east or west of the Prime Meridian, expressed in degrees.
24. Terrain: The physical features of a tract of land, including its elevation, slope and orientation.
25. Aurora: A natural light display in the Earth's sky, predominantly seen in high-latitude regions around the Arctic and Antarctic, caused by the collision of solar wind and magnetospheric charged particles with the atmosphere.
26. Delta: A landform at the mouth of a river where it fans out into multiple channels and deposits sediment, typically forming a triangular shape.

Literary terms:

1. Allegory: A narrative in which characters and events symbolize broader moral or political meanings.
2. Allusion: An indirect reference to a person, place, event or literary work with which the reader is presumably familiar.
3. Ambiguity: The presence of two or more possible meanings in a single passage or text.
4. Analogy: A comparison between two things, typically for the purpose of explanation or clarification.
5. Antagonist: A character or force in conflict with the main character or protagonist, in a story.
6. Apostrophe: A rhetorical device in which a speaker addresses an absent person, an abstract idea or an inanimate object.
7. Assonance: The repetition of vowel sounds within non-rhyming words, particularly in poetry.
8. Ballad: A type of narrative poem that tells a story, often set to music.
9. Cacophony: A harsh, discordant mixture of sounds used in literature to convey disorder or tension.
10. Characterization: The process by which an author reveals a character's personality, traits and qualities.
11. Climax: The point of highest tension in a story, where the main conflict reaches its peak.
12. Conceit: An extended metaphor with a complex logic that governs a poetic passage or entire poem.
13. Conflict: The struggle between opposing forces that drives the plot of a story.
14. Connotation: The implied or associated meaning of a word beyond its literal definition.
15. Consonance: The repetition of consonant sounds within or at the end of words in a phrase or sentence.
16. Denouement: The final resolution or clarification of a dramatic or narrative plot.
17. Enjambment: The continuation of a sentence or clause across a line break in poetry without a pause.

18. Falling Action: The part of a story following the climax where the tension decreases and the plot moves towards resolution.
19. Foreshadowing: A literary device used to give an advance hint of what is to come later in the story.
20. Irony: A contrast between expectation and reality, often highlighting the opposite of what is meant or expected.
21. Literal: Taking words in their usual or most basic sense without metaphor or allegory.
22. Metonymy: A figure of speech in which one thing is replaced with a word closely associated with it (e.g., 'the crown' for 'the king').
23. Motif: A recurring theme, subject or idea in a literary work.
24. Plot: The sequence of events that make up a story, typically including exposition, rising action, climax, falling action and resolution.
25. Parallelism: The use of similar structures in two or more clauses or sentences.
26. Satire: A genre of literature that uses humour, irony or ridicule to criticize or expose human vices and follies.
27. Rising Action: The series of events that build up to the climax of a story.
28. Soliloquy: A speech in which a character speaks their thoughts aloud, often when alone on stage, revealing inner feelings and thoughts.
29. Theme: The central topic, subject or message explored in a literary work.

Some common everyday greetings:

1. Hello: This is one of the most common and universally recognized greetings in the English language. 'Hello' is used in both formal and informal settings to acknowledge someone's presence or to begin a conversation.
2. Good morning: This is a polite and cheerful way to greet someone at the start of the day. It acknowledges the time of the day and also conveys a sense of optimism.
3. Nice to meet you: A polite and friendly greeting typically used when being introduced to someone for the first time. It is common in both personal and professional settings.
4. Good night: Used before going to end signifying the end of the day's activities and expresses well wishes for a restful and peaceful night.
5. Good evening: A polite and formal greeting used for late afternoon until nighttime. It helps to set a pleasant tone for the interaction and it is used in more formal settings, such as business meetings, dinners, and social events to convey respect and courtesy.

Note: 'Good evening' is used as a greeting and farewell during the nighttime to wish someone well for the remainder of the day. However, 'Good Night' is used specifically to wish someone before they go to sleep. Although not a hard and fast rule, in formal settings we usually end a conversation with 'Good evening' rather than 'Good night.'

Everyday Greetings:

Morning Greetings

- Good morning!
- Have a great day!
- Rise and shine!

Afternoon Greetings

- Good afternoon!
- Hope you're having a good day!
- Enjoy your afternoon!

Evening Greetings

- Good evening!
- How was your day?
- Have a relaxing evening!

Asking for Permission

1. Can I…?
   Example: 'Can I borrow your pen?'
2. May I…?
   Example: 'May I leave early today?'
3. Could I…?
   Example: 'Could I use your phone for a moment?'
4. Is it okay if I…?
   Example: 'Is it okay if I bring a friend to the party?'
5. Do you mind if I…?
   Example: 'Do you mind if I open the window?'
6. Would it be alright if I…?
   Example: 'Would it be all right if I take tomorrow off?'
7. Am I allowed to…?
   Example: 'Am I allowed to park here?'
8. Would you mind if I…?
   Example: 'Would you mind if I joined you for lunch?'
9. Is it alright if I…?
   Example: 'Is it alright if I use your computer?'
10. I was wondering if I could…?
    Example: 'I was wondering if I could have an extension on the deadline?'

Environmental terms:

1. Aquifer: A body of permeable rock that can contain or transmit groundwater.
2. Arenes: Aromatic hydrocarbons that form part of the molecular structure of many pollutants.
3. Atmosphere: The layer of gases surrounding the Earth, essential for life and climate regulation.
4. Biodegradable: Capable of being decomposed by bacteria or other living organisms, thus avoiding pollution.
5. Biomass: Organic material that comes from plants and animals, used as a renewable energy source.
6. Carbon dioxide: A colourless, odourless gas produced by burning carbon and organic compounds and by respiration. It is absorbed by plants in photosynthesis.
7. Carbon monoxide: A colourless, odourless and toxic gas produced by incomplete combustion of carbon-containing materials.
8. Carcinogen: A substance capable of causing cancer in living tissue.
9. Climate: The long-term pattern of weather in a particular area.
10. Coal: A combustible black or brownish-black sedimentary rock used as a fuel.
11. Compost: Decomposed organic material used as a fertilizer.
12. Conservation: The preservation, protection or restoration of the natural environment and wildlife.
13. Contaminant: A substance that makes something impure or unsuitable by contact or mixture.
14. Deforestation: The clearing or thinning of forests by humans.
15. Disposable: Intended to be used once and then thrown away.
16. Diversity: The variety of different species, genetic variability and ecosystems in an area.
17. Ecology: The branch of biology dealing with the relations and interactions between organisms and their environment.

18. Ecosystem: A biological community of interacting organisms and their physical environment.
19. Emission: The act of releasing substances, especially gases or radiation, into the atmosphere.
20. Endangered: A species at risk of extinction.
21. Energy: The capacity to do work, which can be derived from various sources, including renewable and non-renewable resources.
22. Environment: The surroundings or conditions in which a person, animal or plant lives or operates.
23. Erosion: The process by which the surface of the Earth gets worn down by natural forces such as wind and water.
24. Extinct: A species that no longer exists.
25. Fauna: The animals of a particular region, habitat or geological period.
26. Flora: The plants of a particular region, habitat or geological period.
27. Fossil fuel: A natural fuel such as coal or gas, formed from the remains of living organisms.
28. Geothermal: Relating to or produced by the internal heat of the Earth.
29. Habitat: The natural home or environment of an animal, plant or other organism.
30. Hazard: A danger or risk.
31. Inert: A substance that does not react chemically.
32. Organic: Relating to or derived from living matter.
33. Photosynthesis: The process by which green plants and some other organisms use sunlight to synthesize foods with the help of chlorophyll.
34. Pollution: The presence in or introduction into the environment of a substance which has harmful or poisonous effects.
35. Pyrolysis: The thermal decomposition of materials at elevated temperatures in an inert atmosphere.

Different between asking and demanding:

When you ask someone to do something for you, we must keep in mind to make the conversation more polite. Some sentences can sound rude if we don't request them properly. Try to see if you can tell the difference between asking and demanding in the statements below.

A: Can you please help me with this box?
A: Help me carry this box.

B: Could you kindly tell me the way to the temple?
B: Do you know the way to the temple?

C: Please let me know what our plans are for tomorrow.
C: You should tell me the plans for tomorrow.

Asking for directions:

Swathi: Hi, excuse me, can you please help me? I'm a little lost, I think. I want to find the nearest post office.

Amogh: Oh, yes, yes! Actually, you're quite close. From here, walk straight down this street and take a turn by the paan shop.

Swathi: Okay. After that?

Amogh: After that, you'll see a large bookstore on your left. Take the small right at the corner, just past the bookstore.

Swathi: Got it. Turn right.

Amogh: And once you turn right, go down that street and you will see a coffee shop. The post office is on the fourth floor of the same building.

Swathi: Oh thank you so much. This was very helpful.

Amogh: No problem. If you are confused, you can ask anybody here and they'll help.

Swathi: Thank you. I will do that.

Mr, Mrs, and Ms are common titles used before a person's last name to indicate respect and address. Mr is used for men regardless of their marital status. Mrs is used for married women and is paired with their husband's last name or their own. Ms is a neutral title that can be used for women regardless of their marital status, offering a respectful and modern alternative to Mrs or Miss These titles convey the appropriate level of formality and respect in written and spoken communication.

In formal settings the title Mr or Mrs is used before the person's last name. For example: Vasudev Srinivasan may be called Mr Srinivasan or Akhila Gopal may be called Mrs Gopal. However, nowadays it has become common to use Mr or Mrs before the first name as well.

Fill in the blanks with the answers given below:

(zealot, sonorous, expiate, inundate, panacea, delinquent, dirge, truant, boorish, juxtapose, xenophobia, contrite, treason, whittle, laconic)

1. Heavy rains began to __________ the region, causing widespread flooding.
2. He used a knife to __________ the stick into a sharp point.
3. Due to his __________ behaviour, he frequently found himself in trouble with the school authorities.
4. The politician was accused of being __________ in his dealings.
5. His __________ outburst was completely unexpected.
6. The country's __________ made it difficult for immigrants to feel welcome.
7. Many believe that education is the __________ to all societal problems.
8. He sought to __________ his guilt through acts of charity.
9. The __________ sound of the church bell echoed through the valley.
10. The funeral included a solemn __________ sung by the choir.
11. The artist decided to __________ the two contrasting colors on the canvas.
12. The __________ was caught spray-painting graffiti on the walls.
13. Betraying one's country is considered an act of __________.
14. He was known as a __________, willing to do anything for his beliefs.
15. Despite the interviewer's probing questions, the candidate remained ____________, offering only brief and concise responses.

SOLVE THE CROSSWORD

Across

1. an exact copy made, e.g., of a manuscript, picture, etc.
4. of a voice, a musical sound, etc.: to shake or tremble
5. a light umbrella used as a protection against the sun
6. very talkative
7. a military wake-up call, usually by a drum or bugle
9. a source of threatening danger

Down

2. indecently insulting or abusive, and unjustly damaging to the reputation
3. belonging or relating to or having, a sense of touch
5. dry food for livestock
8. the tolling of a bell announcing a death or funeral

Choose the correct answers:

1. His outspoken views against the government led many to label him as a/an __________.
   a) anarchist b) chauffeur c) dwarf
2. The monk lived a/an __________ life, renouncing worldly pleasures and material possessions.
   a) effeminate b) ascetic c) illiterate
3. The politician's __________ rhetoric worried many, as it seemed to incite conflict rather than promote peace.
   a) inert b) bellicose c) indispensable
4. The reporters continued to __________ the celebrity with questions, hoping to get an exclusive comment.
   a) jacket b) menace c) bombard
5. Much to his __________, he realized he had made a critical error in his calculations.
   a) chagrin b) nostalgia c) gratis
6. The customer's __________ behaviour towards the staff was unacceptable and caused quite a scene.
   a) judicious b) churlish c) hypocrite
7. Her __________ in the face of unjust rules inspired others to stand up for their rights as well.
   a) hyperbole b) voyage c) defiance
8. The teacher aimed to __________ her students by introducing them to a wide range of thought-provoking literature.
   a) edify b) lacerate c) mobilize
9. The meeting turned into a/an __________, with everyone shouting and no decisions being made.
   a) monastery b) farce c) optimist
10. Without proper guidance, the new employee began to __________ in his attempts to complete the project.
    a) propel b) retreat c) flounder
11. The sound of the rat __________ on something inside the wall kept us awake all night.
    a) gnawing b) savouring c) venerate

12. The small __________ nestled among the hills was known for its picturesque scenery and quaint charm.
    a) villain b) hamlet c) cynic
13. In medieval times, spreading __________ could lead to severe punishment, including excommunication or even execution.
    a) jargon b) heresy c) hyperbole
14. The knight used his lance to __________ his opponent during the jousting tournament.
    a) boomerang b) compere c) impale
15. The medication remained __________, failing to produce any noticeable effects on the patient's condition.
    a) devious b) inert c) diffuse
16. After weeks of hard work, they decided to take a spontaneous __________ to the countryside for a relaxing break.
    a) innuendo b) jaunt c) lagoon
17. The cunning __________ attempted to cheat his way into the king's favour, but his deception was eventually uncovered.
    a) janitor b) knave c) maiden
18. The stranger gave her a suggestive __________ before quickly walking away.
    a) leer b) medley c) muslin
19. The soldiers were ordered to __________ the entire village, leaving behind a scene of devastation.
    a) peter b) whittle c) massacre
20. She used a pillow to __________ the sound of her crying so that no one would hear her distress.
    a) whisk b) muffle c) anchor
21. As she flipped through the old photo album, a wave of __________ washed over her as she remembered simpler times.
    a) apartheid b) nostalgia c) insolvent
22. The window was covered with a/an __________ curtain, preventing any light from entering the room.
    a) opaque b) sterile c) unisex
23. The zoo's newest exhibit featured a family of __________, including elephants and rhinoceroses.
    a) villains b) pachyderms c) brunettes

24. She had a/an __________ for collecting vintage vinyl records, scouring flea markets and thrift stores for rare finds.
    a) echo b) journey c) penchant
25. The manager offered to refund the customer's money in an attempt to __________ them over the faulty product.
    a) placate b) laminate c) martyr
26. The lawyer was known for his __________ attention to detail, leaving no stone unturned in his case preparations.
    a) obscure b) punctilious c) virulent
27. The internet is filled with dubious health advice from __________ claiming to have miracle cures for every ailment.
    a) pirates b) hinterland c) quacks
28. The king's coronation ceremony was a grand affair, with the royal __________ on full display for all to admire.
    a) herbarium b) laundry c) regalia
29. The judge decided to __________ the suspect to custody until the trial date could be set.
    a) remand b) efface c) jinx
30. Despite her efforts to help, she was unfairly __________ by those who misunderstood her intentions.
    a) mimicked b) obscured c) reviled
31. The professor emphasized the __________ of the topic by discussing its relevance to current events.
    a) salience b) endemic c) err
32. The king held his golden __________ as a symbol of his royal authority during the coronation ceremony.
    a) esteem b) sceptre c) nemesis
33. The fishermen carefully navigated their boat through the __________ of rocks just beneath the surface of the water.
    a) florist b) shoal c) scaffold
34. His frequent grammatical errors were seen as a/an __________ by his colleagues, who prided themselves on their linguistic precision.
    a) toddler b) volition c) solecism
35. As soon as the picnic basket was opened, a/an __________ of bees descended upon the sweet treats.
    a) tutelage b) retreat c) swarm

36. The ship struggled to stay afloat in the midst of the raging __________, with waves crashing against its hull.
    a) tempest b) mosaic c) holocaust
37. The school has a strict policy for dealing with __________ students who regularly skip classes without a valid excuse.
    a) fictitious b) marooned c) truant
38. The rightful king was overthrown by a/an __________ who seized the throne through treachery and deceit.
    a) masochist b) usurper c) atheist
39. The two families were locked in a bitter __________ that had lasted for generations, with no end in sight.
    a) vendetta b) empathy c) lagoon
40. She decided to leave the company of her own __________, without any pressure from her colleagues.
    a) facile b) garrison c) volition
41. The garden trellis was beautifully __________ with blooming roses and ivy.
    a) fanatic b) sadistic c) wreathed
42. She felt a deep __________ for the days spent with her family at their old countryside home.
    a) feud b) reflex c) yearning
43. His uncompromising beliefs and fervent activism led many to view him as a/an __________ in his cause.
    a) renegade b) zealot c) teetotaller
44. His blatant __________ shocked the devout members of the community, who valued religious observance.
    a) impiety b) tirade c) exertion
45. If you fail to secure the premises, you could be held __________ for any damages or theft that occurs.
    a) dormant b) liable c) eligible
46. He lived by the __________, 'Honesty is the best policy,' and always told the truth, no matter the consequences.
    a) maxim b) intuition c) obligatory
47. The old mansion on the hill was __________ for its haunted reputation, attracting thrill-seekers and ghost hunters from far and wide.
    a) notorious b) obese c) conceited

48. The narrator in the story had an __________ perspective, knowing the thoughts and actions of all the characters.
    a) condone b) omniscient c) herculean
49. She sat by the window, gazing out __________ as she contemplated the events of the past year.
    a) prescient b) pensivley c) truculent
50. The old man lived as a/an __________ in the remote cabin in the woods, rarely venturing out into the outside world.
    a) tyrant b) geriatric c) recluse

Scientific terms:

1. Amygdala: A part of the brain involved in emotion regulation, particularly fear and pleasure responses.
2. Anaphylaxis: A severe, potentially life-threatening allergic reaction.
3. Apoptosis: The process of programmed cell death in multicellular organisms.
4. Big Bang: The prevailing theory about the origin of the universe, suggesting it began from an extremely dense and hot state and expanded over time.
5. Black hole: A region of space where the gravitational pull is so strong that nothing, not even light, can escape from it.
6. Capacitor: An electrical component used to store and release energy in a circuit.
7. Centripetal force: A force that keeps an object moving in a curved path, directed toward the centre of the curvature.
8. Centrifugal force: A perceived force that acts outward on a body moving around a centre, arising from the body's inertia.
9. Cognitive dissonance: The mental discomfort experienced by a person who holds two or more contradictory beliefs, values or ideas simultaneously.
10. Endorphin: A type of neurotransmitter in the brain that reduces pain and induces feelings of pleasure or euphoria.
11. Estivation: A period of dormancy or inactivity in animals during hot or dry conditions.
12. Eutrophication: The process by which a body of water becomes overly enriched with nutrients, leading to excessive growth of algae and depletion of oxygen.
13. Fission: A nuclear reaction in which an atomic nucleus splits into smaller parts, releasing a large amount of energy.
14. Genome: The complete set of genes or genetic material present in a cell or organism.
15. Histone: A type of protein that helps package DNA into structural units called nucleosomes.
16. Hypha: A long, branching filamentous structure of a fungus, essential for its growth and nutrient absorption.

17. Ischemia: A condition characterized by insufficient blood flow to a part of the body, often leading to tissue damage.
18. Isomer: Compounds with the same molecular formula but different structures or arrangements of atoms.
19. Megabyte: A unit of digital information storage equal to 1,048,576 bytes (2^20 bytes).
20. Melanoma: A type of skin cancer that develops from melanocytes, the cells that produce pigment.
21. Mitochondrion: An organelle in cells responsible for producing energy through cellular respiration.
22. Nanotube: A cylindrical nanostructure made of carbon atoms, known for its strength, electrical conductivity and unique properties.
23. Neanderthal: An extinct species of humans who lived in Europe and parts of Asia until about 40,000 years ago.
24. Pavlovian: Relating to classical conditioning as demonstrated by Ivan Pavlov, where a neutral stimulus becomes associated with a significant stimulus.
25. Photoelectronic: Relating to the emission of electrons from a material upon exposure to light.
26. Placebo: A substance or treatment with no therapeutic effect, often used as a control in testing new drugs.
27. Prophylaxis: The prevention of disease or infection, often through preventive treatments or measures.
28. Quantum mechanics: The branch of physics that deals with the behaviour of particles at the atomic and subatomic levels.
29. Refraction: The bending of light as it passes from one medium to another with different densities.
30. Theory: A well-substantiated explanation of some aspect of the natural world based on a body of evidence and multiple tested hypotheses.
31. Universal time: A time standard based on Earth's rotation, also known as Greenwich Mean Time (GMT).
32. Vestigial: Referring to structures or organs that have lost most or all of their original function through evolution.
33. Xerophyte: A plant adapted to survive in an environment with little water.

LEVEL 3

LIST OF WORDS

1. À la carte: (adverb) (adjective) of a meal in a restaurant: with each dish priced and ordered separately
2. Abduct: (verb) to take someone away illegally
3. Abet: (verb) to help or encourage someone to do something wrong
4. Abiogenesis: (noun) the natural process by which life arises from non-living matter, such as simple organic compounds
5. Abiosis: (noun) the absence or lack of life; a state in which no living organisms are present
6. Ablation: (noun) the process of removing or destroying material from an object's surface through means such as melting, erosion, vaporization or other forms of physical removal
7. Ablative: (noun) in e.g., Latin: the form or case of a noun, pronoun or adjective which expresses the place, means, manner or instrument of an action
8. Ableism: (noun) discrimination, prejudice or social prejudice against people with disabilities, favouring able-bodied individuals. It encompasses attitudes, actions and social structures that devalue and limit the potential of people with disabilities
9. Aboriginal: (adjective) of inhabitants: earliest known; indigenous
10. Abozzo: (noun) an initial rough sketch or draft of a work of art, typically used in painting or sculpture, where the basic outlines and composition are established before the final details are added

11. Abrade: (verb) to wear down or scrape away the surface of something through friction or rubbing
12. Abrasion: (noun) Atomic area of skin rock, etc. which has been worn away by scraping or rubbing
13. Abrogate: (verb) to cancel (a law, agreement, etc.) formally or officially
14. Abscess: (noun) a collection of pus in a cavity surrounded by inflamed tissue
15. Abscond: (verb) to depart or leave quickly and usually secretly
16. Abstemious: (adjective) of people, habits, etc.: taking food, alcohol, etc. in very limited amounts
17. Abstergent: (noun) a substance that cleanses or purifies by removing dirt, impurities or contaminants
18. Abstruse: (adjective) hard to understand
19. Abut: (verb) of countries, areas of land, buildings, etc.: to join, touch or lean against another
20. Accede: (verb) to take office, especially to become king or queen
21. Acclivity: (noun) an upward slope or incline, particularly on a hill or a piece of terrain
22. Accolade: (noun) a sign or expression of great praise
23. Accost: (verb) to approach someone and speak to them, especially boldly or in a threatening way
24. Accretion: (noun) 1. an extra layer of material which has formed on something else, 2. the process of separate things growing into one
25. Accrue: (verb) to come in addition as a product, result or development; to be added as interest
26. Acculturate: (verb) to adapt to or adopt the cultural traits or social patterns of another group, typically as a result of prolonged contact
27. Accusative: (noun) in certain languages: the form or case of a noun, pronoun or adjective when it is the object of an action
28. Acidulation: (noun) the process of making something slightly acidic or sour, often by adding a small amount of acid

29. Acolyte: (noun) someone who assists a priest; an assistant or attendant
30. Acquiesce: (verb) to accept (something) or agree to it without objection
31. Acquit: (verb) of a court or jury, etc.: to declare a person accused of a crime to be innocent
32. Acrimonious: (adjective) bitter in feeling, temper or speech
33. Acrolect: (noun) the prestigious or standard form of a language variety, typically associated with educated speakers or formal contexts
34. Actuary: (noun) someone who calculates insurance risks, and gives advice to insurance companies, etc. on what premiums to set
35. Acuity: (noun) sharpness or acuteness, e.g., of the mind or vision
36. Ad hoc: (adjective) (adverb) for one particular purpose, situation, etc. only
37. Adamant: (adjective) determined not to change one's mind or opinion
38. Addle: (verb) to confuse or muddle
39. Adduce: (verb) to mention (a fact) as a supporting reason, piece of evidence, etc.
40. Adept: (adjective) skillful at doing it; proficient
41. Adherent: (noun) a follower
42. Adstrate: (noun) a linguistic situation where two or more languages influence each other at the same level without one being dominant over the other
43. Advent: (noun) coming or arrival; first appearance
44. Adverse: (adjective) unfavourable to one's interests
45. Aegis: (noun) protection or patronage
46. Affective: (adjective) pertaining to emotions, feelings or attitudes
47. Affiance: (noun) a solemn pledge or promise, particularly in the context of engagement or betrothal
48. Affidavit: (noun) a written statement, sworn to be true by the person who makes it, for use as evidence in a court of law

49. Affricate: (noun) a consonant sound that begins as a stop (complete closure of the vocal tract) and then releases into a fricative (a sound produced by forcing air through a narrow channel, creating friction)
50. Agape: (adjective) of the mouth: gaping; open wide
51. Agency: (noun) 1. an office or business that provides a particular service, 2. an active part played by someone or something in bringing something about
52. Aggrade: (verb) the process of building up or increasing the level of sediment or material in a riverbed, stream or valley over time
53. Aggrandize: (verb) to make someone or something seem greater than they really are
54. Agnates: (noun) relatives who are related through male lineage or descent, such as a father, brother or son
55. Agnostic: (noun) someone who believes that one can know only about material things and so believes that nothing can be known about the existence of God
56. Agrarian: (adjective) relating to land or agriculture
57. Al dente: (adjective) of pasta and vegetables: cooked so as to remain firm when bitten
58. Alacrity: (noun) quick and cheerful enthusiasm
59. Alibi: (noun) a plea of being somewhere else when a crime was committed; an excuse
60. Aliped: (noun) an organism or creature, especially an insect, that has wings or wing-like structures adapted for walking or movement
61. Alla Prima: an Italian term that translates to 'at first attempt' or 'at once'
62. Allative: (adjective) a grammatical case or form indicating movement towards or direction to a location
63. Allay: (verb) to make (pain, fear, suspicion, etc.) less intense
64. Allegory: (noun) a story, play, poem, picture, etc. in which the characters represent moral or spiritual ideas or messages
65. Allusion: (noun) any indirect reference to something else
66. Alpine: (adjective) belonging or relating to alps or high mountains

67. Altruistic: (adjective) the quality of being selflessly concerned for the well-being of others, often at the expense of one's own interests or needs
68. Amalgamation: (noun) the process of combining or uniting multiple things into one
69. Amatory: (adjective) belonging or relating to or showing, sexual love or desire
70. Ambiparous: (adjective) capable of reproducing by both sexual and asexual means
71. Ambulatory: (adjective) belonging or relating to or designed for walking
72. Ameliorate: (verb) to make or become better
73. Amerce: (verb) to punish someone by imposing a fine or penalty, typically as a result of a legal judgment or verdict
74. Amiable: (adjective) friendly, present, and good-tempered
75. Amity: (noun) friendship; friendliness
76. Amorphous: (adjective) without definite shape or structure
77. Amortize: (verb) to gradually pay off (a debt) by regular payments of money
78. Amphetamine: (noun) a potentially addictive synthetic drug, often used illegally as a stimulant
79. Amplitude: (noun) 1. spaciousness, wide range or extent, 2. abundance, 3. in any quantity that varies in periodic cycles, such as a wave or vibration: the maximum displacement from its mean position, e.g., the angle between the vertical and the peak position in the swing of a pendulum
80. Amygdala: (noun) a small, almond-shaped cluster of nuclei located deep within the brain's temporal lobes, one in each hemisphere
81. Anabasis: (noun) a military expedition or campaign, particularly one involving a journey or march into enemy territory
82. Anachronism: (noun) the attribution of something to a historical period in which it did not exist
83. Anaclitic: (adjective) the dependency or reliance of an individual on another person or object for emotional support and well-being

84. Anagogic: (adjective) pertaining to an interpretation or understanding of something that transcends the literal or surface meaning, leading to a deeper spiritual or mystical understanding
85. Anagram: (noun) a word, phrase or sentence that is formed by changing the order of the letters of another word, phrase or sentence
86. Analect: (noun) a passage or excerpt selected from a larger work, particularly from a collection of writings, such as essays, speeches or sayings

> Words like 'anachronism' are called 'misnomers.' Misnomers refer to words or terms that are inaccurately named or misapplied, often leading to a misunderstanding or a mistaken impression about the object or concept they describe. Anachronism itself specifically refers to something that is out of place in terms of time, such as an object, event or person that appears in a historical context where it does not belong. Misnomers, on the other hand, can involve any kind of naming or classification error.

87. Anaphoric: (adjective) a linguistic element, typically a word or phrase, that refers back to an earlier word or phrase in a sentence or discourse
88. Anathema: (noun) 1. someone or something that is detested or abhorred, 2. a curse
89. Ancillary: (adjective) helping or giving support to something else, e.g., medical services
90. Aneurysm: (noun) a balloon-like swelling in the wall of an artery
91. Angina: (noun) severe pain behind the chest-bone, usually induced by insufficient blood supply to the heart muscle during exertion
92. Animism: (noun) a belief system or worldview that attributes spiritual or supernatural qualities to natural phenomena, such as plants, animals, rivers, mountains and other elements of the natural world
93. Annul: (verb) to declare publicly that a marriage, legal contract, etc. is no longer valid

94. Annular: (adjective) ring-shaped
95. Annunciate: (verb) to announce or declare something formally or officially
96. Anodize: (verb) to coat (an object made of metal, especially aluminium) with a thin protective oxide film by making that object the anode in a cell to which an electric current is applied
97. Antediluvian (adjective) belonging to the time before the flood as described in the Bible
98. Antenuptial: (adjective) something that occurs or exists before marriage
99. Anterograde: (adjective) the inability to form new memories after a particular event or injury, while long-term memories formed before the event remain intact
100. Anthem: (noun) the song of praise or celebration, especially a national anthem
101. Anthology: (noun) a collection of poems, usually by different authors but with some kind of thematic link
102. Anthropic: (adjective) the concept of the Anthropic Principle, which suggests that the observable universe is finely tuned to support the existence of human life
103. Antigen: (noun) any foreign substance that stimulates the body's immune system to produce antibodies
104. Antimatter: (noun) a substance that is composed entirely of antiparticles
105. Aperture: (noun) 1. a small hole or opening, 2. the opening through which light enters an optical instrument such as a camera or telescope
106. Apex: (noun) the highest point or tip
107. Aphyllous: (adjective) plants that lack leaves or have greatly reduced leaves
108. Aplomb: (noun) calm self-assurance and poise
109. Apocalypse: (noun) 1. the last book of the New Testament, also called the Revelation of St John, which describes the end of the world, 2. any revelation of the future, especially future destruction or violence

110. Apocryphal: (adjective) being of doubtful authenticity
111. Apostle: (noun) 1. someone sent out to preach about Christ in the early Church, especially one of the 12 disciples, 2. any enthusiastic supporter of a cause, belief, etc.
112. Apothegm: (noun) a concise and memorable saying or phrase that encapsulates a profound truth or principle
113. Apotheosis: (noun) the action of raising someone to the rank of a god
114. Apparat: (noun) the administrative and bureaucratic machinery or apparatus of a government, organization or institution
115. Appease: (verb) to calm, quieten and pacify, etc., especially by making some kind of concession
116. Appendectomy: (noun) an operation to remove the appendix
117. Apportion: (verb) to share out fairly or equally
118. Apposite: (adjective) suitable; well chosen; appropriate
119. Apposition: (noun) a construction in which a series of nouns or noun phrases have the same grammatical status and refer to the same person or thing and give further information about them or it, e.g., Poppy, the cat
120. Appraise: (verb) to decide the value or quality of (someone's skills, ability, etc.)
121. Approbation: (noun) approval; consent
122. Arbitrage: (noun) the practice of buying and selling assets, currencies or commodities in different markets to exploit price differences and make
123. Archaeologist: (noun) a scientist who studies human history and prehistory through the excavation of artifacts, structures, and other physical remains
124. Ardent: (adjective) 1. enthusiastic, 2. passionate
125. Arduous: (adjective) 1. needing a lot of work, effort or energy, 2. steep
126. Aria: (noun) a long accompanied song for one voice, especially in an opera or oratorio
127. Armature: (noun) 1. the moving part of an electromagnetic device in which a voltage is induced by a magnetic field, 2.

a wire or wooden framework that forms the support for a sculpture as it is being modelled

128. Arraign: (verb) 1. to bring someone (usually someone who is already in custody) to a court of law to answer a criminal charge or charges, 2. to accuse someone
129. Arrears: (noun) an amount or quantity which still needs to be done or paid back
130. Artifice: (noun) a clever trick or a plan
131. Aspersion: (noun) to make a damaging or spiteful remark
132. Asphyxia: (noun) suffocation caused by any factor that interferes with respiration and prevents oxygen from reaching the body tissues, such as choking, drowning or inhaling poisonous gases
133. Aspirate: (verb) 1. to pronounce the 'h' sound in a word or pronounce a word giving this sound its full phonetic value, 2. to withdraw (liquid, gas or solid debris) from a cavity by suction
134. Asseverate: (verb) to state solemnly
135. Assuage: (verb) to make (a pain, sorrow, hunger, etc.) less severe
136. Astringent: (adjective) 1. severe and harsh, 2. of a substance: causing cells to shrink

Some more words that originate from Greek Philosophy are:

- **Eudaimonia**: Often translated as 'happiness' or 'flourishing', it refers to the highest human good, the condition of living in accordance with virtue
- **Aporia**: A state of puzzlement or doubt, often used to describe a philosophical impasse or the feeling of confusion that can lead to deeper inquiry
- **Arete**: Translated as 'virtue' or 'excellence', it signifies the highest quality a person can achieve, particularly in fulfilling one's potential
- **Ethos**: the characteristic spirit, moral nature or guiding beliefs of a person, group or institution
- **Logos**: Refers to reason, word or principle; in philosophy, it denotes the rational principle that governs and develops the universe

137. Ataraxia: (noun) a desirable state of being that leads to a more fulfilling and contented life
138. Atoll: (noun) a circle of coral reef that surrounds a lagoon, and is itself surrounded by open sea
139. Atone: (verb) to make amends for a wrongdoing, crime, sin, etc.
140. Atrophy: (verb) to diminish or die away; to cause to diminish or die away
141. Attenuate: (verb) to weaken or reduce in force, intensity or value
142. Attest: (verb) To be proof of the truth or validity of something
143. Au gratin: (adjective) of a dish: covered with breadcrumbs or grated cheese or a combination of both
144. Augmentative: (adjective) something that serves to increase or enhance the size, extent or intensity of something else
145. Aural: (adjective) relating to the sense of hearing or to the ears
146. Aurora: (noun) the appearance of bands of coloured lights in the night sky, most often observed from the Arctic and Antarctic regions
147. Auspice: (noun) protection; patronage
148. Austere: (adjective) severely simple and plain
149. Avant-garde: (noun) the writers, painters, musicians, etc. whose ideas and techniques are considered the most modern or advanced of their time, regarded collectively
150. Aver: (verb) to state firmly and positively
151. Averse: (adjective) reluctant about or opposed to it
152. Avocation: (noun) a hobby, pastime or leisure activity pursued for enjoyment or personal fulfilment rather than as a primary occupation or source of income
153. Avulsion: (noun) the sudden removal or tearing away of a body part or structure, often as a result of injury or trauma
154. Awry: (adjective) (adverb) 1. twisted to one side, 2. wrong; amiss

155. Azimuth: (noun) in astronomy and surveying: the bearing of an object, e.g., a planet or star, measured in degrees as the angle around the observer's horizon clockwise from north, which is the zero point
156. Badinage: (noun) playful bantering talk
157. Baleful: (adjective) evil; harmful
158. Balk: (verb) to hesitate or refuse to go on, because of some obstacle
159. Ballad: (noun) a poem consisting of verses grouped in threes, with repeated refrain and a short concluding verse
160. Ballast: (noun) heavy material used to keep a ship steady or to weigh down and stabilize a hot air balloon
161. Banal: (adjective) lacking in interest or unoriginal
162. Bane: (noun) the cause of trouble or evil
163. Banister: (noun) a row of posts and the hand-rail they support, running up the side of a staircase
164. Barb: (noun) a point on a hook facing in the opposite direction to the main point
165. Barbiturates: (noun) a salt or ester of a crystalline acid, used as a source of sedative drugs
166. Bard: (noun) a poet
167. Baroque: (noun) a complex decorative style of architecture, art and music, popular in Europe from the late sixteenth century to the early eighteenth century
168. Basilect: (noun) a term used in sociolinguistics to describe a variety of language or dialect that is considered less prestigious or standard compared to other varieties within a speech community
169. Baste: (verb) to pour hot fat or juices over (especially roasting meat) during cooking
170. Bastion: (noun) a kind of tower which sticks out at an angle from a castle wall
171. Bate: (verb) to moderate or restrain one's intensity, typically used in the phrase 'to bate one's breath' which means to catch one's breath or 'to bate one's enthusiasm' which means to restrain or moderate one's excitement or enthusiasm

172. Batten: (noun) a long flat piece of wood used for keeping other pieces in place
173. Beatific: (adjective) expressing or revealing supreme peaceful happiness
174. Beguile: (verb) to charm or captivate
175. Behemoth: (noun) something huge and monstrous
176. Beholden: (adjective) owing a debt or favour to someone or something
177. Behoove: (verb) to be necessary or fitting
178. Belabor: 1. to argue about or discuss at excessive length, 2. to attack or batter someone or something thoroughly, either physically or with words
179. Belated: (adjective) happening or coming late or too late
180. Belay: (verb) to make (a climber) safe by tying their rope to a rock or a wooden or metal pin
181. Beleaguer: (verb) to cause someone bother or worry
182. Benediction: (noun) a prayer giving blessing, especially at the end of a religious service
183. Beneficiate: (verb) the process of improving the quality or value of raw materials, such as ores or minerals, by removing impurities or increasing their concentration of valuable minerals
184. Benign: (adjective) 1. kind, 2. of a disorder: not having harmful effects; of a mild form
185. Bequeath: (verb) to leave (personal property) in a will (to someone)
186. Bevel: (noun) a slopping edge to a surface, meeting another surface at an angle between the horizontal and the vertical
187. Big Bang: (noun) a hypothetical model of the origin of the universe which postulates that all matter and energy were once concentrated into an unimaginably dense state, which underwent a gigantic explosion between 13 and 20 billion years ago
188. Bilious: (adjective) affected by a disorder relating to the secretion of bile
189. Binomial: (noun) an algebraic expression that contains two variables

190. Bivouac (noun) a temporary camp or camping place without tents
191. Brackish: (adjective) of water: slightly salty
192. Braise: (verb) to cook (meat, vegetables, etc.) slowly with a small amount of liquid in the closed dish
193. Bran: (noun) the outer covering of cereal grain, removed during the preparation of white flour
194. Brazier: (noun) 1. a portable metal container for holding burning coal or charcoal, 2. a person who works in brass
195. Breach: (noun) an act of breaking, especially breaking of a law or promise, etc.
196. Brevity: (noun) 1. the use of few words, 2. shortness of time
197. Brigade: (noun) one of the subdivisions in the army, consisting e.g., of a group of regiments, usually commanded by a brigadier
198. Broach: (verb) to raise (a subject) for discussion
199. Brusque: (adjective) of a person or their manner, etc.: blunt and often impolite
200. Bucolic: (adjective) concerned with the countryside or people living there
201. Buffer: (noun) 1. an apparatus designed to take the shock when an object such as a railway carriage hits something, 2. a temporary storage area for data that is being transmitted from the central processing unit to an output device such as a printer
202. Bulwark: (noun) a wall built as a defence, often one made of earth; a rampart
203. Bumptious: (adjective) Irritatingly conceited or self important
204. Buoyant: (adjective) of an object: able to float in or on the surface of a liquid
205. Burgeon: (verb) to grow or develop quickly; to flourish
206. Burnish: (verb) to make metal bright and shiny by polishing
207. Cabal: (noun) a small group formed within a larger body, for secret, especially political, discussion, etc.
208. Cadaver: (noun) a human corpse, especially one used for dissection

209. Cadence: (noun) 1. the rising and falling of the voice in speaking, 2. rhythm or beat
210. Cadre: (noun) 1. a permanent core unit which can be expanded when required e.g., by conscription, 2. an inner group of activists in a revolutionary party, especially a communist one
211. Caesura: (noun) a pause near the middle of a line of verse
212. Calculus: (noun) the branch of mathematics concerned with the differentiation and integration of functions
213. Caliber: (noun) 1. the internal diameter of a gun barrel or tube, 2. quality; standard; ability
214. Caliper: (noun) a measuring device, consisting of two hinged prongs attached to a scale, which is used to measure the linear distance between the prongs
215. Callow: (adjective) young and inexperienced
216. Calorie: (noun) a metric unit denoting the amount of heat required to raise the temperature of one gram of water by 1° celsius
217. Calumny: (noun) an untrue and malicious spoken statement about a person
218. Canard: (noun) a false report or piece of news
219. Candid: (adjective) honest and open about what one thinks; outspoken
220. Canon: (noun) 1. a basic law, rule or principle, 2. a member of the clergy attached to a cathedral
221. Cant: (noun) 1. insincere talk, especially with a false display of moral or religious principles, 2. a slope
222. Cantata: (noun) a musical work which is sung, with parts for chorus and soloists
223. Cantilever: (noun) a beam or other support that projects from a wall to support a balcony, staircase, etc.
224. Canvass: (verb) 1. to ask for votes or support from someone, 2. to find out the opinions of (voters, etc.)
225. Capitulate: (verb) to surrender formally, usually on agreed conditions
226. Captious: (adjective) inclined to criticize and find fault

227. Caramelize: (verb) to change (sugar) into caramel
228. Carapace: (noun) the hard thick shell that covers the upper part of the body of some tortoises, turtles and crustaceans
229. Carcinogen: (noun) any substance capable of causing cancer
230. Cardinal: (noun) one of a group of leading clergy, who elect and advise the pope
231. Cartoon: (noun) 1. a humorous drawing in a newspaper, etc., often ridiculing someone or something, 2. a film made by photographing a series of drawings, each showing the subjects in a slightly altered position, giving the impression of movement when the film is run at high speed
232. Castigate: (verb) to criticise or punish severely
233. Cataclysm: (noun) an event, especially a political or social one, causing tremendous change or upheaval
234. Catalyst: (noun) any substance that accelerates a chemical reaction
235. Cataract: (noun) an opaque area within the lens of the eye that produces blurring of vision
236. Catharsis: (noun) a term that originally comes from Greek drama and refers to the purging or release of emotional tensions, particularly through the experience of powerful or intense emotions such as pity, fear or sorrow
237. Cathexis: (noun) a term used in psychoanalysis, particularly in theories of Sigmund Freud, referring to the investment of mental or emotional energy into a person, object or idea
238. Caucus: (noun) a small dominant group of people taking independent decisions within a larger organization
239. Caudle: (adjective) relating to, resembling or in the position of a tail
240. Causative: (adjective) producing an effect
241. Cauterize: (verb) to destroy (tissue) by the direct application of a heated instrument or a caustic chemical
242. Cavil: (verb) to make trivial objections to something
243. Celerity: (noun) quickness; rapidity of motion or thought
244. Censure: (noun) severe criticism or disapproval
245. Chameleon: (noun) lizard whose granular skin changes colour rapidly in response to changes in its environment

246. Chastise: (verb) 1. to scold someone, 2. to punish someone severely, especially by beating
247. Chatoyant: (adjective) a gemstone that exhibits a reflective, cat's-eye effect
248. Chattel: (noun) any kind of movable property
249. Chauvinism: (noun) an unreasonable belief, especially if aggressively expressed, in the superiority of one's own nation, sex, etc.
250. Chemotherapy: (noun) the treatment of a disease or disorder by means of drugs or other chemical compounds
251. Cherub: (noun) an angel, represented in painting and sculpture as a winged child
252. Chiaroscuro: (noun) the management of light and shade in a picture
253. Chicanery: (noun) clever talk intended to mislead
254. Chimerical: (adjective) something that is wildly fanciful, highly imaginative or fantastical
255. Choleric: (adjective) someone who is easily angered, irritable or quick-tempered
256. Chorale: (noun) a hymn tune with a slow dignified rhythm
257. Chronic: (adjective) of a disease or symptoms: long lasting, usually of gradual onset and often difficult to treat
258. Cipher: (noun) a secret code
259. Circuitous: (adjective) indirect
260. Circumspect: (adjective) prudent, wary
261. Citadel: (noun) a fortress built close to or within a city, for its protection and as a place of refuge
262. Clandestine: (adjective) kept secret; surreptitious
263. Clarion: (noun) an old kind of trumpet with a shrill sound
264. Cleric: (noun) a clergyman or clergywoman
265. Cloistered: (adjective) secluded
266. Clout: (noun) 1. a blow or cuff, 2. influence or power
267. Cloy: (verb) to become distasteful through excess, especially of sweetness
268. Coalesce: (verb) to come together to form a single mass
269. Coalition: (noun) a combination of temporary alliance, especially between political parties

270. Cochlea: (noun) in the inner ear of vertebrates: a hollow spirally coiled structure which converts the vibrations of sound waves into nerve impulses
271. Coda: (noun) a passage added at the end of a movement or piece to bring it to a satisfying conclusion
272. Codeine: (noun) a morphine derivative that relieves pain and has a sedative effect
273. Coefficient: (noun) 1. a number of other constant factors placed before a variable to signify that the variable is to be multiplied by that factor, 2. a number or parameter that is a measure of a specified property of a particular substance under certain conditions
274. Cognomen: (noun) a Roman's third name, often in origin an epithet or nickname, which became their family name
275. Coherence: (noun) the quality of being logical, consistent and unified
276. Cohort: (noun) 1. in the ancient Roman army: one of the ten divisions of a legion, 2. a group of people sharing a common quality or belief
277. Colander: (adjective) a perforated bowl used to drain water from cooked vegetables, etc.
278. Collage: (noun) a design or picture made up of pieces of paper, cloth, photographs, etc.
279. Collegial: (adjective) a cooperative and collaborative relationship among colleagues, often within a professional, academic or organizational setting
280. Colloquial: (adjective) of language or vocabulary: informal; used in familiar conversation rather than informal speech or writing
281. Colophon: (noun) a publisher's ornamental mark or device
282. Comestible: (noun) something to eat
283. Commensurate: (adjective) in equal proportion to something; appropriate to it
284. Commodious: (adjective) comfortably spacious
285. Comorbidity: (noun) a term used in medicine to describe the simultaneous presence of two or more diseases or medical conditions in a patient

286. Compendium: (noun) 1. a concise summary; an abridgement, 2. a collection of board games, puzzles, etc. in a single container
287. Complaisant: (adjective) eager to please; obliging
288. Complicity: (noun) the state of being an accomplice in a crime or wrongdoing
289. Comport: (verb) to behave in a specified way
290. Compound interest: (noun) interest calculated on the original sum of money borrowed and on any interest already accumulated
291. Compulsion: (noun) the act of compelling or condition of being compelled
292. Concede: (verb) 1. to admit to be true or correct, 2. to give or grant, 3.to yield or give up
293. Concerto: (noun) a composition for an orchestra and one or more solo performers
294. Concierge: (noun) a warden or caretaker of a block of flats, especially one who lives on the premises
295. Concomitant: (adjective) accompanying because of or as a result of something else
296. Concourse: (noun) in a railway station, airport, etc.: a large open area where people can gather
297. Conditioning: (noun) the process of training or accustoming a person or animal to behave in a certain way or to accept certain circumstances
298. Conduit: (noun) a channel, pipe, tube or duct through which a fluid, a liquid or a gas, may pass
299. Confabulate: (verb) to talk, discuss or confer
300. Confectionery: (noun) sweets, biscuits and cakes

> The word 'colloquial' comes from the Latin word 'colloquium,' meaning 'conversation' or 'conference.' It refers to informal language used in everyday speech rather than in formal writing or speech. Colloquial expressions often include idioms, slang, and regional dialects, making language more relatable and accessible. For example, saying 'gonna' instead of 'going to' or 'y'all' instead of 'you all' are colloquial usages.

301. Confederate: (noun) 1. a member of a confederacy, 2. friend or an ally; an accomplice or a fellow conspirator
302. Conflate: (verb) to blend or combine (two things, especially two different versions of a text, story, etc.) into a single whole
303. Conifer: (noun) an evergreen tree or shrub with needle-like leaves, which produces its pollen and seeds in cones, e.g., pine, spruce, etc.
304. Conjugal: (adjective) relating to marriage or to the relationship between husband and wife
305. Conjugate: (verb) to give the inflected parts of (a verb), indicating number, person, tense, mood and voice
306. Connote: (verb) to imply or suggest an additional meaning or idea beyond the literal definition of a word or phrase
307. Consanguinity: (noun) relationship by blood
308. Conservatory: (noun) 1. a greenhouse for plants, 2. a school specializing in the teaching of music
309. Consommé: (noun) a type of thin clear soup made usually from meat stock
310. Consonance: (noun) the state of agreement
311. Contagion: (noun) the transmission of a disease by direct physical contact with an infected person
312. Contingency: (noun) 1. something liable, but not certain, to occur, 2. something dependent on a chance future happening
313. Contraband: (noun) smuggled goods
314. Contrapposto: (noun) used in art to describe a stance where a figure stands with most of its weight on one foot, causing the shoulders and arms to twist off-axis from the hips and legs
315. Contusion: (noun) a bruise
316. Conundrum: (noun) confusing problem
317. Convergence: (noun) the process of coming together or the state of meeting at a common point
318. Copious: (adjective) plentiful
319. Coquettish: (adjective) a playful, flirtatious and teasing behaviour, often intended to attract attention or admiration
320. Cordillera: (noun) a system or chain of mountain ranges, often extending over a large area and typically consisting of parallel ranges

321. Cornea: (noun) in vertebrates: the convex transparent membrane that covers the front of the eyeball
322. Cornucopia: (noun) 1. in painting, sculpture, etc.: a horn full to overflowing with fruit and other produce, used as a symbol of abundance, 2. an abundant supply
323. Corollary: (noun) something that directly follows from another thing that has been proved
324. Corona: (noun) the outer atmosphere of the Sun, consisting of a halo of hot luminous gases visible during a total solar eclipse
325. Corporeal: (adjective) relating to the body as distinct from the soul; physical
326. Corpulence: (noun) state of being excessively fat or obese
327. Cosecant: (noun) for a given angle in a right-angled triangle: a function that is the ratio of the length of the hypotenuse to the length of the side opposite the angle under consideration; the reciprocal of the sine of an angle
328. Cosmogony: (noun) a theory or account of the origin and development of the universe or the cosmos
329. Cosmology: (noun) the scientific study of the origin, nature, structure and evolution of the Universe
330. Coterie: (noun) a small exclusive group of people who have the same interests
331. Countervail: (verb) to counteract, offset or balance the effect of something with an opposing force or influence
332. Coup: (noun) 1. a brilliantly successful move, 2. the sudden, usually violent, overthrow of a government
333. Couvade: (noun) a cultural practice in which a man takes on the symptoms, behaviour or rituals associated with pregnancy and childbirth, often during his partner's labour and delivery
334. Covert: 1. (adjective) secret; concealed, 2. (noun) a shelter for animals
335. Crampon: (noun) A spiked iron attachment for climbing boots, to improve grip on ice or rock
336. Craven: (adjective) cowardly; cringing
337. Cream: (noun) the yellowish fatty substance that rises to the surface of milk and yields butter when churned

338. Crepuscular: (adjective) 1. relating to or like twilight; dim, 2. denoting animals that are active before sunrise or at dusk
339. Crimp: (verb) 1. to press into small regular ridges; to corrugate, 2. to thwart or hinder
340. Crop: 1. (noun) a plant cultivated for food, fodder or raw materials, 2. (verb) to cut short
341. Cryogenics: (noun) the branch of physics concerned with very low temperatures, and of the phenomena that occur at such temperatures
342. Cuboid: 1. (noun) a solid body having six rectangular faces, the opposite faces of which are equal, 2. (adjective) resembling a cube in shape
343. Cuisine: (noun) 1. a style of cooking, 2. the range of food prepared and served at a restaurant, etc.
344. Culinary: (adjective) relating to cookery or the kitchen
345. Cumulative: (adjective) increasing in amount, effect or strength with each successive addition
346. Cupidity: (noun) greed for wealth and possessions
347. Curmudgeon: (noun) a bad-tempered or mean person
348. Cursive: (adjective) of handwriting: having letters which are joined up rather than printed separately
349. Cusp: (noun) a point formed by the meeting of two curves corresponding to the point where the two tangents coincide
350. Cuticle: (noun) the outer layer of cells in hair, and the dead hardened skin at the base of fingernails and toenails
351. Cyanosis: (noun) a bluish discoloration of the skin usually caused by a lack of oxygen in the blood
352. Cynosure: (noun) the focus of attention; the centre of attraction
353. Cytology: (noun) the study of the structure and function of individual cells in plants and animals
354. Damp: (adjective) slightly wet
355. Dapper: (adjective) smart in appearance and lively in movement
356. Dearth: (noun) a scarceness or lack
357. Debark: (verb) to disembark or unload passengers or cargo from a ship or aircraft

358. Debauch: (verb) to cause or persuade someone to take part in immoral, especially sexual, activities or excessive drinking
359. Debenture: (noun) a type of loan to a company or government agency which is usually made for a set period of time and carries a fixed rate of interest
360. Debonair: (adjective) especially of a man: charming, elegant, and well-mannered
361. Debut: (noun) the first public appearance of a performer
362. Decadence: (noun) a falling to low standards in morals, art, etc.
363. Decanter: (noun) an ornamental bottle with a stopper, used for decanted wine, sherry, etc.
364. Decedent: (noun) in legal and formal contexts to refer to a deceased person, especially one who has recently passed away
365. Decibel: (noun) a unit equal to one tenth of a bel, used for comparing levels of power, especially sound
366. Deciduous: (adjective) shedding leaves once a year
367. Decimate: (verb) to destroy a large part or number of something
368. Declension: (noun) in certain languages: any of various sets of forms taken by nouns, adjectives or pronouns to indicate case, number and gender
369. Decorous: (adjective) socially correct or acceptable; showing proper respect
370. Decrypt: (verb) to convert encoded or encrypted information into its original, readable form
371. Defect: 1. (noun) a flaw or fault, 2. (verb) to leave one's country, political party, etc. especially to go to or join an opposing one
372. Deft: (adjective) skillful, quick and neat
373. Deign: (verb) to do something in a way that shows that one considers the matter unimportant or beneath one's dignity
374. Deism: (noun) Belief in the existence of God without acceptance of any religion or message revealed by God to man
375. Deity: (noun) a god or goddess
376. Deleterious: (adjective) harmful or destructive

377. Deliquesce: (verb) especially of salts: to dissolve slowly in water absorbed from the air
378. Demur: (verb) to object or show reluctance
379. Demure: (adjective) quiet, modest and well-behaved
380. Denouement: (noun) the final part of a story or plot, in which uncertainties, problems and mysteries are solved
381. Denude: (verb) to make someone or something completely bare
382. Deplete: (verb) to reduce greatly in number, quantity, etc., 2. to use up (money, resources, etc.)
383. Deploy: (verb) 1. to position (troops) ready for battle, 2. to organize and bring (resources, arguments, etc.) into use
384. Depraved: (adjective) morally corrupted
385. Derailment: (noun) the act of a train or other vehicle leaving its tracks or deviating from its intended path
386. Derivative: (adjective) not original; derived from or copying something else
387. Desiccate: (verb) to remove moisture from something or to dry thoroughly
388. Despot (noun) someone who has great or total power, especially if cruel or oppressive
389. Desultory: (adjective) jumping from one thing to another with no plan, purpose or logical connection
390. Determinism: (noun) the theory that whatever happens has to happen and could not be otherwise
391. Detritus: (noun) bits of rubbish left over from something
392. Dialectic: (noun) the establishing of truth by discussion
393. Dictum: (noun) 1. a formal or authoritative statement of opinion, 2. a popular saying
394. Diffidence: (noun) a lack of confidence or self-assurance, often accompanied by feelings of shyness, timidity or hesitation in social situations
395. Dilatory: (adjective) slow in doing things; inclined to or causing delay
396. Diminutive: (adjective) very small
397. Dint: (noun) a dent

398. Discursive: (adjective) of spoken or written style: wandering from the main point; moving from point to point
399. Disoblige: (verb) to refuse or fail to do a favour for someone, to inconvenience or offend someone or to act in a way that is contrary to someone's wishes or expectations
400. Dispatch: (verb) to send (mail, a person, etc.) to a place
401. Dissemble: (verb) to conceal or disguise (true feelings or motives)
402. Dissociative: (adjective) a psychological state or disorder characterized by a disruption in the normal integration of consciousness, memory, identity or perception of self and environment
403. Dissolute: (adjective) indulging in pleasures considered immoral
404. Distrait: (adjective) thinking of other things
405. Dither: (verb) to act in a nervously uncertain manner
406. Diurnal: (adjective) 1. daily, 2. during the day
407. Diverge: (verb) to separate and go in different directions
408. Docile: (adjective) easy to manage or control
409. Dodecahedron: (noun) a solid geometric figure with 12 faces
410. Doggerel: (noun) badly written poetry
411. Dolt: (noun) a stupid person
412. Dour: (adjective) 1. sullen, 2. stern
413. Dowel: (noun) a wooden peg, especially used to join two pieces by fitting into corresponding holes in each
414. Dowry: (noun) an amount of wealth handed over by a woman's family to her husband in marriage
415. Doxology: (noun) a Christian hymn, words or expression praising God
416. Dredge: (verb) to clear the bottom of or deepen (the sea or a river) by bringing up mud and waste
417. Dross: (noun) 1. waste coal, 2. scum that forms on molten metal
418. Dubious: (adjective) 1. feeling doubt, 2. arousing suspicion; potentially dishonest or dishonestly obtained
419. Dupe: (verb) to trick or deceive

420. Duress: (noun) the influence of force or threats
421. Ebb: (verb) of the tide: to move back from the land
422. Ecclesiastical: (adjective) relating to the church or the clergy
423. Ecumenical: (adjective) bringing together different branches of the Christian Church
424. Eddy: (noun) the current of water running back against the main stream or current, forming a small whirlpool
425. Edict: (noun) an order issued by any authority
426. Edifice: (noun) a building, especially an impressive one
427. Effervescent: (adjective) something that bubbles, fizzes or gives off gas, often in an energetic or lively manner
428. Effete: (adjective) 1. lacking strength or energy, 2. made weak by too much protection or refinement
429. Efficacious: (adjective) producing or certain to produce, the intended result
430. Efficacy: (noun) to the ability or capacity of something to produce a desired effect or result
431. Effluent: (noun) liquid industrial waste or sewage released into a river, the sea, etc.
432. Efflux: (noun) the process of flowing out
433. Effrontery: (noun) shameless rudeness
434. Egregious: (adjective) outrageous; shockingly bad
435. Elasticity: (noun) the extent to which something can change or stretch in response to an external force or influence, and then return to its original shape or size once the force is removed
436. Elixir: (noun) in medieval times: a liquid chemical preparation believed to have the power to give people everlasting life or to turn base metals into gold
437. Elocution: (noun) the art of speaking clearly and effectively
438. Emaciated: (adjective) extremely thin, especially because of illness or starvation
439. Emanate: (verb) of an idea, etc.: to emerge or originate
440. Emanating: (verb) the action of something issuing or spreading out from a source, typically in the form of energy, light, sound or an abstract quality

441. Embalm: (verb) to preserve (a dead body) from decay
442. Embark: (verb) to go or put on board a ship or aircraft
443. Embellish: (verb) 1. to make (a story, etc.) more interesting by adding details which may not be true, 2. to beautify something with decoration
444. Embolism: (noun) the blocking of a blood vessel by an air bubble, a blood clot, etc.
445. Embolus: (noun) any obstruction in a blood vessel, especially a blood clot
446. Emboss: (verb) to carve or mould a raised design on (a surface)
447. Embroil: (verb) to involve in a dispute or argument
448. Embryology: (noun) the scientific study of embryos
449. Emetic: (adjective) making one vomit
450. Eminent: (adjective) famous and admired
451. Emollient: (adjective) 1. softening or soothing the skin, 2. advocating a calmer, more peaceful attitude
452. Emolument: (noun) money earned or otherwise gained through a job or position e.g., salary or fees
453. Empirical: (adjective) based on experiment, observation or experience, rather than on theory
454. Empiricism: (noun) the theory or philosophy stating that knowledge can only be gained through experiment and observation
455. Emulsify: (verb) to make or become an emulsion
456. Enamor: (verb) to be filled with love or admiration for someone or something
457. Enculturation: (noun) the process by which individuals learn and acquire the cultural norms, values, beliefs and behaviours of their society or social group
457. Enervate: (verb) to take energy or strength from something
459. Engender: (verb) to produce or cause (especially feelings or emotions)
460. Enigma: (noun) 1. a puzzle or riddle, 2. a mysterious person
461. Ennui: (noun) boredom or discontent caused by a lack of activity or excitement

462. Entanglement: (noun) a state in which two or more things become deeply interrelated or interconnected in a complex and often inseparable manner
463. Enthrall: (verb) to fascinate
464. Entrepreneur: (noun) someone who engages in business enterprises, often with some personal financial risk
465. Entropy: (noun) a measure of the amount of disorder in a system or of the unavailability of energy for doing work
466. Enunciate: (verb) 1. to pronounce words clearly, 2. to state something formally
467. Enzyme: (noun) a specialized protein molecule that acts as a catalyst for the biochemical reactions that occur in living cells
468. Ephemeral: (adjective) lasting a short time
469. Epidermis: (noun) the outermost layer of a plant or animal, which serves to protect the underlying tissues from infection, injury and water loss
470. Epigram: (noun) 1. a witty or sarcastic saying, 2. a short poem with such an ending
471. Epitaph: (noun) an inscription on a gravestone
472. Epithet: (noun) an adjective or short descriptive phrase which captures the particular quality of the person or thing it describes
473. Epoch: (noun) a major division or a period of history or of a person's life, etc., usually marked by some important event
474. Equestrian: (adjective) belonging or relating to horse riding or horses
475. Equilibrium: (noun) 1. a state in which the various forces acting on an object or objects in a system balance each other, 2. a calm and composed state of mind
476. Equine: (adjective) belonging or relating to or like, a horse or horses
477. Equipoise: (noun) a state of balance
478. Erudite: (adjective) showing or having a great deal of knowledge
479. Escheat: (noun) the handing over of property to the state or a feudal lord in the absence of a legal heir

480. Eschew: (verb) to avoid, keep away from or abstain from something
481. Espionage: (noun) the activity of spying
482. Espouse: (verb) to adopt or give one's support to (a cause, etc.)
483. Etch: (verb) 1. to make designs on (metal, glass, etc.) using an acid to eat out the lines, 2. to make a deep or irremovable impression
484. Ethereal: (adjective) 1. having an unreal lightness or a delicateness, 2. heavenly or spiritual
485. Ethnocentric: (adjective) relating to or holding the belief that one's own cultural tradition or racial group is superior to all others

> An epigram is a brief, witty statement often used to convey a sharp observation, such as Oscar Wilde's famous quip, 'I can resist everything except temptation.'
>
> An epitaph is an inscription on a tombstone in memory of the deceased, often capturing a summary of their life or a final message, like the humorous epitaph on comedian Rodney Dangerfield's grave, 'There goes the neighbourhood.'
>
> An epithet is a descriptive term or phrase expressing a characteristic of the person or thing mentioned, often used in literature, such as Alexander the Great, which highlights his conquests and stature.

486. Ethos: (noun) the typical spirit, character or attitudes of (a group or community)
487. Euphemism: (noun) a mild or inoffensive term used in place of one considered offensive or unpleasantly direct
488. Euphemism: (noun) the use of a mild, indirect or vague expression in place of one that is considered harsh, offensive or unpleasant
489. Euphonic: (adjective) pleasing to the ear
490. Eustress: (noun) to positive or beneficial stress that motivates and energizes an individual, leading to improved performance, productivity or personal growth
491. Evanescent: (adjective) quickly fading; short-lived
492. Evince: (verb) to show or display something, usually a personal quality clearly

493. Evocative: (adjective) something that has the power to evoke or stir up strong emotions, memories or sensations in a person
494. Ewe: (noun) a female sheep
495. Exacerbate: (verb) to make (a bad situation, anger or pain, etc.) worse or more severe
496. Exchequer: (noun) the government department in charge of the financial affairs of a nation
497. Exculpate: (verb) to free someone from guilt or blame
498. Exigency: (noun) Urgent need; an emergency
499. Exiguous: (adjective) scarce or meagre
500. Existentialism: (noun) a philosophy that emphasises freedom of choice and personal responsibility for one's own actions
501. Exorbitant: (adjective) of prices or demands: very high, excessive or unfair
502. Expedient: (adjective) suitable or appropriate
503. Expletive: (noun) a swear word or curse
504. Explicate: (verb) 1. to explain, especially a literary work, in depth with close analysis of particular points, 2. to unfold or develop (an idea, a theory, etc.)
505. Exponential: (adjective) denoting a function that varies according to the power of another quantity, i.e., a function in which the variable quantity is an exponent
506. Expunge: (verb) 1. to cross out or delete something (e.g., a passage from a book), 2. to cancel out or destroy something
507. Extirpate: (verb) to destroy completely; to uproot
508. Extol: (verb) to praise enthusiastically
509. Extort: (verb) to obtain money, information, etc. by threats or violence
510. Extrapolation: (noun) the process of estimating or projecting data or trends beyond the observed or known range, based on existing information or patterns
511. Extricate: (verb) to free someone or something from difficulties
512. Exude: (verb) 1. to give off or give out (an odour or sweat), 2. to show or convey (a quality, characteristic, etc.) by one's behaviour

513. Façade: (noun) 1. the front of a building, 2. a false appearance that hides the reality
514. Facet: (noun) 1. a face of a cut jewel, 2. an aspect e.g., of a problem, topic or someone's personality
515. Facetious: (adjective) of a personal remark, etc.: amusing or witty, especially unsuitably so
516. Facilitate: (verb) to make something easy or easier to do
517. Factitious: (adjective) 1. deliberately contrived rather than developing naturally, 2. insincere; false
518. Factotum: (noun) a person employed to do a large number of different jobs
519. Fallacious: (adjective) something that is based on a mistaken belief or deceptive reasoning, leading to an incorrect conclusion or argument
520. Fallow: (adjective) of land: left unplanted after ploughing, to recover its natural fertility
521. Fatuous: (adjective) foolish, especially in a self-satisfied way; empty-headed
522. Fault: (noun) 1. a flaw or defect in an object, 2. responsibility for something wrong
523. Febrile: (adjective) relating to fever; feverish
524. Feculent: (adjective) something that is foul, polluted or contaminated, especially with waste matter or impurities
525. Feint: (noun) in boxing, fencing, etc.: a mock attack; a movement intended to deceive or distract up one's opponent
526. Fell: 1. (verb) to cut down (a tree); to knock someone or something, 2. (noun) a hill, moor or upland tract of pasture or moorland, 3. (adjective) destructive; deadly
527. Fenestration: (noun) the arrangement of windows in a building
528. Fervid: (adjective) full of fiery passion or zeal
529. Festoon: (noun) a decorative chain of flowers, ribbons, etc.: looped between two points
530. Fetid: (noun) having a strong disgusting smell
531. Fetter: (noun) a chain or shackle fastened to a prisoner's ankle

532. Fiduciary: (noun) someone who holds something in trust
533. Figurative: (adjective) 1. not literal, 2. of writing, etc.: full of figures of speech, especially metaphor
534. Filch: (verb) to steal something small or trivial
535. Fillet: (noun) a piece of meat without bone, taken as an undercut of the sirloin or the fleshy part of the thigh
536. Fiscal: (adjective) of or relating to government finances or revenue
537. Flambe: (adjective) of food: soaked in a spirit, usually brandy and set alight before serving
538. Flange: (noun) a broad flat projecting rim, e.g., round a wheel, added for strength or for connecting with another object or part
539. Fledgling: (noun) a young bird that has just grown its feathers and is still unable to fly
540. Flippant: (adjective) not serious enough about grave matters
541. Florid: (adjective) over-elaborate
542. Flotsam: (noun) goods lost by shipwreck and found floating on the sea
543. Flout: (verb) 1. to defy (an order, convention, etc.) openly; to disrespect authority, etc., 2. to jeer
544. Foible: (noun) a slight personal weakness or eccentricity
545. Foist: (verb) to inflict or impose something unwanted on somebody
546. Foliage: (noun) the green leaves on a tree or plant
547. Foment: (verb) to encourage or foster (ill feeling, etc.)
548. Foppish: (adjective) someone, usually a man, who is excessively concerned with his appearance,

The term 'figurative' derives from the Latin word 'figurativus,' meaning metaphorical. It describes language that uses figures of speech, such as metaphors, similes, and personification, to create vivid imagery and express ideas in imaginative ways. Unlike literal language, which states facts directly, figurative language conveys meanings beyond the ordinary by invoking comparisons and evoking emotions. For instance, saying 'time is a thief' illustrates how time can stealthily take moments from our lives, without implying that time is an actual thief

mannerisms and fashion, often to the point of being overly flamboyant or affected

549. Forage: (noun) a crop grown as feed for livestock
550. Foray: (noun) 1. a raid or attack, 2. a venture; an attempt
551. Forensic: (adjective) 1. belonging or relating to courts of law or to the work of a lawyer in court, 2. concerned with the scientific side of legal investigations
552. Forestall: (verb) to prevent something by acting in advance
553. Forge: (noun) a furnace for heating metal, especially iron, prior to shaping it
554. Fracas: (noun) a noisy quarrel or brawl
555. Franchise: (noun) 1. the right to vote, especially in a parliamentary election, 2. an agreement by which a business company gives someone the right to market its products in an area, 3. a right, privilege, exemption from a duty, etc. granted to a person or organization
556. Fraudulent: (adjective) involving deliberate deception; intended to deceive
557. Fraught: (adjective) causing or feeling anxiety or worry
558. Frenetic: (adjective) distracted or wildly energetic
559. Fresco: (noun) a picture painted on a wall, usually while the plaster is still damp
560. Friable: (adjective) easily broken; easily reduced to powder
561. Fricative: (adjective) of a sound: produced partly by friction, the breath being forced through a narrowed opening
562. Frond: (noun) a large compound leaf, especially of a fern or palm
563. Fugue: a style of musical composition in which a theme is introduced in one part and developed as successive parts take it up
564. Fulcrum: (noun) the point on which a lever turns, balances or is supported
565. Fulminate: (verb) to utter angry criticism or condemnation
566. Functionary: (noun) someone who works as a minor official in the government, etc.
567. Funereal: (adjective) 1. associated with or suitable for funerals, 2. mournful; dismal

568. Furl: (verb) of flags, sails or umbrellas: to roll up
569. Fustian: (noun) 1. a kind of coarse twilled cotton fabric with a nap, 2. a pompous and unnatural style of writing or speaking
570. Gaffe: (noun) a socially embarrassing action or remark
571. Gainsay: (verb) to deny or contradict
572. Galvanize: (verb) 1. to stimulate or rouse to action, 2. to coat (a metallic surface, usually iron or steel) with a thin layer of zinc, in order to protect it from corrosion
573. Gambit: (noun) a chess move made early in the game, in which a pawn or other piece is sacrificed in order to gain an overall advantage
574. Gamble: (verb) to play games of chance for money or other stakes, usually with the hope of winning
575. Gamification: (noun) to the process of applying elements of game design and mechanics to non-game contexts, such as business, education, marketing or health, to engage users and drive desired behaviours
576. Gamut: (noun) the whole range of anything, e.g., a person's emotions
577. Garish: (adjective) unpleasantly bright or colourful
578. Garner: (verb) to collect and usually store (information, knowledge, etc.)
579. Gastronomy: (noun) the appreciation and enjoyment of good food and wine
580. Gauche: (adjective) ill-at-ease; awkward in social situations
581. Genomics: (noun) the study of genomes
582. Geodesic: (adjective) denoting an artificial structure composed of a large number of identical components, especially a dome
583. Geriatric: (adjective) for or dealing with old people
584. Gerontology: (noun) the scientific study of old age, the ageing process and the problems of elderly people
585. Gerrymander: (verb) to arrange or change the boundaries of (one or more electoral constituencies) as so as to favour one political party
586. Gesticulate: (verb) to make gestures, especially when speaking

587. Gilded: (adjective) something that has been covered with a thin layer of gold or has the appearance of being made of gold
588. Glazier: (noun) someone whose job is to fit glass in windows, doors, etc.
589. Glib: (adjective) speaking or spoken readily and persuasively, but neither sincere nor reliable
590. Glissando: (noun) the effect produced by sliding the finger along a keyboard or a string
591. Glower: (verb) to stare angrily
592. Glutinous: (adjective) like glue; sticky
593. Gnome: (noun) a fairy-tale creature, usually in the form of a small misshapen old man, who lives underground, often guarding treasure
594. Gossamer: (noun) a delicate, sheer and lightweight fabric or material, typically made from silk, fine cotton or synthetic fibers
595. Graft: (noun) 1. a piece of plant tissue that is inserted into a cut in the outer stem of another plant, 2. the transfer or transplantation of an organ or tissue from one individual to another or to a different site within the same individual
596. Grandiloquent: (adjective) spoken or written in a pompous style
597. Grandiose: (adjective) exaggeratedly impressive or imposing, especially on a ridiculously large scale
598. Gravity: (noun) the observed effect of the force of attraction that exists between two massive bodies
599. Guild: (noun) 1. a medieval association of merchants or craftsmen for maintaining standards and providing mutual support, 2. the name used by various modern societies clubs and associations
600. Guise: (noun) 1. pretence, 2. external appearance in general
601. Hackneyed: (adjective) of a word, phrase, etc.: meaningless and trite through too much use
602. Halcyon: (adjective) peaceful, calm and happy
603. Hallow: (verb) to make or regard as holy
604. Hallucinogens: (noun) a drug that causes hallucination

605. Hamartia: (noun) a term used in Greek tragedy to refer to a fatal flaw or error in judgment that leads to the downfall or destruction of a tragic hero
606. Hapless: (adjective) unlucky; unfortunate
607. Harangue: (noun) a loud forceful speech either to attack people or to try to persuade them to do something
608. Harbinger: (noun) a person or thing that announces or predicts something to come
609. Harlequin: (noun) a humorous character from traditional Italian plays who wears a black mask and a brightly coloured, diamond-patterned costume
610. Harp: (noun) a large upright musical instrument with a series of strings stretched vertically across it, played by plucking the strings
611. Heathen: (noun) someone who does not adhere to a particular religion, especially when regarded by a person or community that does follow that religion
612. Hedge: (noun) a boundary formed by bushes and shrubs planted close together, especially between fields
613. Hedging: (noun) practice of minimizing risk or uncertainty by taking actions that protect against adverse outcomes or fluctuations in value
614. Heedless: (adjective) taking no care
615. Hegemony: (noun) authority or control, especially of one state over another within a confederation
616. Herald: (noun) a person who announces important news or an officer whose task it is to make public proclamations and arrange ceremonies
617. Hermaphrodite: (noun) a person, plant or animal that has both male and female reproductive organs
618. Hermetic: (adjective) perfectly closed or sealed so as to be airtight
619. Hermitage: (noun) the dwelling place of a hermit
620. Heterodox: (adjective) something that deviates from established beliefs, norms or doctrines, especially in the context of religion, philosophy or economics

621. Heuristics: (noun) mental shortcuts or rules of thumb that people use to make decisions, solve problems or form judgments quickly and efficiently
622. Hew: (verb) to cut, fell or sever something using an axe, sword, etc.
623. Hiatus: (noun) an opening or gap; a break in something which should be continuous
624. Hibernal: (adjective) referring or belonging to the winter; wintry
625. Hirsute: (adjective) hairy; shaggy
626. Hoary: (adjective) white or grey with age
627. Homeostasis: (noun) tendency of living organisms to maintain internal stability and balance, despite external changes or fluctuations in their environment
628. Homonyms: (noun) a word with the same sound and spelling as another but with a different meaning
629. Hospice: (noun) a home that specializes in the care of the sick, especially the terminally ill
630. Hovel: (noun) a small, dirty, rundown dwelling
631. Hubris: (noun) arrogance or overconfidence, especially when likely to result in disaster or ruin
632. Hull: (noun) 1. the frame or body of a ship or airship, 2. the outer covering or husk of certain fruit and seeds, especially the pods of beans and peas
633. Humus: (noun) a dark-brown organic material produced in the topmost layer of soil due to the decomposition of plant and animal matter
634. Husbandry: (noun) the farming business
635. Hyperbola: (noun) the curve produced when a plane cuts through a cone so that the angle between the base of the cone and the plane is greater than the angle between the base and the sloping side of the cone
636. Hyperventilate: (verb) the act of breathing at an abnormally rapid rate, which leads to an excessive intake of oxygen and a decrease in carbon dioxide levels in the blood

637. Hypnosis: (noun) an induced state of deep relaxation, in which the mind responds to external suggestions and can recover subconscious memories
638. Hypodermic: (adjective) 1. of a drug: injected under the skin, 2. of a syringe: designed for use under the skin
639. Hypotenuse: (noun) the longest side of a right-angled triangle, opposite the right angle
640. Ichthyology: (noun) the study of fishes
641. Icosahedron: (noun) a solid figure with 20 faces
642. Idiom: (noun) an expression with the meaning which cannot be derived from the meanings of the words which form it
643. Igneous: (adjective) 1. relating to or like fire, 2. of a rock: formed by the solidification of molten magma
644. Ignominious: (adjective) something or someone deserving or causing public disgrace or shame
645. Ignominy: (noun) public shame, disgrace or dishonour
646. Illiberal: (adjective) narrow-minded; prejudiced
647. Illicit: (adjective) not permitted by law, rule or social custom
648. Illustrious: (adjective) distinguished
649. Imbricate: (adjective) something that is arranged in an overlapping pattern, resembling scales, tiles or shingles
650. Imbroglio: (noun) a confused and complicated situation
651. Imbue: (verb) to inspire someone, especially with ideals or principles
652. Immanent: (adjective) something that is inherent, existing or operating within
653. Immiscible: (adjective) of liquids, e.g., oil and water: forming separate layers and not mixing when shaken together
654. Immutable: (adjective) unable to be changed
655. Impasse: (noun) a situation with no possible progress or escape
656. Impassive: (adjective) incapable of feeling and expressing emotion
657. Impasto: (noun) in painting and pottery
658. Impeach: (verb) to charge someone with a serious crime, especially against the state

659. Impecunious: (adjective) having little or no money
660. Impenitent: (adjective) not sorry for having done something wrong
661. Impetration: (noun) the act of earnestly requesting or petitioning for something, often through formal or solemn means
662. Impetuous: (adjective) acting or done hurriedly and without due consideration
663. Impious: (adjective) lacking respect or proper reverence
664. Importunate: (adjective) persistent or excessively demanding
665. Impresario: (noun) someone who organizes public concerts, etc.
666. Impressionism: (noun) in art, music or literature: a nineteen century style aiming to give a general impression of feelings and events rather than a formal treatment of them
667. Imprimatur: (noun) permission to print or publish a book, now especially one granted by the Roman Catholic Church
668. Imprudent: (adjective) lacking good sense or caution
669. Impudent: (adjective) insolent or impertinent
670. Impugn: (verb) to call into question or raise doubts about (the honesty, integrity, etc. of someone or something)
671. Inadvertent: (adjective) 1. not deliberate, 2. not paying attention
672. Inane: (adjective) without meaning or point
673. Incandescent: (adjective) white-hot; glowing with intense heat
674. Incessant: (adjective) going on without stopping
675. Inchoate: (adjective) at the earliest stage of development; just beginning; unfinished; rudimentary
676. Inchoative: (adjective) something that is in an initial stage or just beginning to develop
677. Incipient: (adjective) beginning to exist
678. Inclement: (adjective) of weather: stormy or severe
679. Incongruous: (adjective) out of place
680. Incontinence: (noun) the lack of voluntary control over urination or defecation

681. Incubus: (noun) an evil male spirit which is supposed to have sexual intercourse with sleeping women
682. Inculcate: (verb) to teach or fix (ideas, habits, etc.) firmly in their mind by constant repetition
683. Incumbent: (adjective) 1. imposed as a duty or responsibility on them, 2. currently occupying a specified position or office
684. Indelible: (adjective) unable to be removed or rubbed out
685. Indemnify: (verb) to provide somebody with security and protection against (loss and misfortune)
686. Indict: (verb) to accuse someone of or charge them formally with, a crime, especially in writing
687. Indigent: (adjective) very poor
688. Indite: (verb) compose, write or put into words, often used in a formal or literary context
689. Indolence: (noun) habitual laziness or avoidance of activity or exertion
690. Ineluctable: (adjective) unavoidable, irresistible or inescapable
691. Inertia: (noun) 1. the tendency of an object to be inert, 2. The state of not wanting to move, act or think
692. Inevitable: (adjective) unable to be avoided; certain to happen
693. Ingenue: (noun) a naive or innocent young woman, especially in literature, theatre or film
694. Ingenuous: (adjective) innocent and childlike, especially in being incapable of deception
695. Ingratiate: (verb) to gain or try to gain somebody's favour or approval
696. Innumerate: (adjective) having no understanding of mathematics
697. Inscrutable: (adjective) hard to understand or explain
698. Insidious: (adjective) 1. developing gradually without being noticed but causing great harm, 2. attractive but harmful
699. Insolent: (adjective) rude or insulting; showing a lack of respect
700. Insouciant: (adjective) without cares or worries; light-hearted
701. Insular: (adjective) 1. relating to an island or its inhabitants, 2. narrow-minded

702. Insurgency: (noun) an uprising or rebellion
703. Integration: (noun) the process of combining or incorporating separate parts or elements into a unified whole
704. Interdict: (noun) an official order forbidding someone to do something
705. Interference: (noun) 1. the act or process of interfering, 2. the interaction between two or more waves of the same frequency
706. Interpolate: (verb) to add (words) to a book or manuscript, especially to make the text misleading or corrupt
707. Intonation: (noun) the rise and fall of the pitch of the voice in speech
708. Intransigent: (adjective) refusing to change or compromise one's beliefs
709. Intravenous: (adjective) located within or introduced into a vein or veins
710. Intrepid: (adjective) bold and daring; brave
711. Invective: 1. (noun) sarcastic or abusive language or a denunciation or critical attack using such words, 2. (adjective) characterized by such an attack
712. Inveigh: (verb) to trick, deceive or persuade them into doing it
713. Inveterate: (adjective) of a habit, etc.: firmly established
714. Invidious: (adjective) likely to cause envy, resentment or indignation, especially by being or seeming to be unfair
715. Involution: (noun) involving or being involved or entangled
716. Iota: (noun) 1. the ninth letter of the Greek alphabet, 2. a very small amount
717. Irrefragable: (adjective) impossible to refute or disprove
718. Irresolute: hesitating or doubtful; not able to take firm decisions
719. Isotope: (noun) one of two or more atoms of the same chemical element that contain the same number of protons but different number of neutrons in their nuclei
720. Iteration: (noun) to the process of repeating or performing a series of steps or actions, typically with the aim of achieving a desired result or refining a solution

721. Jaded: (adjective) tired or bored
722. Jeer: (verb) to mock or deride (a speaker, performer, etc.)
723. Jeopardy: (noun) danger of harm, loss or destruction
724. Jetsam: (noun) 1. goods jettisoned from a ship and washed up on the shore, 2. Flotsam
725. Jingoism: (noun) over-enthusiastic or aggressive patriotism
726. Jocose: (adjective) playful; humorous
727. Jocular: (adjective) of a person: given to joking; good-humoured
728. Jostle: (verb) to push and shove; to push against someone roughly
729. Joule: (noun) In the SI system: the unit of work and energy
730. Jubilant: (adjective) showing and expressing triumphant joy
731. Juggernaut: (noun) 1. a very large articulated lorry, 2. a mighty force sweeping away and destroying everything in its path
732. Julienne: 1. (noun) a clear soup with shredded vegetables, 2. (adjective) vegetables in thin strips; shredded
733. Juncture: (noun) 1. a joining; a union, 2. a point in time especially a critical one
734. Junket: (noun) 1. a dessert made from sweetened and curdled milk, 2. a feast or celebration, 3. a trip made by government officials, businessmen, etc. which they do not pay for themselves
735. Jurisdiction: (noun) 1. the right or authority to apply laws and administer justice, 2. the district or area over which this authority extends
736. Jut: (verb) to stick out; to project
737. Karat: (noun) another spelling of Carat
738. Ken: (verb) 1. to know, 2. to understand
739. Kindle: (verb) 1. to start or make something start burning, 2. of feelings: to stir or be stirred
740. Kinetic: (noun) the branch of mechanics concerned with moving objects, their masses and the forces acting on them
741. Kiosk: (noun) 1. a small booth or stall for the sale of sweets, newspaper, etc., 2. a public telephone box

742. Kismet: (noun) 1. the will of Allah, 2. faith or destiny
743. Knead: (verb) 1. to work (dough) with one's fingers and knuckles into a uniform mass, 2. to massage (flesh) with firm finger movements
744. Knurled: (adjective) a surface that has small, raised, and often roughened or textured patterns, typically in the form of small ridges or bumps
745. Kraft: (noun) a type of strong brown wrapping paper

> Many terms used in French cuisine have become staples in the culinary world, reflecting the influence of French gastronomy. Words like 'soufflé,' meaning 'to puff up,' describe a light, fluffy baked dish made with egg whites. 'Béarnaise' is a rich sauce made of clarified butter, egg yolks and herbs, while 'crêpe' refers to thin pancakes that can be filled with sweet or savoury ingredients. 'Mirepoix' is a mixture of diced vegetables used as a flavour base in soups and stews.

746. Labefaction: (noun) the act or process of weakening, shaking or causing to collapse
747. Lachrymose: (adjective) 1. prone to crying, 2. of a novel, play, film, etc.: likely to make someone cry
748. Lackey: (noun) a servile follower, 2. old use of male servant especially a footman or valet
749. Lacuna: (noun) a gap or a space where something is missing especially in printed text
750. Laity: (noun) the people who are not members of a particular profession, especially the clergy
751. Lampoon: (noun) an attack usually in the form of satirical prose or verse, on someone or something
752. Languish: (verb) 1. to spend time and hardship or discomfort, 2. to grow weak
753. Larceny: (noun) theft of personal property
754. Larder: (noun) a cool room or cupboard for storing food
755. Largess: (noun) 1. generosity, 2. gifts, money, etc. given generously
756. Lash: (noun) 1. a stroke of blow, usually made by a whip as a form of punishment, 2. the flexible part of a whip, 3. an eyelash

757. Lathe: (noun) a machine tool used to cut, drill or polish a piece of metal, wood or plastic that is rotated against its cutting edge
758. Leach: (verb) to make liquid seep through (ash, soil, etc.), in order to remove substances from that material
759. Leaven: (noun) substance especially yeast added to dough to make it rise, 2. anything which is an influence and cause change
760. Legerdemain: (noun) skillful or deceptive manipulation or trickery, especially in performing magic tricks or sleight of hand
761. Lethargic: (noun) lack of energy
762. Lexicon: (noun) 1. a dictionary especially one for Arabic, Greek, Hebrew and Syriac, 2. the vocabulary of terms as used in a particular branch of knowledge or by a particular person group, etc.
763. Libelous: (adjective) a statement or publication, that is defamatory or harmful to someone's reputation
764. Libertine: (noun) someone who is not bound by the generally accepted codes of morality
765. Libidinous: (adjective) lustful
766. Libido: (noun) sexual desire
767. Libretto: (noun) the words or text of an opera, oratorio or musical
768. Licit: (adjective) lawful; permitted
769. Lien: (noun) a right to keep someone's property until a debt has been paid
770. Ligature: (noun) 1. anything that binds or ties, 2. a slur, 3. a character formed from two or more characters joined together
771. Ligneous: (adjective) reassembling or composed wood
772. Limpid: (adjective) of water, eyes, etc.: clear; transparent
773. Lineaments: (noun) a distinguishing feature, especially on the face
774. Lionize: (verb) to treat someone as a celebrity or hero
775. Lipid: (noun) any of a group of organic compounds, mainly oils and fats, that occur naturally in living organisms and are generally insoluble in water

776. Lissome: (adjective) graceful and supple and shape or movement
777. List: (noun) a series of names, numbers, prices, etc. printed out written down or said one after the other
778. Lithe: (adjective) supple and flexible
779. Littoral: (adjective) on or near the shore of a lake
780. Liturgy: (noun) The standard form of service in a church
781. Livid: (adjective) 1. extremely angry, 2. having the greyish colour of lead, 3. a bruise: black and blue, 4. pale, ashen
782. Locution: (noun) 1. a style of speech, 2. an expression, word or phrase
783. Lodestone: (noun) 1. a form of magnetite which exhibits polarity, behaving, when freely suspended, as a magnet, 2. a magnet, 3. something that attracts
784. Loiter: (verb) to wait around, especially furtively, 2. to stand around or pass time doing nothing
785. Lope: (verb) to run with long bounding steps
786. Loquacious: (adjective) very talkative
787. Lout: (noun) someone usually a teenager male, whose behaviour, especially in public, is considered unacceptable
788. Lugubrious: (adjective) sand and gloomy
789. Lumber: (noun) disused articles of furniture or odds and ends that are no longer used and which have been stored away
790. Luminous: (adjective) 1. full of or giving out light, 2. glowing in the dark
791. Lurid: (adjective) glaringly bright especially when the surroundings are dark
792. Macabre: (adjective) causing fear or anxiety
793. Macerate: (verb) to break up or make something break up or become soft by soaking it
794. Machination: (noun) crafty scheme or plot, especially a sinister one
795. Maculated: (adjective) something marked or spotted with stains, blemishes or discolorations
796. Madrigal: (noun) an unaccompanied part song popular in the sixteenth and seventeenth centuries

797. Maelstrom: (noun) a powerful and turbulent whirlpool or a chaotic and violent situation
798. Magnanimous: (adjective) having or showing admirable generosity of spirit towards another person or people
799. Magnify: (verb) to make something appear larger, example by using a microscope or telescope, 2. to exaggerate something
800. Magniloquent: (adjective) outspoken in a grand or pompous style
801. Maim: (verb) to wound (a person or animal) seriously, especially to disable, mutilate or cripple them
802. Maladroit: (adjective) clumsy; tactless
803. Malfeasance: (noun) wrongdoing; the committing of an unlawful act especially by a public official
804. Malignant: (adjective) 1. of a person: feeling or showing hatred or the desire to do harm to another or others, 2. Malignant (noun) especially of a cancerous tumour: of a type that especially if left untreated destroys the surrounding tissues and may spread elsewhere in the body
805. Malingerer: (verb) to pretend to be ill, especially in order to avoid having to work
806. Mandate: 1. (noun) a right or authorization given to a nation, person, etc. to act on behalf of others, 2. (verb) to give authority or power to someone or something
807. Marquee: (noun) a very large tent used for a circus, parties, etc.
808. Marshal: (noun) 1. a high ranking officer in the armed forces, 2. an official who organizes or controls crowds at public events
809. Masochism: (noun) the practice of driving sexual pleasure from pain or humiliation inflicted by another person
810. Masonry: (noun) 1. structures made from stone and brick, 2. the craft of stoneman
811. Mastectomy: (noun) the surgical removal of a women's breast
812. Masthead: (noun) 1. the top of a ship's mast, 2. the title of a newspaper or periodical, and other information such as logo, price and place of publication, printed at the top of its front page

813. Masticate: (verb) to chew (food)
814. Materialism: (noun) excessive interest in or devotion to material possession and financial success
815. Matrilineal: (adjective) a social system, family structure or kinship system in which lineage, inheritance or descent is traced through the maternal line
816. Matrix: (noun) a square or rectangular arrangement of symbols or numbers, in rows or columns, used to summarize relationships between different qualities, etc.
817. Matutinal: (adjective) something relating to or occurring in the early morning or dawn
818. Maudlin: (adjective) especially of a drunk person: foolishly sad or sentimental
819. Maverick: (noun) 1. an unbranded stray animal, especially a calf, 2. a determinedly independent person; a non-conformist
820. Medium: 1. something by or through which an effect is produced, 2. a particular category of materials seen as a means of expression, e.g., watercolours, photography or clay
821. Medulla: (noun) the central part of organ or that differs in structure or function from the outer layer, e.g., the pith of a plant stem
822. Mellifluous: (adjective) of sounds, speech, etc.: having a smooth sweet flowing quality
823. Mendacity: (noun) the quality of being untruthful or deceitful
824. Mendicant: (noun) a monk who is a member of an order that is not allowed to own property and is therefore entirely dependent on charity
825. Mercenary: 1. (adjective) excessively concerned with the desire for personal gain, especially money; hired for money, 2. a soldier available for hire by a country or a group
826. Mercurial: (adjective) 1. relating to or containing mercury, 2. of someone or their personality, mood, etc.: lively, active and unpredictable
827. Meridian: (noun) an imaginary line on the Earth's surface passing through the poles at right angles to the equator; a line of longitude

828. Metaphysics: (noun) the branch of philosophy dealing with the nature of existence and the basic principles of truth and knowledge
829. Mete: (verb) to give out or dispense something, especially punishment
830. Mettle: (noun) 1. courage, determination and endurance, 2. personal qualities
831. Mezzanine: (noun) in a building: a small storey between two main floors
832. Miasma: (noun) 1. a thick foul-smelling vapour, 2. an evil influence or atmosphere
833. Midden: (noun) 1. a rubbish heap, a pile of dung, 2. an untidy mess
834. Mien: (noun) an appearance, expression or manner, especially one that reflects a mood
835. Milieu: (noun) a social environment or set of surroundings
836. Militate: (verb) of facts, etc.: to have a strong influence or effect
837. Minion: (noun) an employee or follower, especially one who is subservient
838. Minstrel: (noun) in the Middle Ages: a travelling singer, musician and reciter of poetry, etc., 2. in the USA and Britain: any of a group of white-skinned entertainers made up to look black, who superficially performed song and dance routines of Black origin
839. Misconstrue: (verb) to interpret something wrongly or mistakenly
840. Misogynist: (noun) someone who holds strong prejudices or dislikes against women, often expressing contempt or hostility towards them
841. Missive: (noun) a letter, especially a long or official one
842. Mitigate: (verb) to make pain, anger, etc. less severe
843. Mnemonic: (noun) a device or form of words, often a short verse, used as a memory aid
844. Modulate: (verb) to alter the tone or volume of a sound or one's voice

845. Molecule: (noun) the smallest particle of an element or compound that can exist independently and participate in a reaction, consisting of two or more atoms bonded together
846. Mollify: (verb) to make someone calmer or less angry
847. Momentum: (noun) 1. continuous speed of progress, 2. the force that an object gains in movement
848. Monopoly: (noun) 1. the right to be or the fact of being, the only supplier of a specified commodity or service, 2. exclusive position or control of anything
849. Montage: (noun) 1. the process of creating a picture by assembling and piercing together elements from other pictures, photographs, etc., and mounting them onto canvas,, etc., 2. a film sequence made up of short clips or images superimposed, dissolved together, etc., especially one used to condensed events that take place over a long period
850. Moratorium: (noun) an agreed temporary break in an activity
851. Mordant: (adjective) sharply sarcastic or critical
852. More: 1. (adjective) greater, 2. (adverb) used to form the comparative form of many adjectives and most adverbs, especially those of two or more syllables, 3. (adverb) to a greater degree; with a greater frequency, 4. (adverb) again, 5. (pronoun) a greater or additional, number or quantity of people or things
853. Morpheme: (noun) any of the grammatically or lexically meaningful units forming or underlying a word, not divisible themselves into smaller meaningful units
854. Morphology: (noun) the study of morphemes and the rules by which they combine to form words
855. Mortgage: (noun) a legal agreement by which a building society or bank, etc. (the mortgagee) grants a client (the mortgagor or mortgager) a loan for the purpose of buying the property, ownership of the property being held by the mortgagee until the loan is repaired
856. Motif: (noun) 1. on clothing, etc.: a single design or symbol, 2. a shape repeated many times within a pattern, 3. in the

arts: something that is often repeated throughout a work or works, e.g., a theme in a novel

857. Motile: (adjective) of a living organism: capable of independent spontaneous movement
858. Motley: (adjective) made up of many different kinds
859. Multifarious: (adjective) consisting of many different kinds
860. Multiparous: (adjective) of a mammal: producing several young at one birth
861. Munificent: (adjective) extremely generous
862. Myelin: (noun) a soft white substance that forms a thin insulating sheath around the nerve fibres of vertebrates
863. Myriad: (noun) an exceedingly great number
864. Nadir: (noun) the point on the celestial sphere directly opposite the zenith
865. Natal: (adjective) connected with birth
866. Natty~~: (adjective) 1. of clothes: flashily smart, 2. clever~~ ingenious
867. Nebula: (noun) a luminous or dark patch in space representing a mass of dust or particles
868. Nebulous: (adjective) lacking distinct shape, form or nature
869. Necromancy: (noun) 1. divination or prophecy through communication with the dead., 2. black magic; sorcery
870. Nefarious: (adjective) wicked; evil
871. Negotiable: (adjective) open to discussion
872. Neophyte: (noun) a beginner
873. Nepotism: (noun) the favouring of one's relatives or friends, especially in making official appointments

> A morpheme can be a word, like 'book', or a part of a word, such as a prefix or suffix. They are units that cannot be broken down further, unlike syllables. For example, in the word 'unhappiness', there are three morphemes: 'un-' (a prefix meaning 'not'), 'happy' (the root word), and '-ness' (a suffix indicating a state or condition). Morphemes are crucial in the study of linguistics because they help in understanding how words are formed and how meaning is constructed in language.

874. Nettle: (noun) a plant covered with hair that stings if touched
875. Neurosis: (noun) a mental disorder that causes obsessive fears, depression and unreasonable behaviour
876. Neutrino: (noun) a stable subatomic particle that has no electric charge, virtually no mass, and travels at or near the speed of light
877. Nexus: (noun) a connected series or group
878. Nib: (noun) the writing point of a pen, especially a metal one with a divided tip
879. Niggling: (adjective) something small or trivial, yet persistent and annoying
880. Nihilism: (noun) the rejection of moral and religious principles
881. Nocturne: (noun) a dreamy piece of music, usually for the piano
882. Noisome: (adjective) disgusting; offensive; stinking
883. Nomad: (noun) A member of a people without a permanent home, who travel from place to place seeking food and pasture
884. Nonagon: (noun) a nine-sided figure
885. Nonplus: (verb) to puzzle; to disconcert
886. Nostalgic: (adjective) sentimental longing or wistful affection for the past, often accompanied by fond memories or emotions associated with particular people, places or experiences
887. Noxious: (adjective) harmful; poisonous
888. Nugatory: (adjective) worthless; trifling; ineffective; futile; invalid
889. Nuptial: (adjective) relating to marriage
890. Obdurate: (adjective) hard-hearted; stubborn; difficult to influence or change
891. Obeisance: (noun) a bow or other expression of obedience or respect
892. Obelisk: (noun) a tall tapering, usually four-sided, stone pillar with a pyramidal top
893. Obfuscate: (verb) to darken or obscure (something)

894. Oblong: (adjective) rectangular with adjacent sides of unequal length
895. Obloquy: (noun) abuse, blame or censure
896. Obsequies: (noun) funeral rites
897. Obsidian: (noun) a volcanic glass, usually black
898. Obstreperous: (adjective) noisy and hard to control
899. Obviate: (verb) to prevent or remove (a potential difficulty or problem, etc.) in advance
900. Occipital: (adjective) relating to or in the region of the back of the head
901. Octahedron: (noun) a solid figure with eight plane faces
902. Ode: (noun) a lyric poem with lines of different lengths and complex rhythms, addressed to a particular person or thing
903. Odious: (adjective) extremely unpleasant or offensive
904. Odorous: (adjective) something that has a noticeable or distinct smell, often pleasant or unpleasant
905. Officious: (adjective) someone who is excessively eager to offer unsolicited advice, assistance or opinions, often in a domineering or intrusive manner
906. Oligopoly: (noun) a situation in which there are few sellers of a particular product or service, and a small number of competitive firms control the market
907. Ombudsman: (noun) an official appointed to investigate complaints against public authorities, government departments or the people who work for them
908. Omnivorous: (adjective) an organism, typically an animal, that has a diet consisting of both plant and animal matter
909. Ontology: (noun) the branch of metaphysics that deals with the nature and essence of things or of existence
910. Oracular: (adjective) something related to or resembling an oracle, which is a person or thing regarded as an authoritative source of wisdom, knowledge or prophecy
911. Ordinal: (noun) a service book
912. Ordinate: (noun) on a graph: the second of a pair of numbers x and y, known as the y-coordinate, which specifies the distance of a point from the horizontal or x-axis

913. Ornithology: (noun) the scientific study of birds and their behaviour
914. Oscillating: (adjective) describe something that moves back and forth or alternates between two states of positions in a regular or rhythmic manner
915. Osmosis: (noun) the movement of a solvent, e.g., water, across a semipermeable membrane from a more dilute solution to a more concentrated one
916. Ostentatious: (adjective) describe behaviour, actions or displays that are intended to attract attention, impress others or show off one's wealth, status or importance in a flashy or flamboyant manner
917. Ostinato: (adjective) frequently repeated
918. Ostracize: (verb) to exclude (someone) from a group or society, etc.
919. Overture: (noun) an orchestral introduction to an opera, oratorio or ballet
920. Ovoid: (adjective) egg-shaped
921. Pabulum: (noun) bland or insipid intellectual material, entertainment or sustenance
922. Palate: (noun) the roof of the mouth; the sense of taste
923. Palette: (noun) a handheld board with a thumb hole, on which an artist mixes colours
924. Palliate: (verb) to ease the symptoms of a disease without curing it
925. Pandemic: (adjective) describing a widespread epidemic of a disease, one that affects the whole country, continent, etc.
926. Pantomime: (noun) a Christmas entertainment usually based on a popular fairy tale which songs, dancing, comedy acts, etc.
927. Paradigm: (noun) an example, model or pattern
928. Paragon: (noun) someone who is the model of excellence
929. Parallax: (noun) the apparent change in the position of an object, relative to a distant background when it is viewed from two different positions
930. Parallelogram: (noun) a two-dimensional four-sided figure, in which opposite sides are parallel and equal in length, and opposite angles are equal

931. Paramour: a lover
932. Paraphrase: (noun) a restatement of something using different words
933. Parathyroid: (noun) an infectious disease, similar to but milder than typhoid fever, caused by a bacterium
934. Parboil: (verb) to boil something until it is partially cooked
935. Pariah: (noun) someone scorned and avoided by others
936. Parietal: (adjective) relating to or forming the wall of a bodily cavity, e.g., the skull
937. Parity: (noun) equality in status, e.g., in pay
938. Parlance: (noun) a particular style or way of choosing words
939. Parochial: (adjective) of tastes, attitude, etc.: concerned only with local affairs; narrow, limited or provincial in outlook
940. Parody: (noun) a comic version or satirical imitation of a work or the style, of a particular writer, composer, etc.
941. Partisan: (noun) an enthusiastic supporter of a party, person, cause, etc.
942. Pasteurize: (verb) to partially sterilize (food, especially milk) by heating it to a specific temperature for a short period before rapidly cooling it
943. Pastiche: (noun) a musical, artistic or literary work in someone else's style or in a mixture of styles
944. Paternal: (adjective) 1. referring, relating or appropriate to a father, 2. of a relation or ancestor: related on one's father's side
945. Pathology: (noun) the branch of medicine concerned with the study of the nature of diseases
946. Pathos: (noun) a quality in a situation, etc., especially in literature, that moves one to pity
947. Patina: (noun) a coating formed on a metal surface by oxidation
948. Patrilineage: (noun) a system of kinship or social organization in which descent, inheritance and family membership are traced through the male line
949. Patronize: (verb) to treat someone condescendingly
950. Paucity: (noun) smallness of quantity; a scarcity or lack
951. Peccadillo: (noun) a minor misdeed

952. Pecuniary: (adjective) relating to, concerning or consisting of money
953. Pedagogy: (noun) the science, principles or work of teaching
954. Pejorative: (adjective) of a word or expression: disapproving, derogatory, disparaging or uncomplimentary
955. Pellucid: (adjective) transparent; absolutely clear in expression and meaning
956. Penance: (noun) repentance or atonement for an offence or wrongdoing or an act of repentance
957. Penitent: (adjective) regretful for wrong one has done, and feeling a desire to reform
958. Penumbra: (noun) the lighter outer shadow that surrounds the dark central shadow produced by a large unfocused light-source shining on an opaque object
959. Penurious: (adjective) someone who is extremely poor or impoverished, often to the point of lacking basic necessities such as food, shelter or clothing
960. Peonage: (noun) a system of labour or servitude in which workers are bound to their employers through debt or other forms of coercion
961. Percolate: (verb) to undergo or subject (a liquid) to the process of filtering, oozing and trickling
962. Perdition: (noun) everlasting punishment after death; hell
963. Perdurable: (adjective) something that is extremely durable, long-lasting or enduring
964. Peregrination: (noun) a journey, especially one that is long, meandering or undertaken with a sense of exploration or adventure
965. Peremptory: (adjective) of an order: made in expectation of immediate compliance
966. Perennial: (adjective) referring or relating to a plant that lives for several to many years
967. Perfidy: (noun) Betrayal or deceitfulness.
968. Perfunctory: (adjective) done merely as a duty or routine, without genuine care or feeling
969. Peripatetic: (adjective) travelling about from place to place

970. Peripeteia: (noun) a sudden or unexpected reversal of fortune or circumstance, especially in a literary or dramatic work
971. Peristalsis: (noun) In hollow tubular organs, e.g., the intestines: the waves of involuntary muscle contractions that force the contents of the tube, e.g., food, further forward
972. Perjure: (verb) to forswear oneself in a court of law, i.e., lie while under oath
973. Permutation: (noun) any of several different ways in which a set of objects or numbers can be arranged
974. Pernicious: (adjective) harmful, destructive, deadly
975. Peroration: (noun) the concluding section of a speech, in which the points made are summed up
976. Pertinacious: (adjective) determined in one's purpose
977. Pervade: (verb) to spread or extend throughout something; to affect throughout something
978. Pervious: (adjective) something that is permeable or capable of being penetrated or passed through
979. Pestiferous: (adjective) something that is causing or likely to cause annoyance, trouble or harm, especially in a persistent or insidious manner
980. Petulant: (adjective) ill-tempered
981. Phalanx: (noun) in ancient Greece: a body of infantry in close-packed formation

Similarly, the word Maternal is an adjective that means relating to mother or motherhood; inherited from or related to mother's side of the family.

982. Philatelist: (noun) a person who collects and studies postage stamps
983. Phlegmatic: (adjective) of a person: calm; not easily excited
984. Phoneme: (noun) the smallest unit of sound in a language that has significance in distinguishing one word from another
985. Phonetic: (adjective) referring or relating to the sounds of a spoken language
986. Pidgin: (noun) a type of simplified language used especially for trading purposes between speakers of different languages, commonly used in the East and West Indies, Africa and Americas

987. Pilfer: (verb) to steal in small quantities
988. Pious: (adjective) religiously devout; dutiful
989. Pique: (verb) 1. to hurt someone's pride; to offend or nettle them, 2. to arouse (curiosity or interest)
990. Pitch: 1. (verb) to set up (a tent or camp), 2. (noun) A line in sales talk, especially one often made use of, 3. (noun) the degree of highness or lowness of a note that results from the frequency of the vibrations producing it
991. Piton: (noun) a metal peg or spike with an eye for passing a rope through, hammered into a rock face as an aide to climbers
992. Placebo: (noun) a substance that is administered as a drug but has no medical content, either given to a patient for its reassuring and therefore beneficial effect (the placebo effect) or used in a clinical trial of a real drug, in which participants who have been given a placebo serve as untreated control subjects for comparison with those actually given the drug
993. Plenary: (adjective) full; complete
994. Plenitude: (noun) abundance; profusion; completeness; fullness
995. Plethora: (noun) a large or excessive amount
996. Ploy: (noun) a stratagem, dodge or manoeuvre to gain an advantage
997. Pluvial: (adjective) relating to or characterized by rain; rainy
998. Poach: 1. (verb) to cook (an egg without its shell) in or over boiling water, 2. to catch (game or fish) illegally on someone else's property
999. Polemic: (noun) a controversial speech or piece of writing that fiercely attacks or defends an idea, opinion, etc.
1000. Politic: (adjective) 1. of a course of action: prudent; wise; shrewd, 2. of a person: cunning, crafty
1001. Polity: (noun) 1. a politically organized body such as a state, church or association, 2. any form of political institution or government
1002. Polyglot: 1. (adjective) speaking, using or written in many languages, 2. (noun) someone who speaks many languages

1003. Polynomial: (noun) of an expression: consisting of a sum of terms each containing a constant and one or more variables raised to a power
1004. Polyphony: (noun) the style of musical composition in which each part or voice has an independent melodic value
1005. Portend: (verb) to warn of (usually something bad); to signify or foreshadow it
1006. Poseur: (noun) someone who behaves in an affected or insincere way, especially to impress others
1007. Positivism: (noun) a school of philosophy maintaining that knowledge can come only from observable phenomena and positive facts

> Pidgin languages are simplified forms of communication that develop between groups of people who do not share a common language. These languages typically arise in situations of trade, colonization or contact between speakers of different native languages. Pidgins often have simplified grammar, limited vocabulary and borrow words from multiple languages. Despite their rudimentary structure, pidgins serve as effective tools for basic communication and can facilitate interactions between diverse groups. Over time, some pidgins may evolve into creole languages with more complex grammar and expanded vocabulary, becoming fully functional languages in their own right.

1008. Positron: (noun) an antiparticle that has the same mass as an electron, and an equal but opposite charge
1009. Posterity: (noun) future generations
1010. Postern: (noun) a back door, back gate or private entrance
1011. Postulate: (verb) to assume or suggest something as the basis for discussion; to take it for granted
1012. Potentate: (noun) a powerful ruler; a monarch
1013. Pragmatism: (noun) a practical matter-of-fact approach to dealing with problems, etc.
1014. Preamble: (noun) an introduction or preface, e.g., to a speech or document

1015. Precedent: (noun) a previous incident or legal case, etc., that has something in common with the one under consideration, serving as a basis for a decision in the present one
1016. Precept: (noun) 1. a rule or principle, especially one of a moral kind, that is seen or used as a guide to behaviour, 2. the written warrant of a magistrate
1017. Precocious: (adjective) e.g., of a child: unusually advanced in mental development, speech, behaviour, etc.
1018. Predilection: (noun) a special liking or preference for something
1019. Preeminent: (adjective) better than all others
1020. Preemptive: (adjective) having the effect of pre-empting
1021. Prehensile: (adjective) denoting a part of an animal that is adapted for grasping, e.g., the tail of certain vertebrates
1022. Prepossessing: (adjective) attractive; winning
1023. Presage: (verb) to warn of or be a warning sign of something; to foreshadow
1024. Prescience: (noun) the ability to predict events; foresight
1025. Prevaricate: (verb) to avoid stating the truth or coming directly to the point
1026. Primogeniture: (noun) 1. the fact or condition of being the first-born child, 2. the right or principle of succession or inheritance of an eldest son
1027. Prism: (noun) 1. a transparent block, usually of glass and with triangular ends and rectangular sides, that separates a beam of white light into the colours of the visible spectrum, 2. a solid figure in which the two ends are matching parallel polygons (e.g., triangles or squares) and all other surfaces are parallelograms
1028. Pristine: (adjective) fresh, clean, unused or untouched
1029. Privation: (noun) the condition of not having or being deprived of, life's comforts and necessities; a lack of something particular
1030. Procure: (verb) to manage to obtain something or bring it about
1031. Prodigal: (adjective) headlessly extravagant or wasteful

1032. Proem: (noun) an introduction, prelude or preface, especially at the beginning of a book
1033. Profess: (verb) to make an open declaration of (beliefs, etc.)
1034. Progenitor: (noun) 1. an ancestor, forebear or forefather, 2. the founder or originator of a movement, etc.
1035. Progesterone: (noun) a steroid sex hormone that prepares the lining of the uterus for implantation of a fertilized egg
1036. Prognosis: (noun) an informed forecast of developments in any situation
1037. Prolepsis: (noun) the anticipation and representation of future events or developments as if they had already occurred
1038. Prolific: (adjective) 1. abundant in growth; producing plentiful fruit or offspring, 2. of a writer, artist, etc.: constantly producing new work
1039. Prolix: (adjective) of speech and writing: tediously long winded
1040. Promulgate: (verb) to make (a decree, etc.) effective by means of an official public announcement
1041. Propensity: (noun) a tendency or inclination
1042. Propitious: (adjective) favourable; auspicious; advantageous
1043. Prosaic: (adjective) unpoetic; unimaginative; dull, ordinary and uninteresting
1044. Proscenium: (noun) 1. the part of a stage in front of the curtain, 2. the arch framing the stage and separating it from the auditorium
1045. Proscribe: (verb) to prohibit or condemn something (e.g., a practice)
1046. Proselytize: (verb) to try to convert someone from one faith to another; to make converts
1047. Prosody: (noun) 1. the study of verse composition, especially poetic metre, 2. the study of rhythm, stress and intonation in speech
1048. Prospectus: a brochure giving information about a school or other institution, especially about the courses on offer
1049. Prosthesis: (noun) an artificial substitute for a part of the body that is missing or non-functional, e.g., dentures, an artificial limb or breast or a pacemaker

1050. Protean: (adjective) readily able to change shape or appearance; variable; changeable
1051. Provenance: (noun) the place of origin (of a work of art, archaeological find, etc.)
1052. Proxy: (noun) a person authorized to act or vote on another another's behalf; the agency of such a person
1053. Prurient: (adjective) unhealthily or excessively interested in sexual matters; tending to arouse such unhealthy interest
1054. Pseudonym: (noun) a false or assumed name, especially one used by an author
1055. Pugilism: (noun) the art or practice of boxing or prizefighting
1056. Pugnacious: (adjective) given to fighting; quarrelsome; belligerent or combative
1057. Pulchritude: (noun) beauty
1058. Pullulate: (verb) breed or produce rapidly, to swarm or teem with life or to multiply or increase abundantly
1059. Pulsar: (noun) a star that emits electromagnetic radiation in brief regular pulses, mainly at radio frequency
1060. Pundit: (noun) 1. an authority or supposed authority on a particular subject, especially one who is regularly consulted, 2. a person learned in Hindu culture, philosophy and law
1061. Pungent: (adjective) of a taste and smell: sharp and strong
1062. Purloin: (verb) to steal or pilfer
1063. Purser: (noun) the ship's officer responsible for keeping the accounts and, on a passenger ship, seeing to the welfare of passengers
1064. Purview: (noun) 1. scope of responsibility or concern, e.g., of a court of law, 2. the range of someone's knowledge, experience or activities
1065. Pusillanimous: (adjective) timid, cowardly or faint-hearted
1066. Quadrant: (noun) 1. a quarter of the circumference of a circle, 2. any device or mechanical part in the shape of a 90 degrees arc
1067. Quadratic: (noun) an algebraic equation that involves the square, but no higher power, of an unknown quantity or variable

1068. Quaff: (verb) to drink eagerly or deeply
1069. Quagmire: (noun) 1. an area of soft marshy ground, 2. dangerous, difficult or awkward situation
1070. Quandary: (noun) a state of indecision, uncertainty, doubt or perplexity
1071. Quantum: (noun) an amount of quantity, especially a specified one
1072. Quarantine: (noun) the isolation of people or animals to prevent the spread of any infectious disease that they could be developing
1073. Quarry: (noun) an open excavation for the purpose of extracting stone or slate for building
1074. Quasar: (noun) a highly intense luminous star-like source of light and radio waves that exists thousands of millions of light years outside the Earth's galaxy
1075. Querulous: (adjective) of someone or their disposition: inclined or ready to complain
1076. Queue: (noun) a line of file of people vehicles, etc., especially ones that are waiting for something
1077. Quibble: (verb) to argue over trifles; to make petty objections
1078. Quiescent: (adjective) quiet, silent, at rest or in an inactive state, usually temporarily
1079. Quintessence: (noun) 1. a perfect example or embodiment of it, 2. the fundamental essential nature of something
1080. Quisling: (noun) 1. a traitor, 2. someone who collaborates with the enemy
1081. Quorum: (noun) the fixed minimum number of members of an organization, society, etc. who must be present at a meeting for its business to be valid
1082. Radian: (noun) The SI unit of plane angular measurement defined as the angle that is made at the centre of a circle by an arc whose length is equal to the radius of the circle
1083. Raiment: (noun) clothing
1084. Rancor: (noun) a long lasting feeling of bitterness or dislike
1085. Rapacious: (adjective) 1. greedy, especially for money, 2. of an animal or bird: living by catching prey

1086. Ratify: (verb) to give formal consent to (a treaty, agreement, etc.)
1087. Ratiocination:
1088. Rebuff: (noun) 1. a snub, 2. a refusal or rejection, especially of someone's help, advice, etc.
1089. Rebus: (noun) a puzzle where pictures, etc. represent words or syllables
1090. Recalcitrant: (adjective) not willing to accept authority or discipline
1091. Recapitulate: (verb) to go over the chief points of (an argument, statement, etc.) again
1092. Recidivism: (noun) the habit of relapsing into crime
1093. Reciprocal: (adjective) giving and receiving or given and received
1094. Recompense: (verb) to repay a reward for service, work done, etc.
1095. Recondite: (adjective) of a subject or knowledge: difficult to understand
1096. Reconnaissance: (noun) 1. a survey, e.g., of land or the position of troops, to obtain information about the enemy before advancing, 2. a preliminary survey
1097. Reconnoiter: (verb) to examine or survey (land, enemy troops, etc.) especially with a view to military operations, etc.
1098. Recreant: (noun) someone who is cowardly, disloyal or lacking courage in the face of danger or hardship
1099. Recriminate: (verb) accuse someone of wrongdoing in return, especially as a response to accusations made against oneself
1100. Recumbent: (adjective) lying down
1101. Red herring: (noun) a misleading idea, clue, etc.
1102. Redress: (verb) to set right or compensate for (something wrong)
1103. Reduce: (verb) to make or become less, smaller, etc.
1104. Refectory: (noun) a dining hall, especially one in a monastery or university
1105. Refractory: (adjective) 1. difficult to control; stubborn, 2. of a disease: resistant to treatment, 3. of a material: resistant to heat

1106. Refute: (verb) to prove that (a person, theory, etc.) is wrong
1107. Regalia: (noun) the insignia of royalty, e.g., the crown, sceptre and orb
1108. Regatta: (noun) a meeting for yacht or boat races
1109. Regicide: (noun) 1. the act of killing a king, 2. someone who kills a king
1110. Regime: (noun) 1. a system of government, 2. a particular government or administration
1111. Regiment: (noun) 1. a body of soldiers consisting of several companies, etc., 2. a large number of people or things formed into an organized group
1112. Reimburse: (verb) 1. to repay (money spent), 2. to pay (a person) money to compensate for or cover (expenses, losses, etc.)
1113. Reiterate: (verb) to do or say again or repeatedly
1114. Relegate: (verb) to move down to a lower grade, position, status, etc.
1115. Relief: (noun) 1. the lessening or removal of pain, worry, etc. or the feeling that comes from this, 2. anything lessening pain, worry, boredom, etc.
1116. Remnant: (noun) a remaining small piece or amount of something larger
1117. Rend: (verb) to tear something especially using force or violence
1118. Renege: (verb) to go back on one's word, an agreement, etc.
1119. Repertory: (noun) 1. a repertoire, especially of a theatre company, 2. a storehouse
1120. Repose: (noun) a state of rest, calm or peacefulness
1121. Reprise: (noun) the repeating of a passage or theme
1122. Reprove: (verb) 1. to rebuke, 2. to blame or condemn for a fault, wrongdoing, etc.
1123. Repudiate: (verb) to deny or reject as unfounded
1124. Requiem: (noun) any piece of music composed or performed to commemorate the dead
1125. Requisite: (adjective) required or necessary
1126. Rescind: (verb) to cancel, annul or revoke (an order, law, etc.)

1127. Resolute: (adjective) determined; with a fixed purpose or belief
1128. Resonate: (verb) to resound or cause to resound or echo
1129. Restive: (adjective) restless; nervous
1130. Reticent: (adjective) not saying very much; not willing to communicate
1131. Reticulate: (adjective) like a net or a network, especially in having lines, waves, etc.
1132. Retinue: (noun) the servants, officials, etc. who travel with and attend an important person
1133. Revocable: (adjective) something that can be cancelled, annulled or revoked
1134. Revulsion: (noun) 1. a feeling of complete disgust, distaste or repugnance, 2. a sudden and often violent change of feeling, especially from love to hate
1135. Rhapsodic: (adjective) something that is intensely emotional, enthusiastic or ecstatic, often in a spontaneous or unrestrained manner
1136. Rhombus: (noun) a quadrilateral with four equal sides and two angles greater than and two angles smaller than a right angle
1137. Ribald: (adjective) of language, a speaker, humour, etc.: humorous in an obscene, vulgar or indecently disrespectful way
1138. Rife: (adjective) very common or numerous
1139. Riparian: (adjective) relating to, occurring or living on a riverbank
1140. Risible: (adjective) laughable
1141. Rite: (noun) a formal ceremony or observance, especially a religious one
1142. Rococo: (noun) a style of architecture, decoration and furniture-making originating in France in the early eighteenth century, characterized by elaborate ornamentation and asymmetry
1143. Rookery: (noun) 1. a colony of rooks, 2. a colony of seals and sea birds

1144. Rorschach: a test where a subject is asked to interpret a standard set of ink blots in order to determine personality type, mental state, etc.
1145. Rostrum: (noun) a platform for a public speaker, orchestra conductor, etc.
1146. Rout: (verb) 1. to defeat (an army, a sporting team, etc.) completely, 2. to dig something up, especially with the snout
1147. Roux: (noun) a cooked mixture of flour and fat, usually butter, used to thicken sauces
1148. Ruffian: (noun) a coarse, violent, brutal or lawless person
1149. Ruminate: (verb) to chew the cud, 2. to think deeply about something
1150. Sabotage: (noun) deliberate or underhand damage or destruction, especially for military or political reasons
1151. Sacrosanct: (adjective) something that is regarded as sacred, inviolable or immune from violation or interference
1152. Salient: (adjective) outstanding or prominent
1153. Salubrious: (adjective) promoting health or well being
1154. Salutary: (adjective) bringing or containing a timely warning
1155. Sanction: (noun) 1. official permission or authority, 2. aid; support, 3. an economic or military measure taken by one nation against another as a means of coercion
1156. Sanguine: (adjective) cheerful, confident and full of hope
1157. Sanguineous: (adjective) pertaining to blood or is characterized by the presence of blood
1158. Sardonic: (adjective) mocking or scornful
1159. Sartor: (noun) a tailor or someone who makes or alters clothing, typically as a profession
1160. Saturnine: (adjective) having a grave and gloomy temperament; melancholy in character
1161. Sauté: (verb) to fry lightly for a short time
1162. Savant: (noun) a wise and learned man or woman respectively
1163. Scalar: (noun) a quantity that has magnitude but not direction, such as distance, speed and mass
1164. Scald: (verb) to injure with hot liquid or steam

1165. Scalene: (adjective) of a triangle: having each side a different length
1166. Scandent: (adjective) plants that climb or scramble by means of tendrils, aerial roots or other structures
1167. Scarp: (noun) the steep side of a hill or rock; an escarpment
1168. Schism: (noun) a breach or separation from the main group or into opposing groups
1169. Schizophrenia: (noun) a severe mental disorder characterized by loss of contact with reality, impairment of thought process, a marked personality change, loss of emotional responsiveness and social withdrawal
1170. Scintilla: (noun) a hint or trace; an iota
1171. Scotch: 1. (adjective) of things, especially products, but not usually of people: Scottish, 2. (verb) to ruin or hinder, e.g., plans
1172. Scourge: (noun) a cause of great suffering and affliction, especially to many people
1173. Scurrilous: (adjective) indecently insulting or abusive, and unjustly damaging to the reputation
1174. Secant: (noun) 1. a straight line that cuts a curve at one or more places, 2. for a given angle in a right-angled triangle: the ratio of the length of the hypotenuse to the length of the side adjacent to the angle under consideration; the reciprocal of the cosine of an angle
1175. Secede: (verb) to withdraw formally, e.g., from a political or religious body or alliance
1176. Sect: (noun) a religious or other group whose views and practices differ from those of an established body or from those of a body from which it has separated
1177. Sedentary: (adjective) 1. of work: involving much sitting, 2. of a person: spending much time sitting; taking little exercise
1178. Sedge: (noun) a plant, resembling grass, which grows in bogs, fens, marshes and other poorly drained areas
1179. Sedulous: (adjective) assiduous and diligent; steadily hardworking

1180. Seine: (noun) a large vertical fishing net held underwater by floats and weights, and whose ends are brought together and hauled
1181. Semantic: (adjective) 1. referring or relating to meaning, especially of words, 2. referring or relating to semantics
1182. Senescent: (adjective) growing old; ageing
1183. Sententious: (adjective) 1. fond of using or full of sayings or proverbs, 2. tending to lecture others on morals
1184. Sentient: (adjective) capable of sensation or feeling; conscious or aware of something
1185. Sentry: (noun) a person, usually a soldier, posted on guard to control entry or passage
1186. Sepsis: (noun) the presence of disease-causing microorganisms, especially viruses or bacteria, and their toxins in the body tissues
1187. Sept: (noun) especially in Scotland and Ireland: a clan; a division of a tribe
1188. Sepulchre: (noun) referring or relating to a tomb or burial
1189. Sequester: (verb) to set aside or isolate
1190. Serrated: (adjective) notched like the blade of a saw
1191. Sesquipedalian: (adjective) characterized by long-words; long-winded
1192. Sextant: (noun) a device used in navigation and surveying for measuring angular distances
1193. Shard: (noun) a fragment of something brittle, usually glass or pottery
1194. Shear: (verb) to clip or cut off something, especially with a large pair of clippers
1195. Siccative: (adjective) something with drying or desiccating properties
1196. Sidereal: (adjective) referring or relating to or determined by the stars
1197. Sieve: (noun) a utensil with a meshed or perforated bottom, used for straining solids from liquids or for sifting large particles from smaller ones

1198. Simoon: (noun) a hot, dry and often dusty wind that blows across deserts
1199. Sinewy: (adjective) something as lean, muscular and strong, often with well-defined muscles or tendons
1200. Siphon: (noun) a tube held in an inverted U-shape that can be used to transfer liquid from one container at a higher level into another at a lower level, used to empty car petrol tanks, etc.
1201. Skepticism: (noun) a questioning or doubting attitude towards beliefs, claims or propositions
1202. Slag: 1. (noun) the layer of waste material that forms on the surface of molten metal ore during smelting and refining, 2. to criticize or deride somebody harshly or speak disparagingly about them
1203. Slip: 1. (verb) to lose one's footing and slide accidentally, 2. (verb) to make a slight mistake inadvertently rather than due to ignorance, 3. (verb) to move or cause to move quietly, smoothly and unobtrusively with a sliding motion, 4. (noun) a small strip or a piece of paper
1204. Smidgen: (noun) a very small amount
1205. Solder: 1. (noun) an alloy with a low melting point, applied when molten to the joint between two metals to form an airtight seal, 2. (verb) to join (two pieces of metal) without melting them, by applying solder to the joint between them
1206. Solicitous: (adjective) anxious or concerned about somebody or something, 2. eager to do something
1207. Solipsism: (noun) the theory that one's own existence is the only certainty
1208. Solvency: (noun) the ability to pay one's debts
1209. Somatic: (adjective) referring or relating to the body
1210. Somnambulism: (noun) sleepwalking
1211. Sonata: (noun) a piece of music written in three or more movements for a solo instrument, especially the piano
1212. Sonic: (adjective) relating to or using sound or sound waves
1213. Sortie: (noun) 1. a sudden attack by besieged troops, 2. a short return trip

1214. Spate: (noun) a sudden rush or increased quantity
1215. Specie: (noun) money in the form of coins as opposed to notes
1216. Specious: (adjective) superficially or apparently convincing, sound or just, but really false, flawed or lacking in sincerity
1217. Spectrum: (noun) 1. the band of colours (red, orange, yellow, green, blue, indigo and violet) that is produced when white light is split into its constituent wavelengths by passing it through a prism, 2. any full range
1218. Speculum: (noun) 1. a mirror with a reflective surface, usually of polished metal, 2. a device that is used to enlarge the opening of a body cavity so that the interior may be inspected
1219. Speleology: (noun) 1. the scientific study of caves, 2. the activity or pastime of exploring caves
1220. Spendthrift: (noun) someone who spends money wastefully
1221. Spit: 1. (verb) to expel (saliva) from the mouth, 2. (noun) a long thin metal rod on which meat is skewered for roasting
1222. Squall: 1. (noun) a sudden or short-lived violent gust of wind, usually accompanied by rain or sleet, 2. (verb) to yell
1223. Stalwart: 1. (adjective) strong and sturdy, 2. (noun) a longstanding and committed supporter
1224. Stanchion: (noun) an upright beam or pole that functions as a support
1225. Staunch: 1. (adjective) steadfast; water-tight, 2. (verb) to stop the flow of (something, such as blood from a wound)
1226. Stentorian: (adjective) of a voice: loud and strong
1227. Stethoscope: (noun) an instrument that consists of a small concave disc that has hollow tubes attached to it and which, when it is placed on the body, carries sound
1228. Stigma: (noun) shame or social disgrace
1229. Stipulate: (verb) in a contract, agreement, etc.: to specify as a necessary condition
1230. Stolid: (adjective) showing little or no interest or emotion
1231. Stricture: (noun) a severe criticism
1232. Strident: (adjective) of a sound, especially a voice: loud and harsh

1233. Structuralism: (noun) an approach to various areas of study, e.g., literary criticism and linguistics, which seeks to identify underlying patterns or structures
1234. Strut: 1. (verb) to walk in a proud way, 2. (noun) a bar or rod whose function is to support weight or take pressure
1235. Stultify: (verb) to cause something to be useless, worthless, etc.
1236. Subjugate: (verb) especially of one country, people, etc. in regard to another: to dominate them; to bring them under control
1237. Sublimate: (verb) to channel a morally or socially unacceptable impulse towards something else that is considered more appropriate
1238. Subliminal: (adjective) existing in, resulting from or targeting the area of the mind that is below the threshold of ordinary awareness
1239. Subpoena: (noun) a legal document that orders someone to appear in a court of law at a specified time
1240. Substrate: (noun) 1. the material that a living organism, such as plant, bacterium, etc. grows on or is attached to, 2. the substance that an enzyme acts on during a biochemical reaction
1241. Subterfuge: (noun) a trick or deception that evades, conceals or obscures
1242. Subvert: (verb) to undermine or overthrow (especially a government or other legally established body)

Words that are unpleasant to hear:

- **Poop**: Solid waste matter discharged from the bowels
- **Pee**: Urine, liquid waste matter excreted by the kidneys
- **Vomit**: Eject matter from the stomach through the mouth
- **Snot**: Nasal mucus
- **Pus**: A thick, yellowish or greenish liquid produced in an infected tissue
- **Booger**: Dried nasal mucus
- **Scum**: A layer of dirt or froth on the surface of a liquid

1243. Succour: (noun) 1. help or relief in time of distress or need, 2. someone or something that gives this kind of help
1244. Suffrage: (noun) the right to vote in political elections
1245. Supercilious: (adjective) arrogantly disdainful or contemptuous
1246. Superfluous: (adjective) more than is needed or wanted
1247. Supine: (adjective) lying on one's back; lazy
1248. Surety: (noun) 1. someone who agrees to become legally responsible for another person's behaviour, debts, etc., 2. security, usually in the form of a sum of money, against loss, damage, etc. or as a guarantee that a promise will be kept
1249. Surfeit: (noun) 1. an excess, 2. the stuffed or sickened feeling that results from any excess, especially overeating
1250. Surgent: (adjective) something rising or increasing rapidly, often with energy or intensity
1251. Surrogate: (noun) someone or something that takes the place of another
1252. Sybarite: (noun) someone devoted to a life of luxury and pleasure
1253. Syllogism: (noun) an argument in which a conclusion, whether valid or invalid, is drawn from two independent statements using logic
1254. Symbiosis: (noun) a close association between two organisms of different species, usually to the benefit of both partners, and often essential for mutual survival
1255. Synapse: (noun) a junction between two nerve cells, consisting of a minute gap across which impulses pass by diffusion of a neurotransmitter
1256. Syncretism: (noun) the merging or blending of different cultural or religious traditions, beliefs or practices to create a new and often distinct system
1257. Syndicate: 1. (noun) any association of people or groups working together on a single project, 2. an association of criminals organising widespread illegal activities
1258. Syndrome: (noun) 1. a group of symptoms whose appearance together usually indicates the presence of a particular disease

or disorder, 2. a pattern or series of events, observed qualities, etc. characteristic of a particular problem or condition

1259. Synergy: (noun) a phenomenon in which the combined action of two or more things is greater than the sum of the individual effects of each
1260. Syntax: (noun) the positioning of words in a sentence and their relationship to each other
1261. Systemic: (adjective) relating to or affecting the whole body
1262. Tableau: (noun) a moment or scene in which the action is frozen for dramatic effect
1263. Taboo: (noun) something forbidden or disapproved of for religious reasons or by social custom
1264. Taciturn: (adjective) saying little; quiet and uncommunicative
1265. Tack: (noun) 1. a short nail with a sharp point and a broad flat head, 2. a long loose temporary stitch, 3. a direction; course of action or policy
1266. Tactile: (adjective) belonging or relating to or having, a sense of touch
1267. Tantamount: (adjective) producing the same effect or result as; equivalent to
1268. Taxidermy: (noun) the art of preparing, stuffing, and mounting the skins of dead animals birds, etc. so that they present a lifelike appearance

> The word 'syllogism' originates from the Greek 'syllogismos,' meaning 'inference' or 'deduction.' In logic, a syllogism is a form of deductive reasoning that consists of two premises and a conclusion, each of which is a categorical proposition. One classic example of a syllogism is: 'All humans are mortal (major premise), Socrates is a human (minor premise), Therefore, Socrates is mortal (conclusion).' Developed by ancient Greek philosophers like Aristotle, syllogisms form the foundation of logical reasoning and are used to demonstrate the validity of arguments. Despite its technical nature, the concept of syllogism has permeated various fields, including philosophy, mathematics and rhetoric, shaping our understanding of logical thought and argumentation.

1269. Temerity: (noun) 1. rashness or impetuosity, 2. boldness or impudence
1270. Tempera: (noun) 1. a method of painting using an emulsion, 2. this emulsion or a painting produced using it
1271. Temporal: (adjective) 1. relating to time, 2. relating to worldly or secular life rather than to religious or spiritual life
1272. Tendentious: (adjective) characterized by a particular bias, tendency or underlying purpose
1273. Tendril: (noun) a long shoot-like extension that some climbing plants use for attaching themselves to objects for support
1274. Terrarium: (noun) 1. a container in which small land animals are kept, 2. a sealed jar in which plants are grown
1275. Tetrahedron: (noun) a solid figure with four triangular plane faces
1276. Thermal: (adjective) 1. relating to, caused by or producing heat, 2. of clothing: designed to prevent the loss of heat from the body
1277. Thrombosis: (noun) an abnormal congealing of the blood within a blood vessel, causing a blood clot
1278. Timbre: (noun) the distinctive quality of the tone produced by a musical instrument or voice, as opposed to pitch and loudness
1279. Timorous: (adjective) very timid; frightened
1280. Tinnitus: (noun) an abnormal ringing, buzzing, etc. noise in the ears, not caused by external sound
1281. Titular: 1. (adjective) having the title of an office or position, but none of the authority or duties, 2. relating to a title
1282. Tocsin: (noun) an alarm bell or warning signal
1283. Tome: (noun) a large, heavy and usually scholarly book
1284. Torpor: (noun) the state of being sluggish and dull
1285. Torque: (noun) a force that causes an object to rotate around on an axis; a necklace made of metal twisted into a band, worn by the ancient Britons and Gauls
1286. Torsion: (noun) twisting by applying force to one end while the other is held firm or twisted in the opposite direction

1287. Tort: (noun) any wrongful act, other than breach of contract, for which an action for damages or compensation may be brought
1288. Tortuous: (adjective) 1. full of twists and turns, 2. devious or involved
1289. Totem: (noun) 1. in Native American culture: a natural object, especially an animal, that is the sign and usually spirit guardian of a tribe or an individual, 2. an image or representation of this
1290. Touchstone: (noun) a hard black flint-like stone used for testing the purity and quality of gold and silver alloys
1291. Toxicology: (noun) the scientific study of poisons
1292. Traduce: (verb) to say or write unpleasant things about (someone or something)
1293. Transcribe: (verb) 1. to write or type out (a spoken or written text), 2. to transliterate, 3. to arrange (a piece of music) for an instrument or voice that it was not originally composed for, 4. to transfer (data) from one computer storage device to another
1294. Transgress: (verb) 1. to break or violate (divine law, a rule, etc.), 2. to go beyond or overstep (a limit or boundary)
1295. Trapezium: (noun) any four-sided geometric figure that is not a parallelogram
1296. Treatise: (noun) a formal piece of writing that deals systematically and in depth with a subject
1297. Trenchant: (adjective) incisive; penetrating; forthright; vigorous
1298. Tribalism: (noun) 1. the system of tribes as a way of organizing society, 2. the feeling of belonging to a tribe, racial group, etc., especially when leading to violence
1299. Tribulation: (noun) great sorrow, trouble, affliction, misery, etc.
1300. Tripe: (noun) 1. parts of the stomach of a cow or sheep, used as food, 2. nonsense; rubbish
1301. Tropism: (noun) the change of direction of an organism especially a plant or plant part, in response to an external stimulus such as gravity, light or heat

1302. Troubadour: (noun) 1. one of a group of lyric poets in Southern France and North Italy between the eleventh and thirteenth centuries who wrote about love, 2. a poet or singer, especially one whose topic is love
1303. Truncate: (verb) to cut a part from (a tree, word, piece of writing, etc.), especially in order to shorten
1304. Truss: (noun) 1. a framework supporting a roof, bridge, etc., 2. a belt, bandage, etc. worn to support hernia, 3. a bundle of hay or straw, 4. a cluster of flowers or fruit
1305. Truss: (verb) 1. to tie up or bind tightly, 2. to support with a truss
1306. Tryst: (noun) 1. an arrangement to meet someone, especially a lover, 2. the meeting itself
1307. Tufa: (noun) a white, spongy porous rock that forms in a calcium carbonate encrustation in areas around springs, streams, etc.
1308. Tundra: (noun) a vast relatively flat treeless zone lying to the south of the polarized cap in America and Eurasia with permanently frozen subsoil
1309. Turbid: (adjective) 1. of liquid, etc.: cloudy; not clear, 2. of writing, the construction of an argument, etc.: confused; disordered; unclear
1310. Tureen: (noun) a large deep dish with a cover that food, especially soup or vegetables, is served from
1311. Turgid: (adjective) swollen; inflated or distended
1312. Turpitude: (noun) vileness, depravity
1313. Tyranny: (noun) 1. the use of cruelty, injustice, suppression, etc. to enforce authority or power, 2. absolute, cruel and oppressive government by a single tyrant or a group of tyrannical people; a state under such government, 3. a cruel, unjust and oppressive act
1314. Ubiquitous: (adjective) existing, found or seeming to be found everywhere at the same time
1315. Umbra: (noun) the shadow cast by the moon on the earth during an eclipse of the sun
1316. Umbrage: (noun) annoyance; offence

1317. Unctuous: (adjective) 1. insincerely and excessively charming, 2. oily; greasy
1318. Undulate: (verb) to move or to make something move in or like waves
1319. Untoward: (adjective) 1. inconvenient; unfortunate, 2. adverse; unfavourable, 3. difficult to manage; unruly or intractable, 4. unseemly; improper
1320. Unwieldy: (adjective) 1. of an object: large and awkward to carry or manage, 2. of a person: clumsy; not graceful in movement; awkward or ungainly
1321. Urbane: (adjective) 1. with refined manners; suave; courteous, 2. sophisticated; civilized; elegant
1322. Ursine: (adjective) relating to or like a bear
1323. Usurp: (verb) 1. to take possession of (e.g., land) or assume (e.g., power, authority, etc.) by force, without right or unjustly, 2. to encroach on something (e.g., someone else's rights, sphere of interest, etc.)
1324. Vacuous: (adjective) 1. unintelligent; stupid, 2. of a look or expression: blank; conveying no feeling or meaning, 3. empty
1325. Vagary: (noun) an unpredictable and erratic act or turn of events
1326. Vainglorious: (adjective) extremely boastful; excessively proud of oneself
1327. Valediction: (noun) 1. the act of saying farewell; a farewell, 2. a valedictory speech, etc.
1328. Vandalize: (verb) to inflict willful and senseless damage (on property, etc.)
1329. Vanguard: (noun) 1. the part of a military force that advances first, 2. a person or group that leads the way, especially by setting standards or forming opinion; a leading position
1330. Variable: (adjective) referring to something that varies or tends to vary; changeable
1331. Variegated: (adjective) of leaves or flowers: marked with patches of two or more colours
1332. Varnish: (noun) 1. an oil-based liquid containing resin, painted on a surface such as wood to give a hard transparent

and often glossy finish, 2. a superficial attractiveness or impressiveness, especially masking underlying shoddiness or inadequacy

1333. Venal: (adjective) 1. of a person: willing to be persuaded by corrupt means, especially bribery, 2. of behaviour: dishonest, corrupt
1334. Vendetta: (noun) 1. a bitter feud in which the family of a murdered person takes revenge by killing the murderer or one of the murderer's relatives, 2. any long-standing bitter feud or quarrel
1335. Venerable: (adjective) deserving respect, especially on account of age or religious association
1336. Ventral: (adjective) 1. denoting the lower surface of an animal that walks on four legs, of any invertebrate or of a structure such as a leaf or wing, 2. denoting the front surface of the body of an animal that walks upright, e.g., a human being
1337. Verdant: (adjective) 1. covered with lush green grass or vegetation, 2. of a rich green colour
1338. Verisimilitude: (noun) the appearance of being real or true
1339. Veritable: (adjective) accurately described as such; real
1340. Vernal: (adjective) relating to or appropriate to spring; happening or appearing in spring
1341. Vertigo: (noun) a whirling sensation felt when the sense of balance is disturbed
1342. Vesicle: (noun) 1. any small sack or cavity, especially one filled with fluid, within a living cell, 2. a small blister
1343. Vespiary: (noun) a nest or colony of wasps
1344. Vest: (noun) an undergarment for the top half of the body
1345. Vestibule: (noun) an entrance hall
1346. Vestigial: (adjective) a structure, organ or behaviour that has lost most or all of its original function through evolution
1347. Viable: (adjective) 1. of a plan, etc.: having a chance of success, 2. of a plant, etc.: able to exist or grow in particular conditions, 3. of a foetus or baby: able to survive independently outside the womb
1348. Vicarious: (adjective) achieved through witnessing the experience of another person; standing in for another

1349. Vicissitude: (noun) an unpredictable change of fortune or circumstance
1350. Victuals: (noun) food; provisions
1351. Vigilante: (noun) an unappointed private citizen who assumes responsibility for keeping order in a community
1352. Vignette: (noun) 1. a decorative design on a book's title page, traditionally of vine leaves, 2. a photographic portrait with the background deliberately faded, 3. a short literary essay, especially one describing a person's character
1353. Vilify: (verb) to say insulting or abusive things about someone or something
1354. Vintner: (noun) a wine-merchant
1355. Viscosity: (noun) a measure of the resistance of fluid to flow, caused by internal friction
1356. Vitreous: (adjective) 1. relating to or consisting of glass, 2. like glass in hardness, sheen or transparency
1357. Vituperate: (verb) to attack someone with abusive criticism or disapproval
1358. Vociferous: (adjective) loud and forceful, especially in expressing opinions; noisy
1359. Voucher: (noun) 1. a ticket or paper serving as proof, e.g., of the purchase or receipt of goods, 2. a ticket worth of specific amount of money, exchangeable for goods or services up to the same value
1360. Vulpine: (adjective) belonging or relating to or resembling, a fox
1361. Waive: (verb) to refrain from insisting upon (something); to voluntarily give up (a claim or right, etc.)
1362. Wangle: (verb) to contrive or obtain something by persuasiveness
1363. Wanton: (adjective) thoughtlessly and needlessly cruel, 2. motiveless, 3. sexually immoral
1364. Warrant: 1. (noun) a written legal authorization for doing something, e.g., searching property, 2. (verb) to justify (something), 3. (verb) to guarantee (goods, etc.) as being of the specified quality or quantity

1365. Waylay: (verb) 1. to lie in wait for and ambush (someone), 2. to delay (someone) with conversation
1366. Wheedle: (verb) to coax or cajole someone, often by flattery
1367. Winch: (noun) 1. a reel or roller round which a rope or chain is wound for hoisting or hauling the heavy loads, 2. a crank or handle for setting a wheel, axle or machinery in motion
1368. Winsome: (adjective) charming; captivating
1369. Wizened: (adjective) shrivelled or wrinkled, especially with age
1370. Yeoman: (noun) a farmer who owned and worked his own land
1371. Yield: (verb) 1. to produce (an animal product, such as meat or milk or a crop), 2. to give or produce (interest, etc.), 3. to give up or give in; to surrender
1372. Yokel: (noun) an unsophisticated country-dweller
1373. Zealous: (adjective) enthusiastic; keen
1374. Zephyr: (noun) a light gentle breeze
1375. Zeppelin: (noun) a cigar-shaped airship
1376. Zest: (noun) 1. keen enjoyment; enthusiasm, 2. something that adds to one's enjoyment of something, 3. the coloured outer layer of the peel of an orange or lemon or the oil contained in it, used for flavouring, 4. piquancy; agreeably sharp flavour

When describing disabilities it is best to avoid passive, victimizing words.

- Instead of saying 'handicapped' or 'disabled' it is best to use 'disabled people/person'.
- When talking about places that cater to disabilities do not use the terms 'disabled friendly' or 'handicapped friendly' but instead use the term 'accessible'. Say 'an accessible parking space', 'an accessible bathroom'.
- Do not use vocabulary that is patronizing or victimizing to people with disabilities. Avoid using terms like 'cripple', 'victim', 'poor', 'unfortunate', 'special needs' or 'retarded'.
- Do not use terms like 'deaf', 'dumb', 'deaf-and-dumb', 'invalid'. Instead say person with a 'visual impairment', 'hearing impairment', 'communication disability'. It is respectful to say 'a person who is blind' or 'a person who is deaf or hard of hearing' or 'person with a speech/ communication disability.'
- When someone has a mental health disability it is best to avoid terms like 'mad', 'hyper-sensitive', 'psycho', 'crazy', 'insane' or 'retard'. Instead say 'a person with a mental health disability'.
- Instead of using terms like 'wheelchair bound' say 'wheelchair user.'
- When someone has a short stature do not use terms such as 'dwarf' or 'midget'. Instead say 'someone of a short stature.'
- When someone has a cognitive disability do not use terms like 'retarded' or 'special needs person'. Instead say 'a person with a cognitive/developmental disability'.

WORD CLUSTERS

Words to describe **Sight**

- I **glanced** at my book to find the answers to the questions asked in the test.
- They **observed** the moon through the telescope.
- The teacher **gazed** at the students while they wrote the exam.
- I **glimpsed** the sun **peeking** out of the clouds.
- They **glared** at each other before the fight.
- I **noticed** a spelling error in her sentences.
- He only **stared** at his food and did not eat it.
- I **witnessed** a crime in my neighborhood on Sunday.

Words to describe **Smell**

- The whole place **stinks** of fish.
- The **fragrance** of the flowers filled the air.
- The **perfume** was aromatic.
- The eggs gave off a **putrid** smell.
- The **sweet-smelling** air pleased her.
- The **pungent** smell was due to the acids.

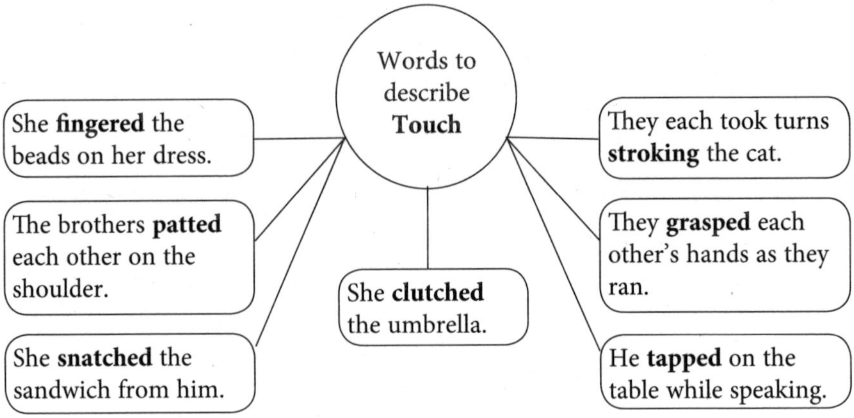
Words to describe **Touch**
She **fingered** the beads on her dress.
The brothers **patted** each other on the shoulder.
She **snatched** the sandwich from him.
She **clutched** the umbrella.
They each took turns **stroking** the cat.
They **grasped** each other's hands as they ran.
He **tapped** on the table while speaking.

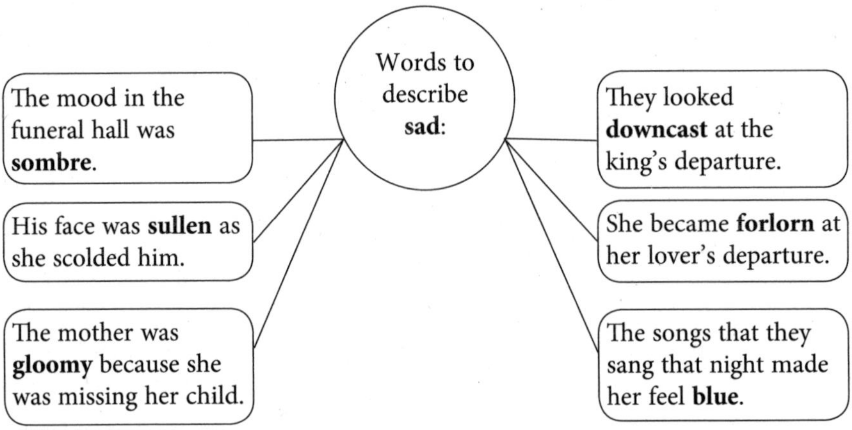
Words to describe **sad**:
The mood in the funeral hall was **sombre**.
His face was **sullen** as she scolded him.
The mother was **gloomy** because she was missing her child.
They looked **downcast** at the king's departure.
She became **forlorn** at her lover's departure.
The songs that they sang that night made her feel **blue**.

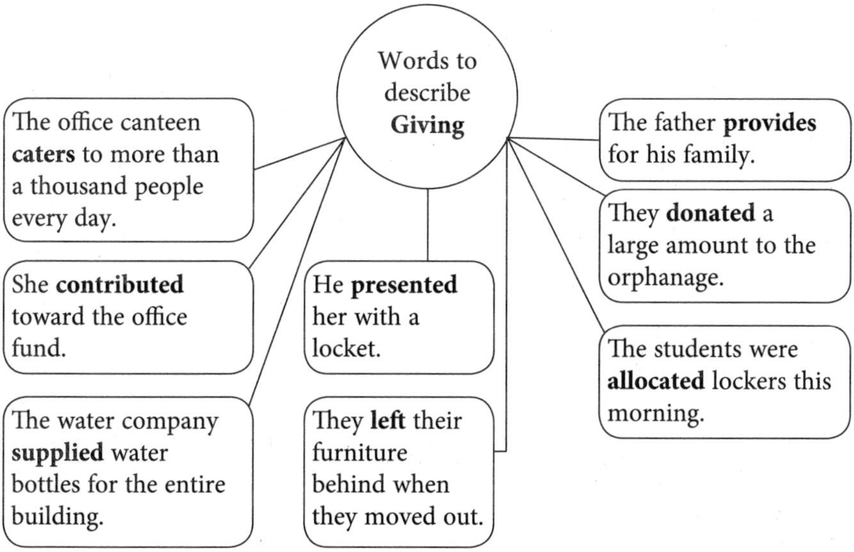
Words to describe **Giving**
The office canteen **caters** to more than a thousand people every day.
She **contributed** toward the office fund.
The water company **supplied** water bottles for the entire building.
He **presented** her with a locket.
They **left** their furniture behind when they moved out.
The father **provides** for his family.
They **donated** a large amount to the orphanage.
The students were **allocated** lockers this morning.

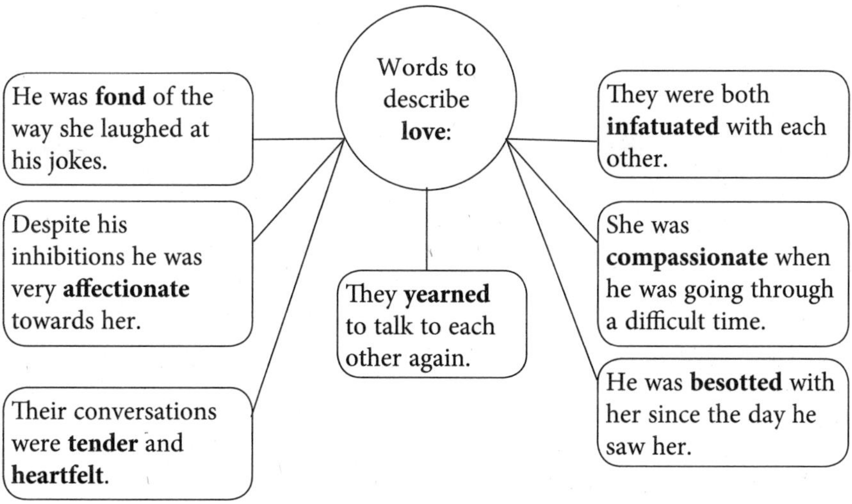
Words to describe **love**:
He was **fond** of the way she laughed at his jokes.
Despite his inhibitions he was very **affectionate** towards her.
Their conversations were **tender** and **heartfelt**.
They **yearned** to talk to each other again.
They were both **infatuated** with each other.
She was **compassionate** when he was going through a difficult time.
He was **besotted** with her since the day he saw her.

Some words you can use instead of said:

- 'I'm home,' he **announced** with enthusiasm.
- 'Yes, I will marry you,' she **answered, in response** to his proposal.
- 'You will have to come with us to the beach,' she **insisted**.
- 'This is a good book,' she **observed**.
- 'Shut up or I will cut you,' he **barked** at his son.
- 'I will never speak of this again, let us go,' she **pleaded** with her kidnapper.
- 'Please finish your homework and we can have pizza,' she **explained** to her son.

Words to describe looking:

- He **examined** his surroundings for any kind of clues.
- She **peeked** into the living room to see if her parents were around.
- They **watched** the sequel in the theatre but did not like it.
- She **glowered** at him after he broke the vase.
- He **glared** at her when she told him she hated him.
- Even though he knew it was wrong, he found himself **ogling** at her constantly.
- As soon as the question papers were distributed, the students began to **scan** them.

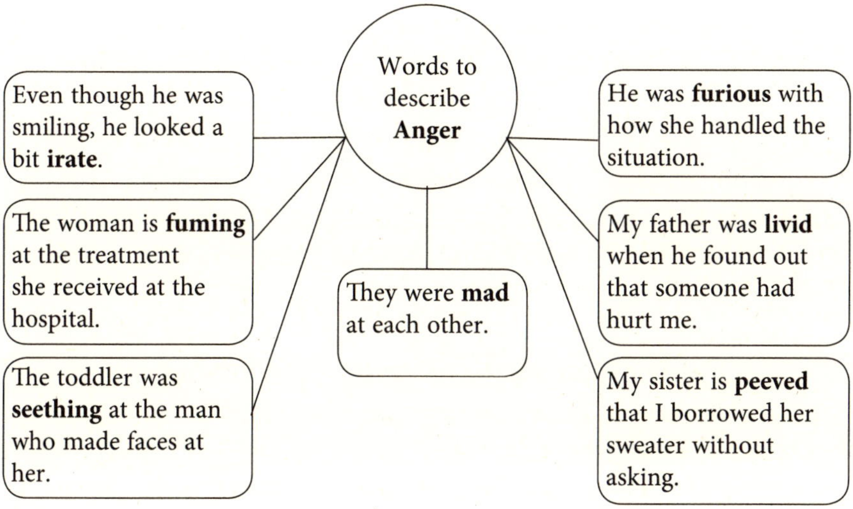
Words to describe **Anger**
Even though he was smiling, he looked a bit **irate**.
The woman is **fuming** at the treatment she received at the hospital.
The toddler was **seething** at the man who made faces at her.
They were **mad** at each other.
He was **furious** with how she handled the situation.
My father was **livid** when he found out that someone had hurt me.
My sister is **peeved** that I borrowed her sweater without asking.

ONOMATOPOEIC WORDS:

1. Bam: A sudden, loud sound, often from a collision or impact.
2. Bash: A heavy blow or strike, often causing a loud noise.
3. Boing: The sound of something elastic bouncing back.
4. Chatter: Rapid, continuous talk or sound, often used for humans talking quickly or animals like monkeys or birds.
5. Chirp: A short, sharp sound made by small birds or insects.
6. Clang: A loud, resonant metallic sound.
7. Clang: (Same as above) A loud, resonant metallic sound.
8. Clash: A loud, harsh noise made by two metal objects striking each other.
9. Clatter: A series of short, sharp sounds as objects fall or hit each other repeatedly.
10. Cliché: A phrase or opinion that is overused and lacks original thought.
11. Clink: A light, sharp ringing sound, typically made by glass or metal objects hitting each other.
12. Clip-clop: The sound of a horse's hooves on a hard surface.
13. Crackle: A series of small, sharp cracking sounds, like a fire burning.
14. Crackle: (Same as above) A series of small, sharp cracking sounds, like a fire burning.
15. Crash: A loud noise caused by a violent collision or fall.
16. Creak: A long, high sound, often made by something under strain, like an old door opening.
17. Dash: A sudden, quick movement, often creating a sound as something rushes.
18. Ding: A small, clear ringing sound, like a bell.
19. Fizz: A sound like that made by effervescent liquid as it bubbles.
20. Giggle: A light, silly laugh.
21. Grumble: A low, continuous noise, often indicating dissatisfaction or anger.
22. Grumpy: Irritable or in a bad mood, often making disgruntled sounds.
23. Grunt: A short, low sound made by an animal or a person, often indicating effort or discomfort.

24. Hiccup: A sudden, involuntary sound made by a spasm of the diaphragm.
25. Mash: To crush or smash something into a pulp or paste, often producing a squishy sound.
26. Moo: The sound a cow makes.
27. Oink: The sound a pig makes.
28. Plop: The sound of something dropping into water or another liquid.
29. Rattle: A rapid series of short, sharp sounds, typically made by something loose or shaking.
30. Smack: A sharp slap or blow, often making a loud sound.
31. Snap: A sudden, sharp cracking sound, like breaking a twig.
32. Sneeze: A sudden, involuntary expulsion of air from the nose and mouth.
33. Splash: The sound of something hitting water or another liquid.
34. Splat: The sound of something soft and wet hitting a surface.
35. Splutter: A series of short explosive sounds, often when trying to speak while laughing or choking.
36. Sprinkle: Lightly scattering small particles or drops.
37. Squeak: A high-pitched, short sound, often made by something small or tight.
38. Squish: A soft, wet, sucking sound made when pressure is applied to something soft and moist.
39. Tinkle: A light, clear, ringing sound, often made by a small bell or similar object.
40. Trickle: The sound of a small flow of liquid.
41. Wheeze: A high-pitched, whistling sound made while breathing, typically due to a respiratory issue.
42. Whip: A sharp, cracking sound made by a whip or something similar.
43. Whistle: A high-pitched sound made by forcing air through a small opening, such as pursed lips.
44. Whizz: A high-pitched, fast-moving sound.
45. Wriggle: A series of twisting movements or sounds made by something squirming.

Practical Usage: Dialogue – Going to the cinema

Yukta: Hi, Shubhali. Want to go watch a movie with me?

Shubhali: Sure, sure. Been a while since I've been to the cinema. What movie are you planning to watch?

Yukta: A new action film that has just come out. It has three Academy Award winners acting in it.

Shubhali: I'm not a huge fan of action movies, dude.

Yukta: Why not? Action movies are so much fun, man. They have everything that a story needs – tension, drama, climax.

Shubhali: I find them extremely boring and chaotic. Could we watch a romantic movie instead? The new one with Shah Rukh Khan as the lead has great reviews. And you like Shah Rukh too, don't you?

Yukta: I like romantic films too, yes, and I have heard great reviews about the Shah Rukh film. Let's go.

Music terms:

1. Adagio: A slow tempo, often used to describe a gentle and leisurely pace.
2. Accelerando: A gradual increase in speed or tempo.
3. Allegro: A fast and lively tempo.
4. Andante: A moderate walking tempo.
5. Aria: A solo vocal piece, typically found in operas.
6. Atonal: Music that lacks a tonal center or key.
7. Bar: A segment of time in a piece of music, marked by bar lines on the staff.
8. Baritone: A male singing voice that is higher than bass but lower than tenor.
9. Berceuse: A lullaby or soothing song.
10. Cadence: A sequence of chords that brings a phrase, section or piece of music to a close.
11. Cantata: A vocal composition with instrumental accompaniment, typically in several movements.
12. Chorale: A harmonized hymn, usually sung by a choir.
13. Chord: A combination of three or more notes played simultaneously.
14. Clef: A symbol at the beginning of a staff that indicates the pitch of the notes.
15. Crescendo: A gradual increase in volume.
16. Elegy: A mournful, melancholic composition.
17. Ensemble: A group of musicians playing together.
18. Flat: A symbol indicating that a note is to be played a half step lower.
19. Harmony: The combination of different musical notes played or sung simultaneously to produce a pleasing sound.
20. Hymn: A religious song or poem of praise to God.
21. Intonation: The accuracy of pitch in playing or singing.
22. Key: The group of pitches or scale, that forms the basis of a music composition.
23. Leitmotif: A recurring musical theme associated with a particular person, place or idea.

24. Major: A scale or key that typically has a happy or bright sound.
25. Octave: An interval between one musical pitch and another with double its frequency.
26. Overture: An instrumental introduction to an opera or other large musical work.
27. Pitch: The frequency of a note determining how high or low it sounds.
28. Quartet: A group of four musicians or a piece composed for four instruments or voices.
29. Scale: A series of notes in ascending or descending order.
30. Sonata: A composition for one or more solo instruments, typically in several movements.
31. Soprano: The highest female singing voice.
32. Symphony: An extended musical composition for orchestra, typically in several movements.
33. Tenor: A male singing voice between baritone and alto.
34. Tempo: The speed at which a piece of music is played.
35. Vibrato: A slight fluctuation in pitch used to enhance or intensify a sound.
36. Waltz: A dance in triple time, typically performed to music in the same rhythm.

Words to express admiration:

Expressing admiration involves using words that convey deep respect, appreciation, and awe for someone's qualities, actions or achievements. Terms like 'commendable', 'inspiring', 'remarkable', and 'extraordinary' highlight the exceptional nature of the person or their deeds. Phrases such as 'I admire your dedication', 'Your talent is unparalleled' and 'You are truly an inspiration' encapsulate heartfelt praise, emphasizing the impact the individual has made.

Sports terms:

1. Boundary: In cricket, a scoring shot where the ball crosses the edge of the field.
2. Duck: In cricket, a score of zero by a batsman.
3. No ball: In cricket, an illegal delivery by the bowler, resulting in a penalty.
4. Powerplay: In limited-overs cricket, a period with fielding restrictions to encourage aggressive batting.
5. Run out: In cricket, when a batsman is dismissed because they fail to make it to the crease before the fielders break the stumps.
6. Bully: In field hockey, a method used to restart play after a stoppage.
7. Dangle: In ice hockey, a skillful manoeuvre to get past an opponent.
8. Hat trick: In various sports, achieving three goals, wickets or successes in a row.
9. Power Play: In ice hockey, a period when one team has a numerical advantage due to an opponent's penalty.
10. Penalty Kill: In ice hockey, the effort to defend against the opponent's power play.
11. Goalkeeper: A player who defends the goal in sports like football, hockey and handball.
12. Penalty Kick: In football, a direct shot on goal from the penalty mark.
13. Yellow Card: In football, a cautionary card shown to a player for a serious infraction.

Words to express dislike:

Words expressing dislike are varied and nuanced, reflecting different degrees and types of aversion. Terms like 'hate' and 'despise' convey strong, intense feelings of animosity, often implying a deep-seated repulsion. Milder expressions, such as 'dislike' and 'distaste', suggest a more subdued but still clear aversion. Words like 'loathe' and 'detest' imply an intense, often visceral, rejection, while 'abhor' conveys a sense of moral or ethical repugnance.

14. Red Card: In football, a card shown to a player for a severe infraction, leading to their expulsion from the game.
15. Clean Sheet: In football, when a team prevents the opposition from scoring.
16. Ace: In tennis, a serve that the opponent cannot touch, resulting in a point.
17. Backhand: In racket sports, a stroke played on the opposite side of the dominant hand.
18. Serve: In tennis and similar sports, the act of starting play by hitting the ball to the opponent.
19. Smash: In racket sports, a powerful overhead shot.
20. Tie break: In tennis, a method of deciding a set when the score is tied at six games each.
21. Shuttlecock: The projectile used in badminton.
22. Net: The barrier over which the ball or shuttlecock must be hit in sports like tennis, badminton, and volleyball.
23. Love: In tennis, a score of zero.
24. Halfcourt: In basketball, the area around the middle of the court.
25. Clinch: In boxing, when two fighters hold each other to prevent punches.
26. Knock Out: In boxing, when a fighter is unable to continue after being hit.
27. Hook: In boxing, a punch delivered in a semi-circular motion.
28. Punch: A blow with the fist.
29. Relay: A race in which each team member runs or swims a portion of the total distance.
30. Track: The surface used for running races in athletics.
31. Hurdle: An obstacle that runners must jump over in certain track events.
32. Discus: An athletic event where a heavy disc is thrown for distance.
33. Shot Put: An athletic event where a heavy spherical object is thrown for distance.

34. Field: The area used for events like long jump, javelin throw and hammer throw in athletics.
35. Sprint: A short-distance running race at maximum speed.
36. Gambit: In chess, a strategy where a player sacrifices material for a positional advantage.
37. Stalemate: In chess, a situation where the player to move is not in check but has no legal moves.
38. Peg: In baseball, a strong, accurate throw, especially from an infielder to a base.
39. Jockey: In horse racing, the rider of a horse.
40. Freestyle: In swimming, a race where competitors can choose any stroke, but usually choose the front crawl.
41. Backstroke: A swimming stroke performed on the back.
42. Carpool: In motorsports, the area where vehicles are parked and maintained during a race event.
43. Anchor: In relay races, the last runner who usually is the fastest.
44. Split: In bowling, a situation where two or more pins are left standing with a gap between them.
45. Stroke: In rowing, the rower who sits closest to the stern of the boat and sets the rhythm.
46. Range: In shooting sports, the area where shooting practice or competition takes place.
47. Marksmanship: The skill of shooting accurately.

Fill in the blanks with the words given below:

(zest, harangue, recumbent, conflate, vernal, festoon, pariah, celerity, umbrage, garish, perjure, jocose, indelible, beleaguer, dour, wizened, noxious, hyperbole, imbue, tendril)

1. In the soft light of the ______________ season, I found myself unexpectedly ________________.
2. Her story made an _________________ impression on the entire group.
3. He contemplated the ________________ of everyday life.
4. Despite his ________________ appearance, his attitude was ______________, which lifted the spirits of those around him.
5. The old man's face was ________________ with wrinkles.
6. The ____________________ smell of chemicals made her dizzy.
7. Her description of the storm's power was filled with __________, making it sound like the end of the world.
8. She approached the project with a new-found ___________, infusing it with her energy.
9. He launched into a lengthy ____________________ criticizing the government's policies.
10. It doesn't help to _____________ different issues as it can lead to misunderstandings.
11. The garden was ____________________ with colourful flowers, each one __________ with the scent of spring.
12. The ____________________ city struggled to withstand the constant onslaught of enemy attacks.
13. Despite her efforts to fit in, she found herself increasingly isolated, eventually becoming a ___________ in her own community, and took ___________ at their rejection.
14. The artwork's colours were so bright and clashing that it appeared ___________, yet amidst the chaos, a delicate ___________ of ivy provided a subtle touch of elegance.
15. He swore under oath that he was innocent, but later evidence revealed that he had ___________ himself in court.

Fill in the blanks with the words given below:

(annul, baleful, deign, emetic, exculpate, fraught, guild, jut, kindle, laity, lithe, magniloquent, malingerer, natal, obfuscate, officious, prolix, quaff, schism, sequester)

1. Despite the mounting evidence against him, he was confident that the new testimony would __________ him, proving his innocence once and for all.
2. The cliff's edge seemed to __________ out over the roaring ocean below, while fog began to __________ the coastline, obscuring landmarks from view.
3. The __________ neighbour always seemed to be meddling in everyone else's affairs, offering unsolicited advice and opinions at every opportunity.
4. The court decided to __________ their marriage, declaring it null and void, effectively erasing any legal recognition of their __________ union.
5. She immediately regretted taking the medication, as it had an __________ effect, causing her to feel nauseous and sick to her stomach.
6. The speaker's __________ style of lecturing exacerbated the existing __________ within the group, as some found it tedious while others appreciated the thoroughness.
7. His speeches were always grandiose and __________, filled with lofty language and grand gestures that captivated his audience.
8. As the sun dipped below the horizon, the campers gathered around the fire, eagerly awaiting the moment to __________ the flames and illuminate the darkness of the night.
9. The discussion among the __________ was __________ with tension as they grappled with complex theological concepts beyond their usual understanding.
10. The queen would rarely __________ to speak to commoners, considering it beneath her dignity to engage with those she deemed beneath her station.

11. After the toast, they raised their glasses and __________ the exquisite wine, savoring its rich flavour with every sip.
12. The jury was __________ during the trial to prevent any outside influence on their deliberations, ensuring a fair and impartial verdict.
13. The cat moved with a __________ grace, its movements fluid and effortless, yet its eyes held a __________ glare, warning of its potential for danger.
14. The medieval town was bustling with artisans, each belonging to their respective __________, dedicated to preserving and promoting their craft.
15. His constant complaints of illness were viewed with suspicion by his colleagues, who began to suspect him of being a __________.

Choose the correct answers:

1. The doctor reassured the patient that the tumour was __________, meaning it was not harmful and did not pose a serious health risk.
   a) benign b) altruistic c) paradigm d) prosthesis
2. The two families had been involved in a bitter __________ for generations, with each side seeking revenge for past wrongs.
   a) sabotage b) coda c) parity d) vendetta
3. The animals ventured into the forest to __________ for food, searching for berries, nuts, and edible plants.
   a) pilfer b) forage c) sauté d) scourge
4. He opened the chess match with an aggressive __________, sacrificing a pawn to gain a strategic advantage early in the game.
   a) sedition b) gambit c) expletive d) sonata
5. The police raided the warehouse and uncovered a large stash of __________ drugs, leading to several arrests.
   a) illicit b) timbre c) mordant d) pastiche
6. The young actress made her __________ on Broadway last night, impressing the audience with her outstanding performance.
   a) placebo b) ploy c) debut d) rebuff
7. The comedian's __________ jokes had the audience in stitches, laughing uncontrollably throughout the show.
   a) risible b) synergy c) thermal d) varnish
8. The __________ smell from the garbage dump made it difficult for the nearby residents to breathe comfortably.
   a) noisome b) vandalize c) conjugate d) ephemeral
9. In the crowded market, shoppers often had to __________ their way through the throngs of people to reach the stalls.
   a) jostle b) impeach c) lethargic d) lash
10. The tech giant's dominance in the industry was so complete that it effectively held a __________ on Internet services.
    a) perennial b) insidious c) monopoly d) declension

11. The archaeologists discovered ancient artifacts crafted from shimmering ________________.
    a) cursive b) masonry c) obsidian d) nettle
12. The detective realized that the suspicious clue was a ________________.
    a) neutrino b) red herring c) panacea d) quibble
13. The director created a brilliant ________________ of the political landscape.
    a) quixotic b) recriminate c) stigma d) parody
14. After being immobilized in a cast for several weeks, his muscles began to ________________.
    a) atrophy b) suffrage c) tripe d) euphonic
15. The pianist performed a breathtaking rendition of Beethoven's famous ________________.
    a) deity b) sonata c) hypodermic d) idiom
16. The spy operated under ________________ conditions and gathered intelligence without detection.
    a) impassive b) malignant c) covert d) neurotic
17. The artist's painting captured the full ________________ of colours and created a mesmerizing visual experience.
    a) opaque b) pastiche c) rancor d) spectrum
18. In some cultures, certain topics such a death or religion are considered ________________.
    a) taboo b) remnant c) sardonic d) siphon
19. The ambitious General plotted to ________________ the throne to seize power for himself.
    a) usurp b) braise c) capitulate d) exigency
20. He helped her because he had an incredible sense of ________________ and understood how she felt.
    a) empathy b) incumbent c) kindle d) largess

Unscramble the following words:

1. eotvgir: a whirling sensation felt when the sense of balance is disturbed
2. lootyixcg: the scientific study of poisons
3. emkciistps: a questioning or doubting attitude towards beliefs, claims or propositions
4. entilibvae: unable to be avoided; certain to happen
5. rahqneliu: a humorous character from traditional Italian plays who wears a black mask and brightly coloured, diamond-patterned costume
6. pyacesloap: any revelation of the future, especially future destruction or violence
7. atveseencn: quickly fading; short-lived
8. hcipnrzehsaoi: a severe mental disorder characterized by loss of contact with reality
9. ocdrntabna: smuggled goods
10. ereiuqu: any piece of music composed or performed to commemorate the dead

Match the following:

1. Gnome	a. not able to be satisfied
2. Tyranny	b. a person who announces important news or an officer whose task it is to make public proclamations and arrange ceremonies
3. Amiable	c. the activity of spying
4. Herald	d. the use of cruelty, injustice, suppression, etc. to enforce authority or power
5. Insatiable	e. the favouring of one's relatives or friends, especially in making official appointments
6. Macabre	f. friendly, present and good-tempered
7. Espionage	g. a fragment of something brittle, usually glass or pottery
8. Nepotism	h. to argue you over trifles; to make petty objections
9. Shard	i. causing fear or anxiety
10. Quibble	j. a fairy-tale creature, usually in the form of a small misshapen old man, who lives underground, often guarding treasure

Answer Key

Recognize the parts of speech below:

1. adjective 2. Verb 3. Subordinating conjunction 4. Adverb
5. Preposition 6. Preposition 7. Interjection 8. Pronoun
9. Pronoun 10. Conjunction

LEVEL 1

Fill in the blanks:

1. amass 2. bedecked 3. bereft 4. censor 5. scrupulous
6. incessant 7. meagre 8. omen 9. paramour 10. relegate
11. rectitude 12. sheath 13. guile 14. yoke

Solve the crossword:

1. congeal 2. jibe 3. novice 4. wheeze 5. tackle 6. cajole
7. harbinger 8. fatal 9. apostle 10. zest

Choose the correct word from the list given:

1. adjourn 2. arid 3. strut 4. besmirch 5. bolster
6. cajole 7. chirp 8. clamour 9. decorum 10. devote
11. derived 12. discomfort 13. dowry 14. effigy
15. elusive 16. epoch 17. fare 18. fervor 19. fortitude
20. gale 21. girdle 22. greive 23. hatcher 24. lark

25. impelled 26. insipid 27. jute 28. knot 29. lauded
30. lump 31. mallet 32. nomad 33. nuisance 34. occult
35. plume 36. prowess 37. quarrelled 38. region
39. reverie 40. scorn 41. seize 42. share 43. shrewd
44. thimble 45. turbulent 46. undergo 47. vain
48. visualize 49. whimsical 50. yield

LEVEL 2

Fill in the blanks:

1. inundate 2. whittle 3. delinquent 4. contrite 5. boorish
6. xenophobia 7. panacea 8. expiate 9. sonorous 10. dirge
11. juxtapose 12. truant 13. treason 14. zealot 15. laconic

Solve the crossword:

1. facsimile 2. scurrilous 3. tactile 4. quaver 5. (across) parasol, (down) provender 6. loquacious 7. reveille 8. knell 9. menace

Choose the correct answers:

1. anarchist 2. ascetic 3. bellicose 4. bombard 5. chagrin
6. churlish 7. defiance 8. mobilize 9. farce 10. flounder
11. gnawing 12. hamlet 13. heresy 14. impale 15. inert
16. jaunt 17. knave 18. leer 19. massacre 20. muffle
21. nostalgia 22. opaque 23. pachyderm 24. penchant
25. placate 26. punctilious 27. quacks 28. regalia
29. remand 30. reviled 31. salience 32. sceptre 33. shoal
34. solecism 35. swarm 36. tempest 37. truant
38. usurper 39. vendetta 40. volition 41. wreathed
42. yearning 43. zealot 44. impiety 45. liable 46. maxim
47. notorious 48. omniscient 49. pensive 50. recluse

Match the following incomplete collocations:

1. g 2. f 3. h 4. i 5. e 6. j 7. a 8. c 9. d 10. b

Complete the following dialogue with the collocations given:

1. take medicine 2. overall effect 3. heavy drinker 4. bitterly disappointed 5. lose my temper 6. dirty laundry

LEVEL 3

Fill in the blanks:

1. vernal 1a. recumbent 2. indelible 3. celerity 4. dour 4a. jocose 5. wizened 6. noxious 7. hyperbole 8. zest 9. harangue 10. conflate 11. festooned 11a. imbued 12. beleaguered 13. pariah 13a. umbrage 14. garish 14a. tendril 15. perjured

Fill in the blanks:

1. exculpate 2. jut 2a. obfuscate 3. officious 4. annul 4a. natal 5. emetic 6. prolix 6a. schism 7. magniloquent 8. kindle 9. laity 9a. fraught 10. deign 11. quaffed 12. sequestered 13. lithe 13a. baleful 14. guild 15. malingerer

Choose the correct answers:

1. benign 2. vendetta 3. forage 4. gambit 5. illicit 6. debut 7. risible 8. noisome 9. jostle 10. monopoly 11. obsidian 12. red herring 13. parody 14. atrophy 15. sonata c 16. covert 17. spectrum 18. taboo 19. usurp 20. empathy

Unscramble the following:

1. vertigo 2. toxicology 3. skepticism 4. inevitable 5. harlequin 6. apocalypse 7. evanescent 8. schizophrenia 9. contraband 10. requiem

Match the Following:

1. j 2. d 3. f 4. b 5. a 6. i 7. c 8. e 9. g 10. h

CHAMBERS FACT SERIES

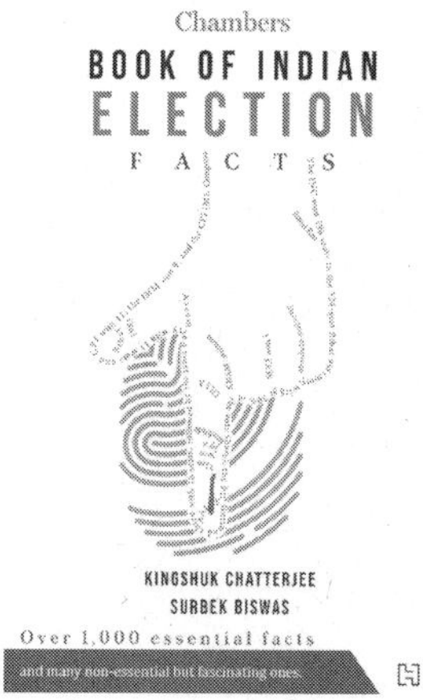

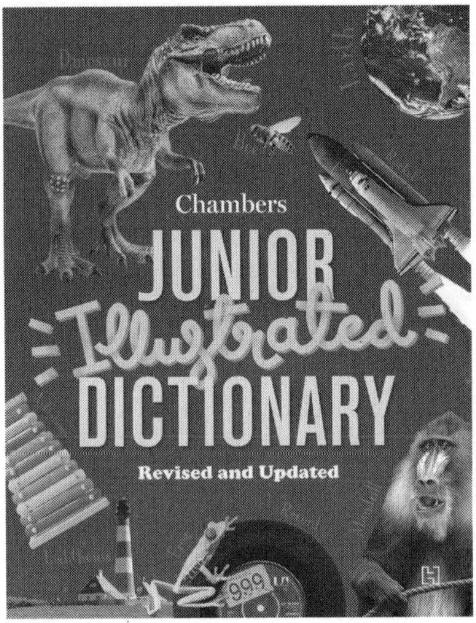

The series covers various subjects that are of professional, academic and general interest. These comprehensive factbooks provide essential facts along with fun-to-read trivia. First time ever here is a set of fact-based books that not only can be your dependable subject references but also are lively and often witty, enough to be your pleasure reading.

Chambers Facts - where facts breathe and even leap at you!